MW00640609

Probability of Intertextual Borrowing

Other Books by Elizabeth Myers

AUTHORSHIP OF 1 PETER AND HEBREWS
New Evidence in Light of Probable Intertextual Borrowing

INTERTEXTUAL BORROWING BETWEEN
1 PETER AND HEBREWS
*Probability of Literary Dependence and the
Most Likely Direction of Borrowing*

PROBABILITY
of

INTERTEXTUAL
BORROWING

A METHODOLOGY
for Determining the Likelihood of Literary
Dependence and the Direction of Borrowing
between New Testament Books

ELIZABETH A. MYERS

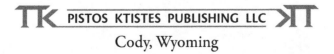
PISTOS KTISTES PUBLISHING LLC
Cody, Wyoming

Probability of Intertextual Borrowing
*A Methodology for Determining the Likelihood of Literary Dependence
and the Direction of Borrowing between New Testament Books*

Published 2020 by
Pistos Ktistes Publishing LLC
1 Adobe Creek Drive
Cody, WY 82414 USA

Cover Design: Elizabeth A. Myers

Cover Graphics: Intersecting strings of parallel Greek texts from Jude 4; Eph 6:21–22; Heb 13:7–8; 1 Thess 4:9–10; 2 Cor 11:12–13; 2 Tim 4:7–8; 2 Pet 2:1; Col 4:7–8; 1 Pet 4:11; Rom 12:9–10; 1 John 4:1; and Jas 1:12–13 NA[28]

Library of Congress Control Number: 2020910969

ISBN (hardback): 978-1-953133-00-7
ISBN (paperback): 978-1-953133-01-4
ISBN (e-book): 978-1-953133-02-1

Contents

PART 1. The Methodology

PART 2. Demonstration of the Methodology

Figures

Tables

Abbreviations

AB	Anchor Bible
AcBib	Academia Biblica
AF	Apostolic Fathers
AJBI	Annual of the Japanese Biblical Institute
BECNT	Baker Exegetical Commentary on the New Testament
BETL	Bibliotheca Ephemeridum Theologicarum Lovaniensium
BHT	Beiträge zur historischen Theologie
Bib	*Biblica*
BibInt	Biblical Interpretation Series
BNTC	Black's New Testament Commentaries
BZ	*Biblische Zeitschrift*
DLNT	*Dictionary of the Later New Testament and Its Developments*

DPL	*Dictionary of Paul and His Letters*
EvQ	*Evangelical Quarterly*
FRLANT	Forschungen zur Religion und Literatur des Alten und Neuen Testaments
HNT	Handbuch zum Neuen Testament
ICC	International Critical Commentary
JBL	*Journal of Biblical Literature*
JSNT	*Journal for the Study of the New Testament*
JSNTSup	Journal for the Study of the New Testament: Supplement Series
JSPSup	Journal for the Study of the Pseudepigrapha Supplement Series
LXX	Septuagint
MT	Masoretic Text
NA^{27}	*Novum Testamentum Graece*, Nestle-Aland, 27th ed.
NA^{28}	*Novum Testamentum Graece*, Nestle-Aland, 28th ed.
NAC	New American Commentary
NCB	New Century Bible
NICNT	New International Commentary on the New Testament
NIGTC	New International Greek Testament Commentary
NIV	New International Version
NTS	*New Testament Studies*
NovT	*Novum Testamentum*
NovTSup	Supplements to Novum Testamentum
PRSt	*Perspectives in Religious Studies*
SB	Sources bibliques
SBLDS	Society of Biblical Literature Dissertation Series

SBLNTGF   Society of Biblical Literature: The New Testament in the
          Greek Fathers

SNTSMS   Society for New Testament Studies Monograph Series

SP   Sacra Pagina

ST   *Studia Theologica*

TRu   *Theologische Rundschau*

VCSup   Supplements to Vigiliae Christianae

WBC   Word Biblical Commentary

WC   Westminster Commentaries

WTT   *Westminster Leningrad Codex*

WUNT   Wissenschaftliche Untersuchungen zum Neuen Testament

Introduction

The curious presence of numerous conceptual and verbal parallels between the books of the New Testament is one of the most enigmatic phenomena of biblical literature. What might explain the presence of these literary parallels? What is the significance of the parallel texts for authenticity and interpretation of the NT writings? The curious phenomenon has raised the intriguing possibility that the authors of NT documents which contain parallel texts, in fact, may have borrowed material from one another. Such a possibility could have far-reaching implications. If parallels between NT documents can be shown to exhibit conclusive evidence of intertextual borrowing, then there are potential implications, not only for matters of origin, such as the date of writing, background of thought, and authorship, but also for exegetical study of the interdependent documents. The true significance of parallel texts for the likelihood of intertextual borrowing, however, has been shrouded in mystery and speculation throughout the history of NT scholarship, primarily due to lack of commonly accepted methods and defensible criteria for evaluating the parallels.

The purpose of this book is to illuminate the long-standing mystery of NT parallels by providing a means of dispelling much of the speculation about their significance. To that end, this book introduces an innovative methodology for determining the likelihood of literary dependence and the most likely direction of borrowing between NT books, the application of which may shed considerable light on interdependent books, their authors, and their intended audiences.

Assessing the nature of the relationship between two documents based on literary parallels is challenging, to say the least. On the one hand, many scholars claim that without explicit indicators of a direct connection it is impossible to discern any more than a possibility that the authors may have had some experience with a common milieu. Claims of direct dependence of one document upon another are frequently dismissed as outstretching the evidence, not only because literary parallels exhibit varying degrees of correspondence, but also because there are no commonly accepted criteria or methods for assessing the nature of the relationship between parallel texts. Alternative theories which claim that intertextual parallels can be explained by the authors' independent use of common traditions have been far more readily accepted in NT scholarship. Common tradition, in fact, is a very popular explanation for intertextual parallels that exhibit a low degree of verbal correspondence. On the other hand, many published NT commentaries and focused studies seem to draw significance from perceived parallels involving NT books. It is not uncommon, for example, to find books and articles in which modern authors comment on presumed redactional practices observed in a NT document, assuming that the NT author borrowed material from another document.

The thorny nature of parallels-analysis is heightened by the fact that the task is a common endeavor in many diverse fields of study. Most, if not all, fields of academic inquiry depend, at least to some degree, on parallels for evaluation of relationships and development of models. For example, in the study of physical sciences, the parallels of interest may include similarities in electrical, material, or chemical properties; for life sciences, parallels in reproductive systems or factors associated with disease may be of more interest; in socio-historical disciplines, interest may be focused on similarities in customs, cultic practices, and symbols. In the case of NT documents, the parallels of interest involve literary forms and conceptual constructs that are conveyed by the written texts. In all cases, the task of evaluating parallels is elusive. Nonetheless, parallels present important and alluring phenomena for many fields of academic inquiry, including NT studies.

Parallels in ancient artifacts are of great importance for understanding the world in which they originated. Whether they entail resemblances of thought, word, or deed, parallels have the potential to open windows of insight in both temporal and logical dimensions. The temporal dimension involves parallels that reflect a genealogical relationship between artifacts over an extended period of time. In this respect, parallels may provide a window through which to view the world on each side of the parallel. Viewed in the temporal dimension, parallels can inform our understanding of how the world represented by one parallel element developed from or into the world represented by the other parallel element. Parallels also offer insight in the logical dimension in that they open a window through which to view the greater system with which the parallel elements interact. A good analogy is the notion of a puzzle. Parallels that can be shown to have a direct connection are like two connected pieces of a puzzle. Each connection helps reveal the bigger picture — the more connections, the clearer the picture. In regard to NT documents, parallels in the logical dimension contribute to our understanding of the greater early Christian discourse in which the documents participate. Thus in both the temporal and logical dimensions, literary parallels may provide important historical-hermeneutical insights that might otherwise be hidden from view.

The scholarly allure of parallels also is unmistakable. Indeed, it is hard to find a more curious phenomenon in the NT than the presence of so many striking intertextual parallels. With the prospect of contributing important historical-hermeneutical insights, it is no wonder that many scholars have ventured into the field seeking to discover and build upon parallels, often with no more than their own intuition as a guide. Indeed, much scholarly ink has been spilled over potential exegetical implications of parallels involving NT books. In the absence of strict controls, or even the most general of guidelines, the results have been inconsistent and often have lacked credibility, so much so that charges of speculation and misuse have been laid upon the field of parallels-study.

Perhaps most notable is the indictment leveled by Samuel Sandmel in his Presidential Address to the annual meeting of the Society of Biblical Literature in 1961. In this frequently quoted speech, Sandmel accuses NT scholarship of "parallelomania," which he describes as "that extravagance among scholars which first overdoes the supposed similarity in passages and then proceeds to describe source and derivation as if implying literary connection flowing in an inevitable or predetermined direction."[1] Although

---

1.   Samuel Sandmel, "Parallelomania," *JBL* 81, no. 1 (March 1962): 1.

the particular details of Sandmel's argument might be disputed, he is right to advise caution in dealing with perceived parallels. The chaotic state of the field has been widely recognized and has prompted attempts to establish clear criteria for classifying parallels and for determining their significance.[2]

The research conducted for this project, however, confirms that the study of parallels still suffers from the lack of sound methodology. Among other things, published studies reveal that there is no consensus either for what constitutes a parallel or for what conclusions may be drawn from parallels. Only rarely are the criteria stated explicitly, and even rarer is the inclusion of underlying rationale for the stated criteria. Most puzzling is the fact that identical criteria often are viewed differently by different scholars — as positive indicators of intertextual borrowing for some and as negative indicators for others. Thus it appears that parallels not only represent potentially valuable pieces of a greater historical-hermeneutical

---

2. Notable for their attention to methodology and criteria for assessing intertextual parallels are the following works: Christopher A. Beetham, *Echoes of Scripture in the Letter of Paul to the Colossians*, BibInt 96 (Leiden, The Netherlands: Brill, 2008), 17–35; Kenneth Berding, *Polycarp and Paul: An Analysis of Their Literary and Theological Relationship in Light of Polycarp's Use of Biblical and Extra-Biblical Literature*, VCSup 62 (Leiden, The Netherlands: Brill, 2002), 27–32; Michael J. Gilmour, *The Significance of Parallels between 2 Peter and Other Early Christian Literature*, AcBib 10 (Leiden, The Netherlands: Brill Academic, 2002), 47–80; Andrew F. Gregory and Christopher M. Tuckett, "Reflections on Method: What Constitutes the Use of the Writings That Later Formed the New Testament in the Apostolic Fathers?" in *The Reception of the New Testament in the Apostolic Fathers*, ed. Andrew F. Gregory and Christopher M. Tuckett (Oxford: Oxford University Press, 2005), 61–82; Richard B. Hays, *Echoes of Scripture in the Letters of Paul* (New Haven: Yale University Press, 1989), 29–32; Dietrich-Alex Koch, *Die Schrift als Zeuge des Evangeliums: Untersuchungen zur Verwendung und zum Verständnis der Schrift bei Paulus*, BHT 69 (Tübingen: Mohr [Siebeck], 1986), 13–15; Wolf-Dietrich Köhler, *Die Rezeption des Matthäusevangeliums in der Zeit vor Irenäus*, WUNT 2.24 (Tübingen: Mohr [Siebeck], 1987), 1–17; Jeffery M. Leonard, "Identifying Inner-Biblical Allusions: Psalm 78 as a Test Case," *JBL* 127, no. 2 (Summer 2008): 246–57; Andreas Lindemann, *Paulus im ältesten Christentum*, BHT 58 (Tübingen: Mohr [Siebeck], 1979), 15–19; William L. Schutter, *Hermeneutic and Composition in 1 Peter*, WUNT 2.30 (Tübingen: Mohr [Siebeck], 1989), 35–36; Kazuhito Shimada, "Is 1 Peter Dependent on Romans?" AJBI 19 (Tokyo: Yamamoto Shoten, 1993), 90–91; Robert H. Stein, *The Synoptic Problem: An Introduction* (Grand Rapids, MI: Baker Books, 1987), 29–42; Michael Thompson, *Clothed with Christ: The Example and Teaching of Jesus in Romans 12.1–15.13*, JSNTSup 59 (Sheffield: Sheffield Academic, 1991), 30–37; Duane Frederick Watson, *Invention, Arrangement, and Style: Rhetorical Criticism of Jude and 2 Peter*, SBLDS 104 (Atlanta, GA: Scholars Press, 1988), 163–87.

puzzle, they are also inherently puzzling. Perhaps that explains the alluring nature of intertextual parallels.

The chaotic state of such a vital and perplexing enterprise calls for a new approach to this old problem. Terence Donaldson is absolutely right when he asserts that what is needed is "a more sober and critical approach to the use of parallels — one characterized by both a concern for rigorous demonstration of the existence of true genealogical parallels, and a more modest and realistic appraisal of what parallels-study can be expected to accomplish."[3] Without a more disciplined approach to the problem, claims of intertextual borrowing based on perceived parallels will continue to invite charges of speculation and misuse.

In the interest of establishing a more disciplined approach to the study of intertextual parallels, this book presents a methodology for determining the likelihood of intertextual borrowing between books of the NT that is based on probability theory and relevant literary indicators. Since the likelihood of literary dependence must first be established before the question of who borrowed from whom is warranted, the methodology is presented in two separate chapters of part 1. A methodology for assessing the likelihood of literary dependence is defined in chapter 1. Here it is shown how the probability of literary dependence between two documents can be determined by examining intertextual parallels for evidence of appropriate indicators and applying probability theory to the data. Chapter 2 follows with a methodology for assessing the most likely direction of borrowing. In a manner similar to that of chapter 1, chapter 2 shows how to determine the probability of borrowing from evidence observed in the intertextual parallels and their host documents. Since each author of two interdependent documents is a potential borrower of the other, the chapter also explains the significance of the probabilities for each directional scenario and identifies the specific combinations that are conclusive for the direction of borrowing.

Usage and reliability of the methodology is then demonstrated in the three chapters of part 2, using both a negative and a positive test case. In chapter 3, the methodology is applied to two NT books that bear little resemblance to one another, namely, James and Philippians. As expected, the analysis produces a soundly negative result which indicates that literary dependence is highly unlikely. Accordingly, investigation of the most likely direction of borrowing, as prescribed in chapter 2, is unwarranted

3. Terence L. Donaldson, "Parallels: Use, Misuse and Limitations," *EvQ* 55 (October 1983): 198.

for James and Philippians. A positive test case follows in chapters 4 and 5. These chapters show how the methodology is applied to Jude and 2 Peter, a pair of NT books that exhibit many striking parallels. In chapter 4 the parallels are evaluated according to the methodology described in chapter 1. For the case of Jude and 2 Peter, a positive result affirms the commonly accepted view that one of these authors borrowed material from the other document. In chapter 5 the same parallels are re-evaluated according to the methodology defined in chapter 2 in order to determine the most likely direction of borrowing. Again, the analysis produces the expected outcome and shows that the author of 2 Peter most likely borrowed from Jude. Thus in both the negative and positive test cases, the methodology is shown to be reliable as the analyses produce the expected results.[4]

As presentation of the methodology commences in chapter 1, readers should note that all English translations are those of the author unless noted otherwise. For the benefit of English-only readers, translations of parallel texts maintain the grammatical features of the Greek and Hebrew texts as much as possible in order to facilitate comparison of the texts and explanation of the analyses. As a matter of convenience, unknown authors of ancient works are referred to with masculine pronouns throughout the book. Finally, the book utilizes the notation of double vertical lines ("||") to indicate a parallel between two texts (e.g., Jude 10 || 2 Pet 2:12).

---

4. A brief overview of an early prototype version of the probability assess-ment methodology appears in an essay by Elizabeh A. Myers entitled, "Probability of Intertextual Borrowing," in *Exploring Intertextuality: Diverse Strategies for New Testament Interpretation of Texts*, ed. B. J. Oropeza and Steve Moyise (Eugene, OR: Cascade Books, 2016), 254–72.

PART 1

The Methodology

CHAPTER 1

Literary Dependence
Assessment Methodology

In order to determine the likelihood that the author of one NT document borrowed material from another document, it is first necessary to establish whether or not a dependent literary relationship is likely to exist between the documents. Only then does it make sense to address the question of who borrowed from whom. For this reason, the methodology is two-stage by design. The current chapter presents stage 1, the methodology for determining the likelihood of a literary connection between two documents, independent of any considerations of directionality. Chapter 2 then follows with stage 2, the methodology for determining the most likely direction of borrowing. The task here in chapter 1 begins by exploring the nature of the intertextual problem and defining a conceptual framework within which the methodology can take shape. This involves examining possible approaches, establishing the preferred approach, identifying criteria for dependence, discovering what constitutes relevant evidence, and selecting appropriate analysis tools and methods. Once the conceptual framework is defined, the methodology takes shape by developing the particular analysis method ("Probability of Literary Dependence") and by specifying how the necessary data is extracted from intertextual parallels ("Scoring Scheme").

Conceptual Framework

General Approach

Despite the problematic nature of parallels described in the introduction, as observable phenomena, they are well suited to scientific methods of investigation. If properly controlled by a suitable method and appropriate parameters, use of a systematic approach may clarify the relational nature of intertextual parallels and yield credible conclusions in regard to literary dependence. To this end, the methodology defined in this chapter employs a systematic approach that is both similar and dissimilar to what has been applied in related areas of intertextual research.

In studies of the use of the OT in the NT, it is most common to see what might be referred to as a "reference" approach. Such an approach classifies parallels according to generally understood definitions of "citation," "quotation," "allusion," or "echo," which are based on the preciseness of the correspondence and perceptions about the author and the intended readers. Although exact definitions can vary, a summary offered by Michael Bird captures the basic idea behind the reference approach:

> Texts can rehearse other texts in a variety of ways. As such, a first point of call will be to define the terms 'citation,' 'allusion,' and 'echo.' By *citation*, I mean a *direct* and deliberate lifting of one text into another with some kind of marker to signify the use of a second text such as 'as it is written,' 'as the Lord said,' or 'as the apostles taught.' An *allusion* is a figure of speech that makes *indirect* extra-textual references by activating awareness of a second text through its particular choice of subject, language, and grammar. Unlike citation, allusion is indirect and requires shared knowledge of a second text between the author and reader in order to be discernible. An *echo* invokes a particular text through the *general* thematic coherence between the subject matter of the two texts. In sum, the key distinguishing features are direct citation, indirect reference, and thematic coherence.[1]

---

1. Michael F. Bird, "The Reception of Paul in the Epistle to Diognetus," in *Paul and the Second Century*, ed. Michael F. Bird and Joseph R. Dodson (New York: T&T Clark International, 2011), 74.

While a reference approach is most typical for evaluating NT use of the OT,[2] it has also been applied to use of the NT in the NT and in other early Christian writings.[3] The methodology presented here is similar in that some of the same criteria are employed for evaluating preciseness of correspondence between parallel elements. The major difference is that conclusions are not based on the likelihood that an author is intentionally drawing the readers' attention to a "referenced" document. Unlike references to the OT, it cannot be assumed that the NT recipients have or are aware of another "referenced" NT document. Accordingly, it cannot be assumed that the author's intention is to "activate awareness of" or "invoke" a particular text with which the reader is assumed to be familiar. Allowance must be made for the possibility that the author is simply leveraging an earlier work or that the author's language and ideology has been shaped by an earlier work, independent of any presumed knowledge on the part of the intended readers. Michael Gilmour draws attention to this issue as he outlines his criteria for determining the significance of parallels. Insisting that "[q]uotations and borrowings are not identical,"[4] Gilmour clarifies the distinction in that the former assumes authorial intention to trigger the readers' awareness, but the latter does not necessarily imply any signal from author to reader that the text has been borrowed. Determinations of

2. For example, Christopher A. Beetham, *Echoes of Scripture in the Letter of Paul to the Colossians*, BibInt 96 (Leiden, The Netherlands: Brill, 2008), 17–24; Richard B. Hays, *Echoes of Scripture in the Letters of Paul* (New Haven: Yale University Press, 1989), 29–32; Dietrich-Alex Koch, *Die Schrift als Zeuge des Evangeliums: Untersuchungen zur Verwendung und zum Verständnis der Schrift bei Paulus*, BHT 69 (Tübingen: Mohr [Siebeck], 1986), 13–15; Stanley E. Porter, "The Use of the Old Testament in the New Testament: A Brief Comment on Method and Terminology," in *Early Christian Interpretation of the Scriptures of Israel: Investigations and Proposals*, ed. Craig A. Evans and James A. Sanders (Sheffield: Sheffield Academic, 1997), 79–96; William L. Schutter, *Hermeneutic and Composition in 1 Peter*, WUNT 2.30 (Tübingen: Mohr [Siebeck], 1989), 35–36.

3. See, e.g., Kenneth Berding, *Polycarp and Paul: An Analysis of Their Literary and Theological Relationship in Light of Polycarp's Use of Biblical and Extra-Biblical Literature*, VCSup 62 (Leiden, The Netherlands: Brill, 2002), 31–32; Bird, "Reception of Paul," 74; Michael Thompson, *Clothed with Christ: The Example and Teaching of Jesus in Romans 12.1–15.13*, JSNTSup 59 (Sheffield: Sheffield Academic, 1991), 30–37.

4. Michael J. Gilmour, *The Significance of Parallels between 2 Peter and Other Early Christian Literature*, AcBib 10 (Leiden, The Netherlands: Brill Academic, 2002), 49.

NT || NT literary dependence, then, cannot be based on the likelihood of an intended reference signal from author to reader.

Another approach that has been used for various types of intertextual studies evaluates intertextual relationships according to quantifiable stylistic features of the written language. Such a stylometric method works by comparing statistical stylistic profiles of the texts in question. In regard to written texts, the method is commonly used to discern authorship of disputed documents. For example, in a study that seeks to determine the authorship of the disputed Federalist Papers (1787–1788), certain common stylistic features of the writings are compared in order to establish which of two authors is most likely to have penned the disputed papers.[5] The basic idea is to compare, based on the selected stylistic features, the relative strength of the relationship of the twelve disputed papers with each of the fifty known to have been written by James Madison and the fifty-six known to have been written by Alexander Hamilton. In the case of the Federalist Papers, there is sufficient comparable data of known authorship by which to make statistically significant assessments of how the twelve disputed papers relate.

Stylometric methods have also been applied to NT documents.[6] Such applications, however, are not completely reliable for establishing who authored the documents. With the possible exception of the Pauline corpus, there are not enough documents known to have been written by the same person with which to make confident comparisons. Even within the Pauline corpus, the possible use of a secretary must be taken into consideration since particular stylistic features might reflect the hand of the secretary rather than the hand of the claimed author.

A stylometric approach has also been applied in the field of NT textual criticism to evaluate relationships between manuscripts. Gerald Donker, for instance, uses a variation of this basic approach in a study of the text of the Apostolos in Athanasius in order to analyze textual relationships between

---

5. Glenn Fung, "The Disputed Federalist Papers: SVM Feature Selection Via Concave Minimization," in *TAPIA '03 Proceedings of the 2003 Conference on Diversity in Computing, Atlanta, GA, October 15–18, 2003* (New York: The Association of Computing Machinery, 2003), 42–46.

6. See, e.g., Anthony Kenny, *A Stylometric Study of the New Testament* (New York: Oxford University Press, 1986); D. L. Mealand, "The Extent of the Pauline Corpus: A Multivariate Approach," *JSNT* 59 (1995): 61–92.

Athanasius and selected Greek NT manuscripts.[7] Donker evaluates the results by using an external standard derived from theoretical data which is intended to approximate data generated from an empirical study.[8] In order to determine the significance of textual dissimilarity between the text of the Apostolos in Athanasius and selected Greek NT manuscripts, Donker first calculates the degree of dissimilarity based on the frequency of disagreements over a set of variant readings. The critical values for statistical significance are then determined by constructing "a normal distribution of probabilities of random agreement (i.e., agreements expected to occur by chance) between two artificial 'pseudo-witnesses.'"[9] In effect, Donker uses a Monte Carlo random manuscript generator to produce comparable data from which to derive the critical values. Assuming that the empirical dissimilarity data also approximates a normal distribution, Donker then applies the theoretical critical values to the Athanasius data to determine the significance of the dissimilarity values for each pairing of manuscripts.

The method established by Karen Jobes for evaluating relationships between books of the Septuagint reflects similar stylometric techniques.[10] Jobes uses syntax criticism to develop what she describes as "a methodology of syntax profiling in order to facilitate the display and interpretation of large quantities of syntactic information and to allow direct comparison of the syntax of the alpha-text with the ό-text of Esther, and then with the two Greek versions of Daniel."[11] Jobes's syntactic profiling method can be used to identify or validate syntactical features that might reflect an underlying Semitic or *koine* influence, or to evaluate relationships between Greek texts by comparing syntactical profiles.

The methodology defined here is similar to stylometric approaches in that analysis is based on observable, measurable features of the text. The main difference is in the criteria used to evaluate significance. Stylometric approaches are generally comparative in nature, evaluating significance

---

7. Gerald J. Donker, *The Text of the Apostolos in Athanasius of Alexandria*, SBLNTGF 8 (Atlanta, GA: Society of Biblical Literature, 2011).

8. Donker, *Text of the Apostolos*, 203–26.

9. Donker, *Text of the Apostolos*, 220.

10. Karen H. Jobes, "Quantitative Methods for Exploring the Relationship between Books of the Septuagint," in *The Bible As Book: The Transmission of the Greek Text*, ed. Scot McKendrick and Orlaith A. O'Sullivan (New Castle, DE: Oak Knoll Press, 2003), 73–95.

11. Jobes, "Quantitative Methods," 80.

via comparison with a known reference. Hence reliability depends, to a large degree, on having a confident basis for comparison which links a particular stylistic profile to the factor of interest (e.g., a particular author or manuscript tradition). Without a sound basis for comparison, the most that can be concluded is the degree to which the stylistic profiles are similar or dissimilar. In the case of NT literary dependence, where a NT author makes direct use of another NT writing in the crafting of his own work, a confident basis for comparison is even less tenable than for NT authorship because there are no undisputed cases of literary dependence between NT documents outside of the Synoptic Gospels. Furthermore, unlike in the case of Donker's study of Greek manuscript relationships, there is no basis for development of a theoretical model that might serve as a reference for comparison. Therefore, the significance of parallel stylistic features must be established on other grounds.

Methods that evaluate the significance of literary parallels based on assumptions regarding authorial intention and reader awareness, or on statistical comparisons with a known reference, rely on external factors for assessing significance. Alternatively, the present methodology evaluates parallels primarily on features of the parallel texts themselves. The likelihood of a literarily dependent relationship is based on the cumulative presence of specific characteristics that are indicators of such a relationship. By focusing evaluation primarily on observable internal indicators, it is possible to avoid the risk of subjective and unreliable conclusions that might result from a "reference" or "stylometric" approach. Focusing on internal indicators does, however, mean that reliability of the method is only as good as the particular indicators that are selected for evaluation.

Identification and selection of an appropriate set of indicators for literary dependence is informed by research that was conducted for this project. With the goal of compiling a database that would be representative of the broad contours of NT intertextual studies, approximately 100 published works were surveyed in search of methods and criteria that have been used to identify and assess the significance of intertextual parallels. The search focused mainly on interdependent relationships involving the NT writings, including studies of the Synoptic Problem, use of the NT in the Apostolic Fathers, and use of the NT in other NT documents. Selected works dealing with the use of the OT in the NT and in the Apostolic Fathers, as well as relevant studies of the manuscript traditions were also included. Although explicit treatments of method and criteria were rarely found in the surveyed works, implicit criteria could frequently be gleaned from the discussions of specific parallels. The resulting database, while by no means comprehensive, paints the landscape of biblical intertextual studies in sufficient detail to expose the more well-traveled paths as well as the major obstacles to be avoided. Specific points of interest are referenced throughout the rest of this chapter and the next.

Having established the general approach of the methodology as based on measurable features of the texts themselves, we now turn to the question of criteria for literary dependence. What is it about a parallel relationship that identifies it as a relationship in which one element developed from the other? The matter of criteria is addressed first by examining the relational possibilities presented by intertextual parallels and then by identifying the basic relational characteristic that is required for literary dependence.

Parallels and the Question of Dependence

Parallel phenomena can indicate many different types of relationships. At one extreme, a parallel may be due to mere coincidence, in which case there is no relationship at all between the paired elements. The elements just happen to resemble one another. At the other extreme, a parallel may be the result of a deliberate act of replication, whereby a second element is created as an exact copy of an original element. In that case, there is a definite relationship between the two elements as one element is directly influenced by the other. In between these two extremes lies a wide range of relational possibilities that might account for parallel phenomena. Since not all parallel relationships reflect dependence of one element upon another, it is necessary to discern the particular type of relationship that must be in place in order for one element to influence the development of another.

Terence Donaldson's examination of the proper use of comparative materials in biblical studies provides a helpful framework for evaluating different types of parallel relationships. The scheme by which he categorizes relationships according to two key parameters is particularly relevant.[12] The first parameter that Donaldson uses to distinguish parallel relationships concerns the mode of influence and whether the elements are genealogically or analogically related. According to Donaldson, a relationship is

---

12. Terence L. Donaldson, "Parallels: Use, Misuse and Limitations," *EvQ* 55 (October 1983): 199–201.

considered genealogical when one element derives from the other in some fashion. Parallels of this nature are characterized as genealogical parallels. In the case of analogical parallels, one element does not derive from the other. Instead, the parallel arises from a common experience of human nature in a similar situation. As an example, Donaldson observes that "the use of ritual washings as a symbol for purification . . . arises so naturally from universal human experience that no true genealogical parallel should be assumed between, say, early Christian baptism and Hindu ceremonies in the Ganges."[13] Such parallel cleansing rituals should be understood as analogically related and not as one ritual having been influenced by the other.

The second parameter that serves to distinguish parallel relationships in Donaldson's scheme is the directness of influence. The main question in regard to directness is whether the parallel reflects a direct connection or an indirect influence through the mediation of some common factor. For literary parallels, direct influence occurs when an author uses his or her personal knowledge of another document in the writing of a new document. Alternatively, when authors make independent use of a shared element through a common religious context, the influence is indirect. The possible permutations of these two key parameters, mode of influence and directness of influence, define the major types of parallel relationships, as shown in figure 1.1.

Directness	*Mode*	
	Genealogical	Analogical
Direct	Literary Dependence	X
Non-direct	Common Source Tradition	Human Nature & Experience

FIGURE 1.1. Major types of parallel relationships

13. Donaldson, "Parallels," 199.

The various combinations of mode of influence and directness of influence result in three major types of parallel relationships.[14] The first relational type, the direct-genealogical relationship, is the kind of relationship that accounts for literary dependence. Donaldson refers to parallels of this type as "stronger genealogical" parallels since they exhibit "a direct, straight-line influence from one element to the other."[15] The second relational type, the non-direct-genealogical relationship, attributes parallels to independent use of common source traditions. Although this case may be described as one of "analogical parallel in common milieu,"[16] it is better to classify this type of parallel relationship as genealogical since there is a genealogical link. Donaldson refers to these types of parallels as "weaker genealogical" parallels because the connection between them is "diffuse and mediated through an indirect process."[17] The third relational type, the non-direct (or non-existent)-analogical relationship, describes cases where parallels arise from common experiences of human nature. Parallels of this type are simply referred to by Donaldson as "analogical" parallels.

In order to discern the significance of intertextual parallels, it is necessary to identify the type of relationship that lies behind the phenomena. This is not a simple task as it requires going beyond the demonstration of similarity of thought, word, or deed. In order to identify a genealogical parallel, either strong or weak, there must be evidence of a relationship between the two elements. For study of the history of religions, Donaldson stresses the need to "provide some reason for believing that religious cargo has passed over the [historical] bridge."[18] The possible existence of such a bridge between religions, according to Donaldson, may be established on geographical and chronological grounds. Such evidence, however, extends beyond the general approach established for the methodology presented in this chapter, unless explicitly indicated in the texts themselves. Since the general approach established here focuses on internal evidence, high demands for evidence are laid upon the texts themselves in order to discern the relational character of parallels. Most demanding is the stipulation that

14. By definition, there is no such thing as a direct analogical relationship. It is possible, however, to find direct-genealogical parallels in a common-milieu situation. Donaldson, "Parallels," 200.

15. Donaldson, "Parallels," 200.

16. Donaldson, "Parallels," 200.

17. Donaldson, "Parallels," 200.

18. Donaldson, "Parallels," 199.

identification of a strong genealogical parallel requires evidence that the connection is *direct*. This, however, can pose an insurmountable challenge if not properly focused.

The task of discerning the nature of the relationship between parallel literary elements can be greatly simplified by streamlining the process to fit the purpose of the study. The primary goal of this methodology is to produce reliable conclusions concerning the likelihood that parallels between two NT documents indicate a relationship of literary dependence of one document upon the other. In other words, in light of the observed parallels, how likely is it that one of the authors employed his knowledge of the other document in the writing of his own document? The specific interest in literary dependence serves to focus analysis on evidence of stronger genealogical parallels. Accordingly, the task may be focused on assessing the *directness* of the parallel relationship. Whereas weak evidence of directness points to weaker genealogical or analogical connections, strong evidence suggests direct literary dependence.

By focusing on the likelihood of literary dependence as evidenced by the directness of the parallel relationship, the task of analysis is simplified in two significant ways. First, it is not necessary to distinguish between the two major types of non-direct parallel relationships, or even to hypothesize underlying common sources, common milieus, or common human experiences that might account for the parallels. For the purpose of this methodology, it is sufficient simply to recognize that the weak evidence of directness offered by such relationships reduces the likelihood of literary dependence. Second, since the primary interest here lies at the level of whole documents, it is not necessary to make a call regarding literary dependence for each individual parallel that is observed between the texts. A direct literary relationship between the two documents can be established with just one direct-connect parallel. Therefore, the minimum criterion for literary dependence is one parallel that derives from a direct literary connection. With this in mind, methodology development is focused on two key questions: (1) What constitutes evidence of directness in literary parallels? and (2) How can the overall probability of literary dependence be determined from such evidence?

Evidence of Directness

Identification of relevant evidence begins by considering different ways in which a direct connection might be indicated between elements. The most obvious way is for one of the elements explicitly to acknowledge a connection. In the case of social relationships, this might appear as an entry in someone's personal journal indicating that a face-to-face meeting with another person occurred on a certain day. For literary relationships, an equivalent example of this type of evidence is the presence of introductory formulae for OT quotations. By introducing a parallel text as having come from Scripture, an author explicitly indicates a direct connection.[19] If all literary parallels were accompanied by introductory formulae, the search for relevant indicators might end here. The fact of the matter is, however, that none of the parallels between NT documents appear with introductory formulae.

The concept of "fingerprinting" presents a different type of evidence that might be suitable. In this case, direct contact may be detected by the presence in one document of literary or theological "fingerprints" belonging to another document or writer. NT fingerprints might appear in the form of language, style, concepts, or usage patterns that are uniquely characteristic of the originating document. Use of such perceived fingerprints to identify cases of literary dependence is not uncommon in published NT studies.[20]

19. Examples of works that advocate introductory formulae as indicators of literary dependence include: Bird, "Reception of Paul," 74–75; Peter H. Davids, "The Pseudepigrapha in the Catholic Epistles," in *The Pseudepigrapha and Early Biblical Interpretation,* ed. James H. Charlesworth and Craig A. Evans, JSPSup 14 (Sheffield: Sheffield Academic, 1993), 240; Gilmour, *Significance of Parallels,* 49; Donald Alfred Hagner, *The Use of the Old and New Testaments in Clement of Rome,* NovTSup 34 (Leiden, The Netherlands: E. J. Brill, 1973), 195; Paul Anthony Hartog, *Polycarp and the New Testament: The Occasion, Rhetoric, Theme, and Unity of the Epistle to the Philippians and Its Allusions to New Testament Literature,* WUNT 2.134 (Tübingen: Mohr [Siebeck], 2002), 174; Jeffery M. Leonard, "Identifying Inner-Biblical Allusions: Psalm 78 as a Test Case," *JBL* 127, no. 2 (Summer 2008): 258; Andreas Lindemann, *Die Clemensbriefe,* HNT 17, Die Apostolischen Väter 1 (Tübingen: Mohr [Siebeck], 1992), 138–39; Gail R. O'Day, "Jeremiah 9.22–23 and 1 Corinthians 1.26–31: A Study in Intertextuality," *JBL* 109 (1990): 264.

20. See, e.g., John Dominic Crossan, *The Birth of Christianity: Discovering What Happened in the Years Immediately after the Execution of Jesus* (New York: HarperSanFrancisco, 1998), 105–6; Paul Ellingworth, "Hebrews and 1 Clement: Literary Dependence or Common Tradition?" *BZ* ns 23, no. 2 (1979): 262–69; Mark S. Goodacre, *Goulder and the Gospels: An Examination of a New Paradigm,* JSNTSup

An example that uses fingerprinting may be found in John Dominic Crossan's approach to discerning the relationship between the Synoptic Gospels, a key part of which involves demonstrating genetic relationships between each pair of Gospel texts. According to Crossan, a genetic relationship may be evidenced by certain characteristics exhibited in the texts:

> *Genetic relationship* means that certain elements of order and content that are characteristically Markan are found in Matthew and Luke. We are not talking of general tradition common to all three gospels but of specific editorial aspects of Markan sequence or style whose presence in those other two texts indicates copying. What we are seeking, as it were, are Markan literary fingerprints or Markan theological DNA present within the gospels of Matthew and Luke.[21]

Crossan understands the Markan *intercalation* or *sandwich* style of storytelling as such a literary fingerprint that indicates a direct connection with both Matthew and Luke.[22]

If NT documents are indeed marked by unique fingerprints, then the appearance of foreign fingerprints that are uniquely characteristic of another work would constitute possible evidence of a direct connection between the two documents. Unfortunately, the fingerprint theory fails to be conclusive with NT documents for the very reason that it is conclusive with human subjects: human fingerprints are verifiably unique to individual humans. The concept of fingerprinting works with human subjects because the uniqueness of human fingerprints has been verified through scientific study. This is not the case with the collection of NT documents that exist today. Although NT documents may exhibit features that are characteristic of the work, uniqueness cannot be verified for at least two reasons. First, the surviving documents represent only a fraction of all the literature that was in circulation during the NT writing period. Thus the appearance of uniqueness is limited to the set of currently available documents. Second, the NT documents available for analysis today are copies of

---

133 (Sheffield: Sheffield Academic, 1996), 42–88; Helmut Koester, "Written Gospels or Oral Tradition?" *JBL* 113 (1994): 297; Craig R. Koester, *Hebrews: A New Translation with Introduction and Commentary*, AB 36 (New York: Doubleday, 2001), 56.

    21. Crossan, *Birth of Christianity*, 105.

    22. Examples of Markan intercalations are found in Mark 3:20–35; 5:21–43; 6:7–30; 11:12–21; 14:1–11; and 14:53–72.

originals that were lost long ago. Based on the myriad of variations evident in the manuscript tradition, there is no guarantee that original fingerprints have survived unaltered. Even if an original fingerprint survived intact, there is no sure way of knowing which manuscripts are marked by the original print. Thus it is unreasonable to assume that direct connections might confidently be traced through literary fingerprints that are presumed to be unique.

Another possibility arises from the notion that a direct relationship implies a one-to-one connection between the paired elements. One-to-one means that the influence is not diffused by multiple contacts, as would be the case with many-to-one or many-to-many relationships. This aspect of direct relationships is significant because it means that directness can be measured by the degree to which a relationship between two parallel elements is exclusive — the higher the degree of exclusivity, the higher the degree of probable directness. Consider, for instance, a classroom full of students. If Elbert comes to school one day with his hair parted on the left instead of the right, he may have been influenced by Albert, who also parts his hair on the left. This reflects a low degree of exclusivity because Elbert might have been influenced by other students with the same hair style. However, if Elbert shows up wearing his hair parted on the left, a blue and yellow striped long-sleeve cotton tee-shirt, a brown leather vest, oversized khaki cargo pants, and black athletic shoes with neon orange laces — an ensemble also worn by Albert, but no other students — then it is highly likely that Elbert was influenced by Albert, either intentionally or as an unconscious result of having spent a lot of time together.[23] This situation reflects a high degree of exclusivity in the relationship because it is unlikely that the influence for such an extensive combination of parallel items came from anyone but Albert.

The example of Albert and Elbert suggests that exclusivity may be indicated in two significant ways. First, since the same ensemble is not worn by any other students, the likelihood that Elbert was influenced by anyone other than Albert diminishes due to the lack of other potential influences. This suggests that exclusivity may be evaluated by measuring the degree of rarity, or how frequently the parallel elements occur in other known

23. For the sake of illustration, it is assumed here that the ensemble originated with Albert rather than Elbert.

sources.[24] In the case of literary parallels, the appearance of the same word
or phrase in two documents reflects a low degree of exclusivity if the word
or phrase occurs frequently in the literature of the period and could have
come from other influences. If, however, the word or phrase is not found
anywhere else in contemporary writings, the degree of exclusivity is quite
high, thus indicating a stronger likelihood of a direct connection between
the two documents.

Second, since the likelihood of exclusive influence upon Elbert by
Albert increases with greater correspondence of parallel items, exclusivity
may also be evaluated by measuring the degree of correspondence evident
between the parallel elements. At the lowest level of individual parallels,
this is reflected in how closely the parallel elements resemble one another.
In Albert's and Elbert's case, the low-level parallels are formed between
the individual pieces of their respective ensembles. For example, the hair
styles form one parallel, the shirts form another parallel, the vests form yet
another parallel, and so on. The case involving Albert and Elbert further
illustrates that correspondence is also evident in common combinations
of lower-level parallel elements. Since both Albert and Elbert exhibit the
same combinations of low-level parallels, their shared ensembles form
another higher-level parallel. Whereas low-level (i.e., low-order) parallels
are formed by individual elements that are held in common, higher-level
(i.e., higher-order) parallels are formed by common combinations of lower-
order parallels. More extensive combinations of parallel elements indicate
higher degrees of exclusivity in the relationship because the likelihood of
influence from elsewhere diminishes. This suggests that exclusivity may be
evaluated by measuring the degree of correspondence evident, not only in

24. Examples of works that advocate rarity of language, form, or concepts
as indicators of literary dependence include: W. K. Lowther Clarke, ed., *The First
Epistle of Clement to the Corinthians* (London: Society for Promoting Christian
Knowledge, 1937), 35; Hagner, *Use of the Old and New Testaments*, 31, 223, 226,
244; Johannes Kahmann, "The Second Letter of Peter and the Letter of Jude: Their
Mutual Relationship," in *The New Testament in Early Christianity: La réception des
écrits néotestamentaires dans le christianisme primitif*, ed. Jean-Marie Sevrin, BETL
86 (Leuven: Peeters & Leuven University Press, 1989), 106; Leonard, "Identifying
Allusions," 251–52; Robert J. Miller, "Is There Independent Attestation for the Trans-
figuration in 2 Peter?" *NTS* 42 (1996): 623–24; C. Leslie Mitton, *The Epistle to the
Ephesians: Its Authorship, Origin and Purpose* (Oxford: Clarendon, 1951), 179–84;
Thompson, *Clothed with Christ*, 31–37; J. W. C. Wand, ed., *The General Epistles of
St. Peter and St. Jude*, WC (London: Methuen & Co. Ltd., 1934), 24–25; Ben With-
erington, III, "The Influence of Galatians on Hebrews," *NTS* 37 (1991): 146, 148.

individual low-order parallels, but also in complex higher-order parallels that are formed by combinations of lower-order parallels. Examples of such complex higher-order literary parallels may include common clusters of parallel words, phrases, or paragraphs.[25] Other examples include common sequences of parallel injunctions or common lists of parallel exempla.[26] It is even possible to find higher-order parallels formed by common rhetorical frameworks that appear in both documents.[27]

Exclusivity appears to be an ideal indicator, not only because it meets the requirement for literary dependence, but also because it is compatible with literary parallels. While the requirement for demonstrating literary dependence is met because of the correlation with *directness*, compatibility with literary parallels derives from the fact that a measure of exclusivity is reflected in both the rarity of individual parallel elements and the degree of correspondence between parallel elements at all levels. Evidence of this type is readily available for intertextual parallels. Thus rarity of occurrence and correspondence of parallel elements provide the necessary evidence for literary dependence. The next question, then, is how can the overall likelihood of literary dependence be determined from such evidence?

25. Common clusters of terms are viewed as indicators of direct literary relationships by Albert E. Barnett, *Paul Becomes a Literary Influence* (Chicago, IL: The University of Chicago Press, 1941), 65–66; Berding, *Polycarp and Paul*, 150–51; Gilmour, *Significance of Parallels*, 52, 90; O'Day, "Jeremiah 9.22–23 and 1 Corinthians 1.26–31," 264–66.

26. The following works highlight common combinations or sequences of parallel elements as evidence of literary dependence: Gilmour, *Significance of Parallels*, 52; Mark S. Goodacre, *The Case Against Q: Studies in Markan Priority and the Synoptic Problem* (Harrisburg, PA: Trinity Press International, 2002), 156–58; Hagner, *Use of the Old and New Testaments*, 184, 188, 197; Werner Georg Kümmel, *Introduction to the New Testament*, rev. ed., trans. Howard Clark Kee (Nashville, TN: Abingdon, 1975), 359, 431; Andrew T. Lincoln, *Ephesians*, WBC 42 (Dallas, TX: Word Books, 1990), xlvii–l; O'Day, "Jeremiah 9.22–23 and 1 Corinthians 1.26–31," 264; Robert H. Stein, *The Synoptic Problem: An Introduction* (Grand Rapids, MI: Baker Books, 1987), 29–42.

27. Examples of studies that look for common rhetorical frameworks as evidence of a direct relationship include: Goodacre, *Case Against Q*, 72, 112; O'Day, "Jeremiah 9.22–23 and 1 Corinthians 1.26–31," 266; Hagner, *Use of the Old and New Testaments*, 188–89, 216–17; Witherington, "Influence," 150.

Probability and the Question of Likelihood

Questions of likelihood concerning a wide range of phenomena have been raised by curious minds for centuries. Whether the goal of the inquisitor is to win at a game of chance or to model a naturally occurring event for medical research, many questions find plausible answers through the use of probability theory. Probability is a branch of mathematics that focuses on analysis of random phenomena, with the basic idea that, over a large number of repeated trials, the outcomes of the trials exhibit a pattern that can be analyzed and predicted. The likelihood of a particular outcome is a function of all possible outcomes. In effect, probability offers an analytical way of discovering and characterizing patterns of order that occur in the world. The theory has its roots in the seventeenth century as French mathematicians Blaise Pascal and Pierre de Fermat set out to analyze and predict games of chance. The basic theory has since developed into more complex concepts that have found applications in many diverse fields of study involving biological, physical, and social phenomena.

While probability has proved to be a fundamental tool in advanced scientific disciplines such as modern genetics and quantum mechanics, applications also abound in common facets of life. For example, insurance companies use probability to analyze lifetime expectancies and accident occurrence rates in order to set insurance premiums and benefits in such a way that will increase the likelihood of long-term profitability. Other useful applications are found in enterprises such as popular opinion polling, rainfall pattern analysis and prediction, information theory, professional gambling, and systems engineering, to name a few. Probability has also been applied to questions of theology and Christian apologetics. An interesting example is found in *The Existence of God* by British philosopher and Christian apologist, Richard Swinburne.[28] In this influential work, Swinburne employs probability, and in particular a probability theorem developed by theologian and mathematician Thomas Bayes (1702–1761), to make a compelling argument for the existence of God. An earlier work that powerfully demonstrates the use of probability regarding the question of faith is Pascal's famous "Wager."[29] Displaying a spirituality that has been described as "an interesting combination of the logic of the professional

---

28. Richard Swinburne, *The Existence of God*, 2nd ed. (New York: Oxford University Press, 2004, first published 1979).

29. Pascal *Pensées* 3.233.

mathematician and the mysticism of a man who had a personal encounter with Christ in 1654,"[30] Pascal analyzes the risk and benefit of wagering one's life on the Christian faith. The argument employs probability along with notions of infinity and finitude to present a compelling case for making the wager. According to Pascal's probability analysis, there is everything to gain and nothing to lose. Although this discussion only scratches the surface of the many ways in which probability has been used to explore questions of likelihood, the noted examples are sufficient to show that it has been widely applied with useful results.

The notion of probability is also not foreign to NT studies. Indeed, questions of likelihood lie at the heart of all studies that attempt to reconstruct or understand historical events or artifacts based on limited available evidence. In the absence of absolute certainty, conclusions must be based on what is deemed to be most likely. The field of New Testament Studies is no exception. For example, tasks of textual criticism seek to identify readings that are most likely to represent the original NT texts; tasks of interpretation seek to discern the meanings most likely intended by the NT authors; and tasks of intertextual studies seek to discern the most likely nature of relationships between ancient texts. All likelihood assessments are based on underlying criteria, which may be subjective or objective. In many published studies of perceived parallels between NT texts, the criteria are largely subjective in that conclusions are based on personal judgments regarding what qualifies as a "parallel," what constitutes evidence of literary dependence, and how to weigh the significance of the evidence. Accordingly, such studies may be rightly characterized as subjective assessments of likelihood. In effect, they are subjective probability analyses. Thus there is a well-established precedent in NT studies for addressing the question of literary dependence as a probability assessment. Due to the subjective nature of such preceding probability assessments, however, the methods employed have been prone to inconsistent and inconclusive results.

In the interest of generating consistent and reliable results, the methodology presented in this chapter prefers a more objective approach to assessing the likelihood of literary dependence. Although some aspects of assessment are necessarily subjective, the overall framework of probability theory provides an objective means of composite analysis. Therefore, the assessment methodology is developed within the objective framework of

30. John R. Tyson, ed., "Blaise Pascal (1623–62)," in *Invitation to Christian Spirituality: An Ecumenical Anthology* (New York: Oxford University Press, 1999), 293.

probability theory, a well-established branch of mathematics that has been applied fruitfully in numerous and diverse fields of study. Probability, in fact, is ideally suited to the phenomena of intertextual parallels because the probability of literary dependence can be derived directly from evidence observed in the parallel texts.

Probability of Literary Dependence

Within the conceptual framework described above, the assessment methodology takes shape by structuring the task as a probability analysis. Since a direct literary relationship between two documents can be established with just one direct-connect parallel, *the objective of the methodology is to determine the overall probability that at least one of the parallels derives from a direct literary connection based on evidence of directness found in the collection of parallels.* As explained earlier, evidence of directness is found in rarity of occurrence and the degree of correspondence between intertextual parallels. Hence the application of probability theory focuses on determining the overall probability of directness based on such evidence.

The Basic Probability Calculation

Since the task at hand requires that the overall probability of a direct literary connection be derived from the evidence observed in individual parallels, the analysis method must provide a way to calculate the overall probability using only the evidence gleaned from all the parallels. This is accomplished through a multi-step calculation that proceeds from evidence of directness exhibited by individual parallels to the probability of literary dependence at the whole document level, as shown in figure 1.2.

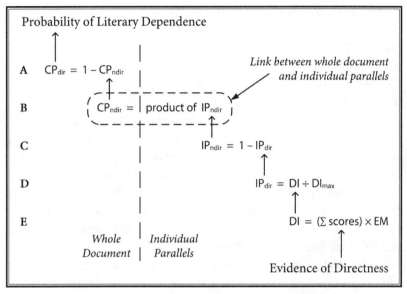

Probability of Literary Dependence

A $\quad CP_{dir} = 1 - CP_{ndir}$

$\quad$ *Link between whole document and individual parallels*

B $\quad CP_{ndir} =$ product of IP_{ndir}

C $\quad IP_{ndir} = 1 - IP_{dir}$

D $\quad IP_{dir} = DI \div DI_{max}$

E $\quad DI = (\Sigma \text{ scores}) \times EM$

Whole Document | *Individual Parallels*

Evidence of Directness

FIGURE 1.2. Calculation of the probability of literary dependence

Given the primary objective, the ultimate parameter of interest is the overall probability that at least one of the parallels derives from a direct literary connection between the two documents. This is the collective probability of directness, denoted as CP_{dir}.[31] The term CP_{dir} is a number between zero and one that represents the probability of directness over the entire collection of parallels. The event that at least one of the parallels is direct is the same as the event that *not all* of the parallels are non-direct. Accordingly, the complement is the event that *all* of the parallels are non-direct. This is denoted as CP_{ndir}. Since the probability of an event is equal to one minus the probability of its complement, $CP_{dir} = 1 - CP_{ndir}$ (figure 1.2, line A).[32]

Recognition of the complement relationship is essential to the analysis because it provides a link between the overall probability of directness at the whole document level and the evidence of directness exhibited by

31. Parameter nomenclature is defined as follows: "CP" = Collective Probability; "IP" = Individual Probability; "DI" = Directness Index; "EM" = Extent Multiplier; and the subscript indicates the event of interest (dir = direct; ndir = non direct; max = maximum).

32. The probability rule of subtraction for complements states that the probability that a certain event *will* occur is equal to one minus the probability that the same event *will not* occur.

individual parallels. This is because CP_{ndir} can be calculated directly from the probabilities of non-directness associated with all of the individual parallels. The term IP_{ndir} denotes the probability that an individual parallel is non-direct in that it derives from non-direct influences. The probability that *all* of the parallels are non-direct is equal to the product of IP_{ndir} for all the parallels (line B).[33] Thus the link between the probability calculation at the whole document level and the probability calculations for individual parallels is made through the complement *non-direct* probabilities. In order to link this to the probability of directness exhibited by individual parallels, the complement relationship is reapplied, only in the reverse direction. The event that a parallel is non-direct is the same as the event that it is *not* direct, the complement of which is that it *is* direct. Thus $IP_{ndir} = 1 - IP_{dir}$, where IP_{dir} denotes the probability that an individual parallel *is* direct in that it derives from a direct influence (line C).[34]

The link to specific evidence of directness is made by defining IP_{dir} as a function of the scores associated with the indicators of directness. This is done through the use of a "Directness Index," denoted DI, which represents the degree of directness for an individual parallel. The DI is equal to the sum of the scores for rarity of occurrence and degree of correspondence, multiplied by an extent multiplier, which accounts for the length of the parallel (line E). The extent multiplier, denoted as EM, is defined below. Specific criteria for assigning scores for the DI are explained in the section, "Scoring Scheme," which follows later in this chapter. The DI is converted to a representative probability value between zero and one by dividing by the maximum possible value, DI_{max} (line D). The resulting value, IP_{dir}, represents the probability of directness for an individual parallel.

Using this method of analysis, the probability of literary dependence between two documents can be computed from the evidence of directness exhibited by all the parallels. The probability of a direct relationship is represented by CP_{dir} over the entire set of intertextual parallels, each of which has a DI value based on observed evidence.

---

33. The probability rule of multiplication for independent events states that the probability that events A and B both occur is equal to the probability that event A occurs times the probability that event B occurs.

34. Berding employs a similar method of computing the probability of literary dependence as a way of demonstrating the cumulative effect of many parallels (*Polycarp and Paul*, 203–4).

Extent Multiplier

The extent multiplier (EM) accounts for the quantity of material involved in a parallel. Since parallels can be based on a solitary word, a combination of words, a sentence, a paragraph, a chapter, or even an entire document, the extent of the parallel text is an important consideration when assessing the overall strength of directness evidence. A high degree of correspondence over a long string of words is more significant than a similarly high degree of correspondence over a short string of words.[35] For this reason, an extent multiplier is applied to the points awarded for all correspondence indicators. The same multiplier is also applied to the points given for rarity of occurrence, but for a different reason. For the purpose of evaluating exclusivity in a parallel relationship, the rarity of a large parallel is not necessarily more significant than a similarly rare small parallel. However, the possibility that parallel texts simply reflect independent use of common vocabulary is probably greater for smaller parallels than for larger parallels. In order to reduce the risk that the authors' possible independent use of common vocabulary artificially inflates the outcome of the analysis in favor of literary dependence, the extent multiplier is also applied to the points awarded for rarity of occurrence.

The extent of a parallel element is defined as the shortest string of basic units that is needed to convey the thought of the parallel element. Basic units are understood as the individual components that constitute the parallel material. For low-order parallels, the basic units are the individual words that make up the parallel expressions. For higher-order parallels, the basic units are the individual low-order parallels that combine to form the parallel clusters. The extent of a parallel element is determined simply by counting the number of basic units in each parallel element and selecting the smaller of the two counts.

The extent multiplier is a number between zero and one that is used to adjust the Directness Index (DI) to be linearly proportional to the extent of the parallel.[36] It is defined as the extent of the parallel (#units) divided

---

35. That more extensive parallels offer stronger evidence of a literary relationship is noted by Gilmour, *Significance of Parallels*, 52, 83, 90; Leonard, "Identifying Allusions," 252–53; Lincoln, *Ephesians*, lv.

36. The main question behind definition of the extent multiplier concerns how the relationship between the extent of the parallel and the strength of directness evidence changes from shorter to longer parallels. If the strength of directness

by the extent range ($\#\text{units}_{max}$). Only parallels whose lengths extend to the high end of the range have a multiplier equal to one and receive full credit for their directness scores. The upper limit of the extent range should be set at a value for which a verbatim parallel of that length would commonly be viewed as evidence of a direct literary relationship. A couple of biblical examples suggest a wide range of possible values for the upper limit of the extent range.

At the low end is the parallel between Eph 6:21–22 and Col 4:7–8, which may be the only NT || NT parallel outside of the Synoptic Gospels that is generally viewed as having derived from a direct literary relationship. The parallel involves thirty-two verbatim words, with the addition of τί πράσσω ("what I am doing") in Eph 6:21 and καὶ σύνδουλος ("and fellow servant") in Col 4:7. Although there is a difference of opinion among scholars regarding who borrowed from whom, a direct literary connection is commonly acknowledged.[37] Even Ernest Best, who attributes the similarities between these two letters to indirect non-literary influences of a common Pauline tradition, concedes, "Yet so far as Eph 6.21–22 and Col 4.7–8 go, one author must have copied from what the other wrote for the possibility of so many words appearing in the same order by chance is too great to be considered a coincidence."[38] Best further adds that "[t]he hypothesis however that one author carried the wording of the other's letter in his mind [memory] and used it as appropriate does not deal with Eph 6.21–22 and Col 4.7–8."[39] C. Leslie Mitton also notes the exceptional nature of the parallel. For Ephesians and Colossians in general, he asserts that

---

evidence rises more sharply at the short end of the extent range, then a logarithmic function might be appropriate. If the strength of directness evidence rises more sharply at the long end of the extent range, then an exponential function might be appropriate. If there is no discernible change in the extent-strength relationship across the entire extent range, then a linear function is probably best. The default position established for this project is that all things are valued equally unless there is a compelling reason to do otherwise. At the present time, there is insufficient data to justify any one of these approaches over the other two. Therefore, a simple linear function is adopted because it best represents the default position by maintaining a constant extent-strength relationship across the entire extent range.

37. So, e.g., Harold W. Hoehner, *Ephesians: An Exegetical Commentary* (Grand Rapids, MI: Baker Academic, 2002), 867–68; Lincoln, *Ephesians*, lv.

38. Ernest Best, "Who Used Whom? The Relationship of Ephesians and Colossians," *NTS* 43, no. 1 (January 1997): 92.

39. Best, "Who Used Whom?" 93.

"[t]he almost entire lack of identical repetition suggests that the similarities are not of the kind we should anticipate if they were the result of one author copying another document open in front of him."[40] Nevertheless, Mitton highlights the exact correspondence found in Eph 6:21–22 and Col 4:7–8 as "an outstanding exception," which "almost suggests that the writer at this point, at any rate, referred to his copy, to make sure that he reproduced it exactly."[41] Given the broad support for this parallel as having derived from a direct literary relationship, it seems that the upper limit of the extent range, #units$_{max}$, might reasonably be set to thirty-two, based on the number of verbatim words in the parallel between Eph 6:21–22 and Col 4:7–8. This, however, does not account for the possibility that scholarly assessment of this parallel is influenced by the presence of many other parallels between Ephesians and Colossians. For this reason, the upper limit of the extent range should be greater than thirty-two.

At the high end of the range of possible values for the upper limit are the parallel Hezekiah narratives found in 4 Kgdms 18:13 — 20:19 LXX (2 Kgs 18:13 — 20:19 English) and Isaiah 36–39 LXX. Although there are differences, the vast extent of verbal similarity leaves no doubt that one of the authors directly leveraged the work of the other document. Since these parallel Greek texts extend for nearly 2,000 words (1,982 in 4 Kingdoms and 1,938 in Isaiah), it is reasonable to assume that setting the upper limit of the extent range to 2,000 would be more than adequate. Thus the value for #units$_{max}$ should be set somewhere between thirty-two and 2,000.

In order to select an appropriate value in the range 32–2,000, it is helpful to consider the length of NT texts that scholars commonly have attributed to the use of a pre-existing source. This includes passages that are believed to reflect early Christian hymns or creeds. According to Richard Longenecker, the most obvious and widely acknowledged early Christian hymns and confessional statements are the passages listed in table 1.1.[42]

The rightmost column of table 1.1 shows the number of Greek words that constitute each of the passages. The data indicates that the length of passages that scholars commonly attribute to sources which pre-date the NT writings ranges from 23 to 112 Greek words. Despite that fact that the

40. Mitton, *Ephesians: Its Authorship, Origin and Purpose*, 58.

41. Mitton, *Ephesians: Its Authorship, Origin and Purpose*, 59.

42. Richard N. Longenecker, "Christological Materials in the Early Christian Communities," in *Contours of Christology in the New Testament*, ed. Richard N. Longenecker (Grand Rapids, MI: Eerdmans, 2005), 71.

underlying sources are only hypothesized, this shows that a NT passage as short as twenty-three words can be understood by scholars as having been borrowed from another source. In fact, five of the twelve hymns are shorter than the parallel between Eph 6:21–22 and Col 4:7–8, and five other hymns are less than two times the length of Eph 6:21–22 ‖ Col 4:7–8. Only two of the hymns have lengths greater than two times the length of Eph 6:21–22 ‖ Col 4:7–8.

TABLE 1.1. Length of NT hymns/creeds

No.	Reference	Number of Words
1	1 Pet 2:22–23	23
2	1 Tim 3:16b	26
3	Rom 1:3b–4	28
4	Gal 4:4–5	28
5	Heb 1:3	30
6	1 Cor 15:3b–5	38
7	Gal 3:26–28	41
8	Rom 11:33–36	53
9	Rom 3:24–26	61
10	Rev 15:3b–4	63
11	Phil 2:6–11	76
12	Col 1:15–20	112

The data in table 1.1 suggests that an appropriate value for $\text{\#units}_{max}$ is much closer to thirty-two than to 2,000, and it probably falls within the range exhibited by the hymns in table 1.1. Since the theological content of these passages contributes to their characterization as leveraged hymns, it is best to set $\text{\#units}_{max}$ at the high end of that range. Therefore, $\text{\#units}_{max}$ is set at 112, the number of Greek words in Col 1:15–20. This is 3.5 times longer than the parallel between Eph 6:21–22 and Col 4:7–8. With the upper limit set at 112, the extent multiplier (EM) is defined as the extent of the parallel (#units) divided by 112.

$$\text{EM} = \frac{\text{\#units}}{\text{\#units}_{max}} = \frac{\text{\#units}}{112}$$

This means that a perfect CP_{dir} value of 1.0 is achievable only if there is a single verbatim parallel that is at least 112 words long and earns the highest possible scores for all the directness indicators. Given the unlikelihood of a 112-word verbatim parallel occurring between NT books, setting the upper limit of the extent range at this value ensures that a high probability of directness can be achieved only with cumulative evidence.[43]

An Illustrative Example

A simple hypothetical example illustrates how the method described above may be used to assess the probability of literary dependence from intertextual parallels. For the purpose of illustrating the basic approach, the indicator scores for each parallel are provided in appendix A rather than in the following discussion. Here it is sufficient simply to observe the DI and the probability calculations. The scores for all the parallels are produced by the scoring scheme that is described in the next section.

Intermediate Calculations
$EM = \#units \div \#units_{max}$
$DI = (\Sigma\ scores) \times EM$
$IP_{dir} = DI \div DI_{max}$
$IP_{ndir} = 1 - IP_{dir}$
$CP_{ndir} = $ product of IP_{ndir}
$CP_{dir} = 1 - CP_{ndir}$

43. The cumulative force of evidence concerning intertextual parallels is well noted by Berding, *Polycarp and Paul*, 203; Michael A. Fishbane, *Biblical Interpretation in Ancient Israel* (New York: Oxford University Press, 1985), 291; Gilmour, *Significance of Parallels*, 56; Andrew F. Gregory, "1 Clement and the Writings That Later Formed the New Testament," in *The Reception of the New Testament in the Apostolic Fathers*, ed. Andrew F. Gregory and Christopher M. Tuckett (Oxford: Oxford University Press, 2005), 151; Hagner, *Use of the Old and New Testaments*, 192–94; Hartog, *Polycarp and the New Testament*, 174; Hays, *Echoes of Scripture*, 30; Kahmann, "Second Peter and Jude," 105; Koch, *Schrift als Zeuge*, 13; Leonard, "Identifying Allusions," 253–55.

To begin the illustration, consider two hypothetical documents that contain three pairs of parallel words that rarely occur in contemporary writings. These parallels are listed in table 1.2.

TABLE 1.2. Probability of directness (3 parallels)

No.	Parallel	Individual			Collective	
		DI	IP_{dir}	IP_{ndir}	CP_{ndir}	CP_{dir}
					1	0
1	word 1	0.125	0.005	0.995	0.995	0.005
2	word 2	0.107	0.004	0.996	0.990	0.010
3	word 3	0.080	0.003	0.997	0.987	0.013

In this simple case, the single-word parallels exhibit various degrees of rarity as well as correspondence in form, meaning, and function. The collective probability of directness, CP_{dir}, begins at zero and increases with each successive parallel that is included in the analysis. The result after analysis of these three short parallels is a CP_{dir} value of only 0.013.

Next, consider the effect of adding three rare parallel phrases which vary in degree of lexical-grammatical correspondence but reflect the same basic meanings and functions.

TABLE 1.3. Probability of directness (6 parallels)

No.	Parallel	Individual			Collective	
		DI	IP_{dir}	IP_{ndir}	CP_{ndir}	CP_{dir}
4	phrase 1	0.777	0.032	0.968	0.955	0.045
5	phrase 2	0.371	0.015	0.985	0.940	0.060
6	phrase 3	0.843	0.035	0.965	0.907	0.093

Based only on the six short parallels listed in tables 1.2 and 1.3, the collective probability of directness between these two hypothetical documents is only 0.093. The likelihood of a direct relationship becomes more probable when three longer clause parallels are included. These parallel clauses exhibit only partial correspondence, and they are somewhat rare in writings of the time period. As shown in table 1.4, with the addition of these three clauses, the value of CP_{dir} rises to 0.288.

TABLE 1.4. Probability of directness (9 parallels)

No.	Parallel	Individual			Collective	
		DI	IP_{dir}	IP_{ndir}	CP_{ndir}	CP_{dir}
7	clause 1	1.518	0.063	0.937	0.850	0.150
8	clause 2	2.057	0.086	0.914	0.777	0.223
9	clause 3	2.000	0.083	0.917	0.712	0.288

Now three additional longer complex-clause parallels may be included in the analysis. These longer parallels are very rare and convey the same basic thoughts. The respective functions, however, are modified, and there is only partial lexical-grammatical correspondence.

TABLE 1.5. Probability of directness (12 parallels)

No.	Parallel	Individual			Collective	
		DI	IP_{dir}	IP_{ndir}	CP_{ndir}	CP_{dir}
10	comp-clause 1	5.234	0.218	0.782	0.557	0.443
11	comp-clause 2	4.942	0.206	0.794	0.442	0.558
12	comp-clause 3	5.089	0.212	0.788	0.349	0.651

With the additional complex-clause parallels, the CP_{dir} value increases to 0.651 (see table 1.5). At this point in the analysis, it is more likely than not that one of these documents is literarily dependent upon the other.

Confidence in such a conclusion rises when higher-order parallels are considered. In this particular case, there are two higher-order parallels, cluster 1 (#13) and cluster 2 (#14), which are formed by combinations of lower-order parallels. The three clause parallels (#7, 8, 9) appear together in parallel cluster 1, but not in the same order. The three complex-clause parallels (#10, 11, 12) appear together in the same order in cluster 2. The three phrase parallels (#4, 5, 6) also are involved in higher-order clusters, but the parallel elements are members of different clusters. The three single-word parallels exhibit a variety of affiliations. Neither of the instances of word 3 (#3) are part of higher-order clusters, one of the instances of word 1 (#1) belongs to a cluster, and both instances of word 2 (#2) are members of different clusters. The effect of the two additional higher-order parallels and the membership affiliations of the lower-order parallels is seen in the

Directness Index (DI) and the collective probability calculations for each successive parallel in table 1.6.

TABLE 1.6. Probability of directness (14 parallels)

No.	Parallel	Individual			Collective	
		DI	IP_{dir}	IP_{ndir}	CP_{ndir}	CP_{dir}
					1	0
1	word 1	0.134	0.006	0.994	0.994	0.006
2	word 2	0.125	0.005	0.995	0.989	0.011
3	word 3	0.080	0.003	0.997	0.986	0.014
4	phrase 1	0.884	0.037	0.963	0.950	0.050
5	phrase 2	0.424	0.018	0.982	0.933	0.067
6	phrase 3	0.986	0.041	0.959	0.895	0.105
7	clause 1	1.920	0.080	0.920	0.823	0.177
8	clause 2	2.512	0.105	0.895	0.737	0.263
9	clause 3	2.643	0.110	0.890	0.656	0.344
10	comp-clause 1	6.484	0.270	0.730	0.479	0.521
11	comp-clause 2	6.406	0.267	0.733	0.351	0.649
12	comp-clause 3	6.446	0.269	0.731	0.257	0.743
13	cluster 1	0.241	0.010	0.990	0.254	0.746
14	cluster 2	0.375	0.016	0.984	0.250	0.750

Consideration of higher-order parallels raises the CP_{dir} value from 0.651 to 0.750. The higher probability arises not only from the addition of two cluster parallels (#13 and #14), but also from the higher DI values reflected in all the parallels that hold some degree of membership in the two cluster parallels. As a result, the probability of directness is fairly high, and it is reasonable to conclude that these hypothetical documents are more likely than not to be related through direct literary dependence.

As demonstrated by this simple example, the likelihood of literary dependence can be addressed objectively using a systematic approach to the phenomena of parallels. Having illustrated the basic probability analysis process with this hypothetical example, attention now turns to the matter of specifying how the necessary data is extracted from individual parallels.

Scoring Scheme

The data required for the probability analysis is derived from intertextual parallels by assigning for each parallel a score that represents the directness of the relationship between its parallel elements. As explained earlier, the degree of directness is based on evidence of exclusivity as reflected in the rarity of individual parallel elements and the degree of correspondence between parallel elements. Accordingly, the scoring scheme is designed to produce a relative quantitative measure for degree of directness as indicated by these types of evidences. This is accomplished by identifying relevant criteria for delineating strength of evidence associated with specific indicators of directness.

Specific Indicators of Directness

Rarity of Occurrence

Rarity of occurrence concerns the degree to which the parallel material is found in other sources, with the idea that other occurrences diminish the probability of an exclusive relationship. The strength of the evidence is inversely proportional to the number of occurrences found in broader literature. As the number of other occurrences increases, the degree of rarity decreases. Conversely, as the number of other occurrences decreases, the degree of rarity increases. This inverse relationship can be represented by a simple ratio between the number of occurrences found in the two documents of interest (#occur_parallel-docs) and the number found in other literature (#occur_other-lit):

$$\frac{\#occur\_parallel\text{-}docs}{\#occur\_other\text{-}lit}$$

If there are no other occurrences of the parallel item outside of the two parallel documents, this expression would result in an illegal operation that attempts to divide by zero. The problem is avoided by including the value for #occur_parallel-docs in the denominator:

$$\frac{\text{\#occur\_parallel-docs}}{\text{\#occur\_parallel-docs + \#occur\_other-lit}}$$

With this basic formula, the maximum value of 1 is produced when the item of interest occurs only in the two parallel documents of interest:

$$\frac{\text{\#occur\_parallel-docs}}{\text{\#occur\_parallel-docs + 0}} = 1$$

The ratio of occurrences decreases toward the minimum value of 0 when the item of interest is so common in other bodies of literature that the total number of occurrences approaches infinity (∞):

$$\frac{\text{\#occur\_parallel-docs}}{\text{\#occur\_parallel-docs} + \infty} \approx 0$$

Intermediate values result when the number of occurrences found in other literature is between 0 and infinity. For example, if a parallel word occurs once in each of the two parallel documents and six times in other writings, the ratio is:

$$\frac{2}{2+6} = 0.25$$

This simple ratio is the basic component of the scoring scheme for rarity of occurrence. Application to the present task is accomplished by defining "# of occurrences" and "other literature" in such a way that the result is representative of the overall rarity of the parallel item within a designated range of literature.

The number of occurrences is defined by two key factors. First, since the rarity of a parallel item between two documents is a function of how frequently the item of interest occurs in other documents, the focus is on occurrences *outside* of the two parallel documents of interest. Multiple *internal* occurrences of the item do not affect the rarity of the item in the broader range of literature; therefore, additional occurrences within one or both of the two parallel documents are not included in the number of occurrences. Second, since the relevant literature for this project includes bodies of literature that contain works by different authors, rarity is based on both the total number of occurrences in a particular body of literature as well as the distribution of those occurrences across the different works contained within that body of literature. Thus, for a particular body of literature, the rarity score includes two components. The first component assesses rarity in terms of the total number of occurrences of the item in an identified body of literature (#occur). The second component assesses rarity in terms of the number of separate works that contain the parallel item within that body of literature (#works):

$$rarity\_body = \#occur\_score + \#works\_score$$

$$= \frac{\#occur\_parallel\text{-}docs}{\#occur\_parallel\text{-}docs + \#occur\_other\text{-}lit} + \frac{\#works\_parallel\text{-}docs}{\#works\_parallel\text{-}docs + \#works\_other\text{-}lit}$$

With this two-part formula, the maximum rarity value associated with a given body of literature (rarity_body) is $1 + 1 = 2$. Since the objective is to assess rarity of a parallel within the broadest scope of literature identified for the assessment, the two-part formula is applied for each body of literature that is included in the broader scope. The total number of points for rarity of the parallel within the base of broader literature is equal to the sum of the two-part formulas for each constituent body of literature:

$$Total\ Rarity\ Points = \sum rarity\_body$$

The scope of writings relevant for a study involving parallels between NT documents includes the major bodies of Greek literature that might have been in circulation when the NT documents were written. In order to allow for the possibility that some NT books might have been written pseudonymously sometime after the death of the original apostles of Jesus Christ, the present methodology recognizes works that can be shown to have originated as late as the first half of the second century as relevant for the study. This includes seven main bodies of Greek literature: the NT, the LXX, the works of Philo, the works of Josephus, the OT Pseudepigrapha, the writings of the Apostolic Fathers, and Greco-Roman literature.[44] It might be argued that the body of literature commonly known as the NT Apocrypha and Pseudepigrapha also applies. Most of these documents, however, appear to be from a later time period, some even as late as the Middle Ages.[45] In recent years some scholars have argued that certain extra-canonical gospels may have originated in the first century (e.g., *Gospel of Peter*); however, the supporting evidence is debatable.[46] Until these extra-canonical works can be shown to have originated prior to the mid-second century, they should not be included in the rarity assessments of NT || NT parallels. Therefore, the formula for rarity in the relevant broader scope of literature has seven parts, each of which has two components of rarity as defined above:

$$
\begin{aligned}
\text{Total Rarity Points} = \ & \text{rarity\_NT} + \text{rarity\_LXX} + \text{rarity\_Philo} + \\
& \text{rarity\_Josephus} + \text{rarity\_OTPseud.} + \\
& \text{rarity\_AF} + \text{rarity\_G-R}
\end{aligned}
$$

The seven major bodies of literature are weighted according to the number of works in each body. For weighting purposes, the number of works equals the number included in BibleWorks for the NT, the LXX, Philo, Josephus, the Pseudepigrapha, and the Apostolic Fathers. For Greco-Roman writings, the number of works is an estimate derived from the list found in Craig Evans's, *Ancient Texts*, prorated to account for the many

---

44. For an excellent overview of the relevant literature, see Craig A. Evans, *Ancient Texts for New Testament Studies: A Guide to the Background Literature* (Peabody, MA: Hendrickson, 2005).

45. Evans, *Ancient Texts*, 257.

46. Evans, *Ancient Texts*, 260–61.

works that survive only in small fragments.[47] The result is an estimated number of Greco-Roman writings that is approximately equal to the sum of works in all six of the other relevant bodies of literature. Accordingly, relative weights are assigned to the seven bodies of literature as follows: 0.05 NT, 0.12 LXX, 0.08 Philo, 0.01 Josephus, 0.15 OT Pseudepigrapha, 0.08 Apostolic Fathers, and 0.51 Greco-Roman literature. The weighted sum of rarity points is equal to the sum of the weighted rarity_body scores:

$$
\begin{aligned}
\text{Weighted Sum} = \ & 0.05 \, (\text{rarity\_NT}) + 0.12 \, (\text{rarity\_LXX}) + \\
& 0.08 \, (\text{rarity\_Philo}) + 0.01 \, (\text{rarity\_Josephus}) + \\
& 0.15 \, (\text{rarity\_OTPseud.}) + 0.08 \, (\text{rarity\_AF}) + \\
& 0.51 \, (\text{rarity\_G-R})
\end{aligned}
$$

With this weighting scheme, the maximum number of points possible for rarity of occurrence is achieved when each of the seven bodies of literature receives the maximum score of 2. In that case, the maximum weighted sum also is equal to 2:

$$
\begin{aligned}
\text{Weighted Sum}_{max} = \ & 0.05 \, (2) + 0.12 \, (2) + 0.08 \, (2) + 0.01 \, (2) + \\
& 0.15 \, (2) + 0.08 \, (2) + 0.51 \, (2) \\
= \ & 2
\end{aligned}
$$

Finally, the total number of points for rarity of occurrence is converted to a relative score that can be used in the analysis. This is done by normalizing it to a ten-point scale (i.e., multiplying by 5):

$$
\text{Total Rarity Score} = 5 \, (\text{Weighted Sum})
$$

By using the scoring scheme defined above, the rarity of a parallel is indicated by a number that represents the parallel item as a proportion of all the occurrences found in other relevant bodies of literature. Parallels that

47. Evans, *Ancient Texts*, 287–98.

are highly conceptual in nature or too complex to permit comprehensive searches earn the default rarity score of zero.

The method for scoring rarity of occurrence is illustrated with the two examples shown in tables 1.7 and 1.8, each of which involves a single-word parallel between Hebrews and 1 Peter. Since exhaustive electronic searches of Greco-Roman literature are rather cumbersome at this point in time, for the purpose of illustration, tables 1.7 and 1.8 reflect the worst-case and best-case scenarios, respectively, for rarity of occurrence in Greco-Roman literature.

TABLE 1.7. Rarity of occurrence: ἀμίαντος ("undefiled," worst case)

Body of Lit.	References	#occur	#works	#occur_score	#works_score	rarity_body	weight	weight_body
parallel docs	1 Pet 1:4; Heb 7:26	2	2					
NT	Jas 1:27	1	1	0.67	0.67	1.33	0.05	0.07
LXX	2 Macc 14:36; 15:34; Wis 3:13; 4:2; 8:20	5	2	0.29	0.50	0.79	0.12	0.10
Philo	15 refs in 10 works	15	10	0.12	0.17	0.28	0.08	0.02
Jos.	J. W. 6:99	1	1	0.67	0.67	1.33	0.01	0.01
OT Pseud.	none	0	0	1.00	1.00	2.00	0.15	0.30
AF	1 Clem. 29:1; 2 Clem. 6:9; Herm. Mand. 2:1:7; Herm. Sim. 5:6:7; 5:7:1	5	4	0.29	0.33	0.62	0.08	0.05
G-R	worst case: ∞	∞	∞	0.00	0.00	0.00	0.51	0.00
							Weighted Sum =	0.55
							Total Rarity Score =	2.75

TABLE 1.8. Rarity of occurrence: ἀντίτυπος ("antitype," best case)

Body of Lit.	References	#occur	#works	#occur_score	#works_score	rarity_body	weight	weight_body
parallel docs	1 Pet 3:21; Heb 9:24	2	2					
NT	none	0	0	1.00	1.00	2.00	0.05	0.11
LXX	none	0	0	1.00	1.00	2.00	0.12	0.24
Philo	*Plant.* 1:133; *Conf.* 1:102; *Her.* 1:181	3	3	0.40	0.40	0.80	0.08	0.06
Jos.	none	0	0	1.00	1.00	2.00	0.01	0.02
OT Pseud.	*Sib. Or.* 1:33, 333; 8:270	3	1	0.40	0.67	1.07	0.15	0.16
AF	*2 Clem.* 14:3 (2×)	2	1	0.50	0.67	1.17	0.08	0.09
G-R	best case: none	0	0	1.00	1.00	2.00	0.51	1.02
							Weighted Sum =	1.70
							Total Rarity Score =	8.51

Degree of Correspondence

Assessment of the degree of correspondence between parallel elements involves both horizontal intertextual evidence and vertical intratextual evidence. In the horizontal dimension, correspondence is evaluated by comparing different aspects of parallel elements *between* two documents. This includes examination of the lexical, grammatical, structural, semantic, and pragmatic features of the parallel material, and noting how closely the elements resemble one another. For scoring purposes, this is done by evaluating five key aspects of the parallels. These include: (1) the collection of basic units (individual components) that make up the parallel material; (2) the grammatical form of the parallel elements; (3) the arrangement or structure of the material; (4) the meanings conveyed by the parallels;

and (5) the function of each parallel element in the greater discourse of its host document.

In the vertical dimension, correspondence is assessed by examining how low-order parallels combine to form higher-order parallels *within* each document. It is important to note whether or not a parallel is part of a higher-order parallel since parallels exhibiting such involvement present stronger evidence of directness in the relationship than do parallels that are isolated from other parallel material. Thus the specific characteristics of correspondence entail five aspects of the horizontal parallel relationship and one aspect of the vertical parallel relationship.

The criteria for scoring the degree of correspondence between parallel elements are derived from what is observed in cases where an interdependent relationship is fairly certain. Use of the OT in the NT, the Synoptic Problem, and the NT and OT manuscript traditions are all good sources of information as each represents a dependent literary relationship of one document upon another. Whether it is a NT author incorporating OT text, one evangelist leveraging the work of another evangelist, or a scribe copying or translating a manuscript exemplar, a dependent relationship of some kind is generally acknowledged. The degree of correspondence in these cases can be divided into three ranges. At one extreme, correspondence is exact — each element is an *identical* copy of the other. While this extreme degree of correspondence is most frequently found in the manuscript tradition, where the intent is to precisely replicate manuscript exemplars, it is also evident in NT use of the OT (e.g., 1 Pet 2:7 || Ps 117:22 LXX), in OT || OT parallels (e.g., the Hezekiah accounts in Isaiah 36–39 LXX || 4 Kgdms 18:13 — 20:19 LXX), and in the Synoptic Gospels. A good example in the Synoptic Gospels involves the curious statement, ὁ ἀναγινώσκων νοείτω, τότε οἱ ἐν τῇ Ἰουδαίᾳ φευγέτωσαν εἰς τὰ ὄρη ("let the reader understand, then those who are in Judea must flee to the mountains"), which is found in both Matt 24:15–16 and Mark 13:14. Identical parallel elements represent the highest degree of verbal correspondence.

At the other extreme, correspondence between parallel text elements might be apparent in concept only, with perhaps a few shared words. In this case, the formal features of the parallel elements bear little resemblance to each other, yet they convey kindred thoughts. Such *paraphrasing* is most evident in NT use of the OT (e.g., Heb 12:18–20 || Exod 19:12–19); however, it is also found in the Synoptics (e.g., Mark 14:3–9; Matt 26:6–13 || Luke 7:36–50) and even in the manuscript tradition (e.g., Isa 38:9–22 LXX || Isa 38:9–22 MT).

Other parallels exhibit various types of transformations that reflect a degree of correspondence somewhere between *identical* and *paraphrastic*. Many of the OT references found in the NT exhibit such transformations, as shown in the examples below. In order to facilitate comparison between parallel texts, the English translations maintain the grammatical features of the Greek and Hebrew texts as much as possible. The first case involves Romans and Isaiah:

v.	Rom 9:27–28	Isa 10:22–23 LXX	v.
27	ἐὰν ᾖ ὁ ἀριθμὸς τῶν υἱῶν Ἰσραὴλ ὡς ἡ ἄμμος τῆς θαλάσσης, τὸ ὑπόλειμμα σωθήσεται·	καὶ ἐὰν γένηται ὁ λαὸς Ἰσραηλ ὡς ἡ ἄμμος τῆς θαλάσσης τὸ κατάλειμμα αὐτῶν σωθήσεται	22a
	"If the number of the sons of Israel be as the sand of the sea, the remnant will be saved;	and if the people of Israel become as the sand of the sea, the remnant of them will be saved;	
28	λόγον γὰρ συντελῶν καὶ συντέμνων ποιήσει κύριος ἐπὶ τῆς γῆς.	λόγον γὰρ συντελῶν καὶ συντέμνων ἐν δικαιοσύνῃ ὅτι λόγον συντετμημένον ποιήσει ὁ θεὸς ἐν τῇ οἰκουμένῃ ὅλῃ	22b–23a
	for the Lord will execute a reckoning on the earth completely and shortly.	for he is completing and shortening a reckoning with righteousness; indeed, God will execute a shortened reckoning on the whole world.	

The quotation here is very similar to the LXX text of Isaiah. The first set of lines exhibit lexical transformations with the use of equivalent nouns, υἱῶν || λαὸς ("sons" || "people"), and the use of equivalent verbs, ᾖ || γένηται ("be" || "become"), in 27a || 22a. Also noteworthy is the transformation evident in the contrasting prefixed prepositions of the composite terms translated above as "remnant" (ὑπόλειμμα || κατάλειμμα). The second set of parallel lines displays synonymous use of the words κύριος || θεὸς ("Lord" || "God") and γῆς || οἰκουμένη ("earth" || "world"). This passage in Romans is preceded by another intriguing reference to the OT, this time to the book of Hosea:

v.	Rom 9:25	Hos 2:25 LXX	v.
25a	καλέσω τὸν οὐ λαόν μου λαόν μου	καὶ ἐλεήσω τὴν Οὐκ-ἠλεημένην	25a
	I will call those who were not my people, my people,	and I will have mercy on her who has not been shown mercy,	
25b	καὶ τὴν οὐκ ἠγαπημένην ἠγαπημένην·	καὶ ἐρῶ τῷ Οὐ λαῷ μου λαός μου εἶ σύ	25b
	and her who has not been beloved, beloved.	and I will say to those who were not my people, you are my people.	

This parallel exhibits a reversal of lines as well as the use of equivalent verbs καλέσω || ἐρῶ ("I will call" || "I will say"). Curiously, the same passage of Hosea is given a different appearance in 1 Peter:

v.	1 Pet 2:10	Hos 2:25 LXX	v.
10a	οἵ ποτε οὐ λαὸς νῦν δὲ λαὸς θεοῦ,	καὶ ἐλεήσω τὴν Οὐκ-ἠλεημένην	25a
	[you] who once were not a people, but now are God's people;	and I will have mercy on her who has not been shown mercy,	
10b	οἱ οὐκ ἠλεημένοι νῦν δὲ ἐλεηθέντες.	καὶ ἐρῶ τῷ Οὐ λαῷ μου λαός μου εἶ σύ	25b
	[who once were] those who had not received mercy, but now are those who have received mercy.	and I will say to those who were not my people, you are my people.	

Again, the lines are reversed, but the Petrine reference reflects a different set of transformations of the Hosea text. Most significant is the grammatical transformation. Whereas Hosea conveys God's words using first-person address and the future tense, the parallel text in 1 Peter employs a direct second-person address and present tense. This creates the perception of a sequential relationship between the parallel texts, where 1 Peter reflects the completion or fulfillment of what is stated in Hosea.

The quotations and allusions noted above demonstrate that at least two NT authors employed various types of transformations in their use of OT passages. The phenomenon however, is not limited to Pauline and Petrine writings. It also appears frequently throughout the NT. A classic example in the Gospels involves the references to Isa 6:9–10 in Mark 4:12, Matt 13:14–15, Luke 8:10, and John 12:40, which exhibit various lexical-grammatical transformations. It should also be noted that NT authors are not necessarily consistent in the transformations they apply to OT passages. This is evident in the repeated quotations of Jer 31:33–34 in Heb 8:10–12 and Heb 10:16–17. These quotations differ, not only from both the LXX and the MT, but also from each other. The author of Hebrews employed different modifications for each instance of the Jeremiah text.

Similar kinds of literary transformations are found in the Apostolic Fathers' use of the OT. Clement of Rome, for instance, provides ample examples for illustration, one of which concerns dual quotations of Job in *1 Clement*. As can be seen in the parallel texts quoted below, the dual quotations found in *1 Clem.* 17:3–4 closely resemble the LXX text of Job.[48] The grammatical relationship between these parallel texts is most evident in the second quotation that appears in *1 Clem.* 17:4, where the question-answer form of Job 14:4–5 is changed to a declarative statement in *1 Clement*. Although not visible in the English translation, the texts are also related through a gender transformation with the words rendered here as "life." The LXX uses the masculine term, βίος, and *1 Clement* uses the feminine term, ζωή. In addition, a nominal case transformation occurs as the nominative μία ἡμέρα ("one day") of Job appears as a genitive μιᾶς ἡμέρας ("one day") in *1 Clement*.

---

48. See the discussion by Hagner in *Use of the Old and New Testaments*, 52.

v.	*1 Clem.* 17:3–4	Job 1:1; 14:4–5 LXX	v.
3	ἔτι δὲ καὶ περὶ Ἰὼβ οὕτως γέγραπται Ἰὼβ δὲ ἦν δίκαιος καὶ ἄμεμπτος ἀληθινός θεοσεβής ἀπεχόμενος ἀπὸ παντὸς κακοῦ	ἄνθρωπός τις ἦν ἐν χώρᾳ τῇ Αὐσίτιδι ᾧ ὄνομα Ιωβ καὶ ἦν ὁ ἄνθρωπος ἐκεῖνος ἀληθινός ἄμεμπτος δίκαιος θεοσεβής ἀπεχόμενος ἀπὸ παντὸς πονηροῦ πράγματος	1:1
	Moreover, concerning Job it is thus written, "And Job was righteous and blameless, true, devout, turning away from every evil."	There was a certain man in the land of Ausitis, whose name was Job, and that man was true, blameless, righteous, devout, turning away from every evil thing.	
4	ἀλλ᾽ αὐτὸς ἑαυτοῦ κατηγορεῖ λέγων Οὐδεὶς καθαρὸς ἀπὸ ῥύπου οὐδ᾽ ἂν μιᾶς ἡμέρας ἡ ζωὴ αὐτοῦ	τίς γὰρ καθαρὸς ἔσται ἀπὸ ῥύπου ἀλλ᾽ οὐθείς ἐὰν καὶ μία ἡμέρα ὁ βίος αὐτοῦ ἐπὶ τῆς γῆς ἀριθμητοὶ δὲ μῆνες αὐτοῦ παρὰ σοί εἰς χρόνον ἔθου καὶ οὐ μὴ ὑπερβῇ	14: 4–5
	Yet he accuses himself, saying, "No one is clean from filth; not even if his life <fem.> lasts but one day <gen.>."	For who can be clean from filth? No one! Even if his life <mas.> on earth is but one day <nom.>...	

Much of the parallel text material between the three Synoptic Gospels also exhibits lexical, grammatical, and structural transformations. A good example involves the account of Jesus healing the paralytic, which is found in all three Synoptic Gospels (Matt 9:3; Mark 2:6–7; Luke 5:21).

Matt 9:3	Mark 2:6–7	Luke 5:21
καὶ ἰδού τινες τῶν γραμματέων εἶπαν ἐν ἑαυτοῖς· οὗτος βλασφημεῖ.	ἦσαν δέ τινες τῶν γραμματέων ἐκεῖ καθήμενοι καὶ διαλογιζόμενοι ἐν ταῖς καρδίαις αὐτῶν· τί οὗτος οὕτως λαλεῖ; βλασφημεῖ· τίς δύναται ἀφιέναι ἁμαρτίας εἰ μὴ εἷς ὁ θεός;	καὶ ἤρξαντο διαλογίζεσθαι οἱ γραμματεῖς καὶ οἱ Φαρισαῖοι λέγοντες· τίς ἐστιν οὗτος ὃς λαλεῖ βλασφημίας; τίς δύναται ἁμαρτίας ἀφεῖναι εἰ μὴ μόνος ὁ θεός;
And behold, some of the scribes said to themselves, "This man is blaspheming."	And some of the scribes were sitting there, questioning in their hearts, "Why does this man speak thus? He is blaspheming! Who can forgive sins but God alone?"	And the scribes and the Pharisees began to question, saying, "Who is this who speaks blasphemies? Who can forgive sins but God only?"

These texts are grammatically related primarily through transformations involving the main verbal ideas conveyed in the first and second parts of each text. In the first part, the verbal terms appear in three different forms: (1) indicative (εἶπαν, "said," Matt 9:3), (2) participle (διαλογιζόμενοι, "questioning," Mark 2:6), and (3) infinitive (διαλογίζεσθαι, "to question," Luke 5:21). The second part involves nominal-verbal transformations between the verb βλασφημεῖ ("blaspheming," Matt 9:3 and Mark 2:7) and the noun βλασφημίας ("blasphemies," Luke 5:21).

Another interesting example of Synoptic texts that display various transformations involves three parallel passages that appear toward the end of Matthew, Mark, and Luke. Here Jesus speaks of things to come:

Matt 24:7	Mark 13:8	Luke 21:11
καὶ ἔσονται λιμοὶ	ἔσονται σεισμοὶ κατὰ τόπους,	σεισμοί τε μεγάλοι
and there will be famines	there will be earthquakes in various places,	and great earthquakes,
καὶ σεισμοὶ κατὰ τόπους·	ἔσονται λιμοί·	καὶ κατὰ τόπους λιμοὶ καὶ λοιμοὶ ἔσονται,
and earthquakes in various places	there will be famines	and in various places famines and plagues, there will be

This set of parallel texts shows a reversal of order between the "famine" clauses and "earthquake" clauses. There is also a syntactical transformation involving the prepositional phrase κατὰ τόπους ("in various places"). Whereas in Matthew the phrase is associated with earthquakes and perhaps famines, in Mark it is associated with earthquakes, and in Luke, the phrase is associated with famines.

The Hebrew and Greek OT manuscript traditions provide additional instances where parallel texts from different manuscripts exhibit varying degrees of correspondence. Intertextual transformations, in fact, are evident in translations as well as transmissions of the text in the same language. A striking example appears in the Hebrew MT and Greek LXX versions of Isa 6:9–10. The differences between the MT and the LXX are easily seen when the parallel lines are read side-by-side.

v.	Isa 6:9–10 MT (WTT)	Isa 6:9–10 LXX	v.
9a	ויאמר לך ואמרת לעם הזה	καὶ εἶπεν πορεύθητι καὶ εἰπὸν τῷ λαῷ τούτῳ	9a
	And he said, "Go and say to this people,	And he said, "Go and say to this people,	

v.	Isa 6:9–10 MT (WTT)	Isa 6:9–10 LXX	v.
9b	שִׁמְעוּ שָׁמוֹעַ וְאַל־תָּבִינוּ	ἀκοῇ ἀκούσετε καὶ οὐ μὴ συνῆτε καὶ	9b
	'Keep on hearing, but do not understand;	'By listening, you will listen, but you will not understand;	
9c	וּרְאוּ רָאוֹ וְאַל־תֵּדָעוּ	βλέποντες βλέψετε καὶ οὐ μὴ ἴδητε	9c
	and keep on seeing, but do not know.'	and looking, you will look, but you will not perceive.'	
10a	הַשְׁמֵן לֵב־הָעָם הַזֶּה	ἐπαχύνθη γὰρ ἡ καρδία τοῦ λαοῦ τούτου	10a
	Make fat the heart of this people,	For the heart of this people has been made fat,	
10b	וְאָזְנָיו הַכְבֵּד	καὶ τοῖς ὠσὶν αὐτῶν βαρέως ἤκουσαν	10b
	and his ears make heavy,	and with their ears they heard heavily,	
10c	וְעֵינָיו הָשַׁע	καὶ τοὺς ὀφθαλμοὺς αὐτῶν ἐκάμμυσαν	10c
	and his eyes make blind,	and their eyes they shut,	
10d	פֶּן־יִרְאֶה בְעֵינָיו	μήποτε ἴδωσιν τοῖς ὀφθαλμοῖς	10d
	lest he see with his eyes,	lest they should see with their eyes,	
10e	וּבְאָזְנָיו יִשְׁמָע	καὶ τοῖς ὠσὶν ἀκούσωσιν	10e
	and with his ears hear,	and with their ears hear,	
10f	וּלְבָבוֹ יָבִין	καὶ τῇ καρδίᾳ συνῶσιν	10f
	and his heart understand	and with their heart understand	
10g	וָשָׁב וְרָפָא לוֹ	καὶ ἐπιστρέψωσιν καὶ ἰάσομαι αὐτούς	10g
	and he turn and be healed."	and turn — and I would heal them."	

This intriguing pair of texts reveals grammatical transformations that have important implications for interpretation of the passage. Most significant are the morphological and syntactical differences that appear in lines 10a–c. Here the LXX uses third-person aorist indicative verbs to declare that the peoples' heart is already fat (ἐπαχύνθη) and they are already impaired in their hearing (ἤκουσαν) and vision (ἐκάμμυσαν); whereas the Hebrew MT employs second-person hiphil imperatives to instruct the prophet to cause their heart to be fat (הַשְׁמֵן), their ears to be heavy (הַכְבֵּד), and their eyes to be blind (הָשַׁע). The verbs in 10b–c also exhibit differences in number. While the Hebrew verbs הכבד ("make heavy") and השע ("make blind") are singular, the corresponding LXX verbs, ἤκουσαν, ("they heard") and ἐκάμμυσαν ("they shut"), are plural. Differences between active and passive voice are also evident in the verbs of 10a. Whereas השמן ("make fat") is active, ἐπαχύνθη ("has been made fat") is passive. Furthermore, a key syntactical difference appears in 10a, where the LXX includes the conjunction γὰρ ("for"), for which there is no parallel in the Hebrew MT. While the expression in 10a MT functions as an imperative for the prophet, the conjunction γὰρ indicates that the parallel LXX expression provides the reason for the people's lack of understanding, namely, that their heart is already fattened. Thus these parallel texts exhibit transformations in verbal mood, voice, person, and number, as well as transformations in syntactical function. The effect is profound in that each version points to a different agent of fattening (i.e., hardening). In the MT, God is responsible for hardening the people's heart so that they will not understand. In the LXX, however, it is the people's already hardened heart that prevents them from understanding. The book of Isaiah offers many more examples of MT ‖ LXX grammatical transformations. See, for instance, the related hardening passages in Isa 38:9–22 and 44:18.

Other interesting examples are found in the Greek NT manuscript tradition, which is replete with evidence of various lexical-grammatical transformations. The phenomenon, in fact, has received much attention from text critics for many years. Even with just the collations that have been completed to date, there are thousands of cases. NT manuscripts exhibit many types of transformations, including those that involve differences in morphology, word order, syntactical structure, prepositional phrases, relative clauses, conjunctions, nouns-pronouns, definite articles, adjectives, and adverbs, as well as additions and omissions of material. Consider, for example, the text of Matt 26:26 as it appears in both codex Alexandrinus and codex Bezae:

v.	Matt 26:26 (02 Codex Alexandrinus)	Matt 26:26 (05 Codex Bezae)	v.
26a	Εσθιοντω‾ δε αυτων	Αυτων δε εσθιοντων	26a
	And while they were eating,	And while they were eating,	
26b	λαβων ο ΙΣ‾ τον αρτο‾	ο ΙΗΣ‾ λαβων αρτον	26b
	Jesus took the bread	Jesus took bread	
26c	και ευχαριστησας εκλασεν	και ευλογησας εκλασεν	26c
	and after giving thanks, broke it	and after blessing it, broke it	
26d	και εδιδου τοις μαθηταις και ειπεν	και δους τοις μαθηταις ειπε‾	26d
	and began giving it to the disciples, and said,	and gave it to the disciples and said,	
26e	Λαβετε φαγετε τουτο εστιν το σωμα μου	Λαβετε φαγεται τουτο εστιν το σω[μα μου]	26e
	Take, eat; this is my body	Take, he will eat; this is my body	

Although these two texts convey the same basic idea, there are noticeable transformations in each of the five lines. In line 26a the order of the three Greek words is reversed, thereby reflecting a chiastic relationship between the two versions of 26a. In line 26b the subject-verb order is switched. The following line, 26c, is identical except for the use of different, yet similar, participles (ευχαριστησας || ευλογησας; "giving thanks" || "blessing"). Line 26d reflects a curious grammatical transformation. Codex Alexandrinus uses an imperfect indicative + και + aorist indicative (εδιδου … και ειπεν) to convey the combined action of giving and saying. Codex Bezae, on the other hand, uses an aorist participle + aorist indicative in what appears to be an attendant circumstance construction (δους … ειπε‾). The last line also exhibits an interesting grammatical transformation with the word "eat." Whereas Alexandrinus employs an aorist active second-person plural imperative (φαγετε), Bezae uses a future middle third-person singular indicative (φαγεται). This example from Matthew is just one of many that demonstrate lexical-grammatical and structural transformations between parallel manuscripts. It is especially noteworthy that these parallels derive from a process that is intended to accurately transmit written texts.

The intriguing examples presented above suggest that various types of transformations are not uncommon in cases where a dependent intertextual relationship is fairly certain. Not surprisingly, the same kinds of transformations are evident in cases where a relationship of literary dependence involving NT documents is strongly suspected by many scholars. Most notable are the relationships between 2 Peter and Jude, and Ephesians and Colossians. Much of the parallel material between 2 Peter and Jude exhibits lexical-grammatical transformations.[49] So too does the bulk of the common material between Ephesians and Colossians.[50] Writings of the Apostolic Fathers give further evidence since many parallels with NT writings reflect similar kinds of intertextual transformations.[51]

Although cases of lexical, grammatical, and structural transformations are plentiful in parallels involving the OT, the NT, and other early Christian writings, their significance for establishing exclusivity in a literary relationship is often overlooked. Many scholars focus on the intertextual differences rather than on the lexical-grammatical relationships between parallels and, as a result, conclude that parallels are most likely due to imprecise memory citation[52] or independent use of a common oral tradition.[53] However, based

49. See, e.g., Jude 4 || 2 Pet 2:1, 3; Jude 6 || 2 Pet 2:4; Jude 7 || 2 Pet 2:6; Jude 9 || 2 Pet 2:11; Jude 10 || 2 Pet 2:12; Jude 12–13 || 2 Pet 2:13, 17.

50. Some of the more notable instances include: Eph 1:4 || Col 1:22; Eph 1:6–7 || Col 1:13–14; Eph 1:8 || Col 1:9; Eph 2:2f || Col 3:7; Eph 2:5–6 || Col 2:12–13; Eph 2:16 || Col 1:20; Eph 2:20f || Col 2:7; Eph 3:2 || Col 1:25; Eph 3:5 || Col 1:26; Eph 4:15–16 || Col 2:19; Eph 4:17–24 || Col 3:5–11; Eph 5:19–20 || Col 3:16–17; Eph 5:22ff || Col 3:18ff.

51. Among the many examples are: 1 Clem. 27:2 || Heb 6:18; 1 Clem. 36:2–6 || Heb 1:3–13; 1 Clem. 49:5 || 1 Cor 13:4–7; Did. 1:2b || Matt 7:15; Diogn. 5:16 || 2 Cor 6:8–10; Pol. Phil. 3:3 || Gal 4:26.

52. Examples of works that attribute grammatically transformed parallels to memory citation or reminiscence include: Crossan, Birth of Christianity, 107–8; Martin Hengel, The Four Gospels and the One Gospel of Jesus Christ: An Investigation of the Collection and Origin of the Canonical Gospels (Harrisburg, PA: Trinity Press International, 2000), 129; C. Leslie Mitton, Ephesians, NCB (London: Oliphants, 1976), 12; Wand, St. Peter and St. Jude, 25.

53. Attribution of grammatically transformed parallels to independent use of common hypothetical traditions is quite common in published studies. See, e.g., Paul J. Achtemeier, 1 Peter: A Commentary on First Peter, Hermeneia (Minneapolis, MN: Fortress, 1996), 12–23; Harold W. Attridge, The Epistle to the Hebrews: A Commentary on the Epistle to the Hebrews, Hermeneia (Philadelphia, PA: Fortress, 1989), 28–31; Crossan, Birth of Christianity, 104–5; John H. Elliott, 1 Peter, AB 37B (New Haven: Yale University Press, 2001), 20–40; Leonhard Goppelt, A Commentary

on the characteristics observed in parallels that are commonly recognized as reflecting a direct dependent relationship, the present methodology acknowledges various degrees and types of correspondence as significant for assessing exclusivity in an intertextual relationship. The highest degree of correspondence is evident when parallel elements are identical. Lesser degrees of correspondence are represented when parallel elements exhibit transformations similar to those noted in the examples above. The lowest degree of correspondence is found in parallels that are paraphrastic in nature and show little or no verbal correspondence. Accordingly, the criteria for scoring the five aspects of the horizontal parallel relationship reflect stronger and weaker degrees of correspondence, as explained below.

Correspondence of Basic Units

Correspondence of basic units is assessed by observing the collections of individual words that make up the parallel material in low-order multi-word parallels and seeing how closely the collections match. Of particular interest is the presence of identical and/or related basic units. Since word morphology is addressed with another indicator (see below), evaluation of basic units focuses mainly on the particular morphemes or roots that are employed in the texts. Basic units are considered *identical* if the roots are identical. Basic units are considered *related* if they reflect some kind of commonly recognized association. For example, at the lexical level, words may be associated as synonyms (e.g., stone-rock), antonyms (e.g., hot-cold), hierarchical classes (e.g., fruit-apple), or natural pairs (e.g., man-woman).

Since multi-word parallels can include multivariate combinations of identical, related, and unrelated basic units, correspondence scores are assigned according to the mathematical formula shown below. For this methodology, the evidence presented by identical basic units is considered

---

on *1 Peter*, ed. Ferdinand Hahn, trans. John E. Alsup (Grand Rapids, MI: Eerdmans, 1993), 26–37; Erich Grässer, "Der Hebräerbrief, 1938–63," *TRu* ns 30, no. 2 (1964): 195–97; L. D. Hurst, *The Epistle to the Hebrews: Its Background of Thought,* SNTSMS 65 (Cambridge: Cambridge University Press, 1990), 130; Michael Mees, "Die Hohepriester-Theologie des Hebräerbriefes im Vergleich mit dem Ersten Clemensbrief," *BZ* ns 22, no. 1 (1978): 115–24; Edward Gordon Selwyn, "Essay II: Bearing of Evidence on the Supposed Dependence of 1 Peter on Other Epistles," in *The First Epistle of St. Peter: The Greek Text with Introduction, Notes and Essays* (London: Macmillan & Co. Ltd., 1955), 365–466; Ceslas Spicq, "La Iᵃ Petri et le témoignage évangélique de Saint Pierre," *ST* 20 (1966): 37.

twice as strong as the evidence offered by related basic units.[54] Parallels that
are identical in all of their basic units earn the highest score of two. Parallels
that exhibit mixed degrees of correspondence for their basic units earn a
score between zero and two. For single-word parallels and higher-order
parallel clusters, zero points are awarded for correspondence of basic units.
This is because single-word parallels by definition correspond, and higher-
order parallels by definition presume the presence of common lower-order
parallels that are assessed individually for lexical correspondence.

$$\text{score} = \frac{2\ (\#\ \text{identical units}) + 1\ (\#\ \text{related units})}{\#\ \text{total units in the longest of the two parallel elements}}$$

Correspondence of Grammatical Constructs

Grammatical correspondence involves the morphological and syntactical
characteristics of the grammatical constructs contained in the parallel texts.
For the purpose of this methodology, a grammatical construct is defined
as a particular instantiation of a lexical root or a syntactical component.
Morphologically, this includes different forms of words for word class, tense,
conjugation, voice, person, gender, number, definiteness, case, or other
morphological features. In regard to syntax, primary interest is in the relationship between the basic units and the parts of speech played by parallel
components. Syntactical constructs include all the basic components that
make up a sentence such as subject, predicate, clause, and phrase.

Correspondence is assessed by observing how closely the morphology
and syntax of the parallel constructs match. As with correspondence of
basic units, multi-construct parallels can reflect multivariate degrees of
grammatical correspondence. If two parallel constructs exhibit the same
morphology and syntax, then the constructs are considered *identical*. This

54. The default position established for this methodology is that all things
are valued equally unless there is a compelling reason to do otherwise. In regard
to lexical correspondence, the difference between identical and related basic units
should be taken into account. The research conducted for this study, however, does
not indicate a particular formula for valuing the relative strength of the evidence.
For this reason, the present methodology assigns a mid-point value for related terms.
Thus the coefficient for the number of identical units is 2, and the coefficient for the
number of related units is 1.

reflects the highest degree of grammatical correspondence. Lesser degrees of grammatical correspondence are evident when parallel constructs exhibit morphological and/or syntactical transformations. For example, parallel constructs may exhibit subject-object, nominal-verbal, positive-negative, or adjectival-adverbial syntactical transformations, as well as various types of morphological transformations. A contrast in grammatical mood may also be present. Parallel constructs are considered grammatically *equivalent* if they exhibit morphological and/or syntactical transformations.

Since extensive parallels can reflect various degrees of grammatical correspondence for their constituent constructs, correspondence scores are assigned according to the formula shown below.[55] Parallels that are identical in all of their grammatical constructs earn the highest score of two, whereas zero points are awarded for parallels that lack any grammatical correspondence. Parallels that show mixed degrees of correspondence, earn a score between zero and two.

$$\text{score} = \frac{2 \, (\# \text{ identical constructs}) + 1 \, (\# \text{ equivalent constructs})}{\# \text{ total constructs in the longest of the two parallel elements}}$$

55. For the same reason given in the previous note regarding correspondence of basic units, the present methodology assigns a mid-point value for equivalent grammatical constructs. Thus the coefficient for the number of identical constructs is 2, and the coefficient for the number of equivalent constructs is 1.

An example of a multi-line parallel that exhibits different types of grammatical equivalences may be observed in the following excerpts taken from 2 Peter and Jude:

v.	2 Pet 2:12	Jude 10	v.
12a	Οὗτοι δὲ	Οὗτοι δὲ	10a
	But these,	But these,	
12b	ὡς ἄλογα ζῷα γεγεννημένα φυσικὰ εἰς ἅλωσιν καὶ φθορὰν	ὅσα μὲν οὐκ οἴδασιν βλασφημοῦσιν,	10b
	like unreasoning animals, born instinctive unto capture and destruction,	all that they do not know, they blaspheme,	
12c	ἐν οἷς ἀγνοοῦσιν βλασφημοῦντες,	ὅσα δὲ φυσικῶς ὡς τὰ ἄλογα ζῷα ἐπίστανται,	10c
	about things of which they are ignorant, blaspheming,	and all that, instinctively, like unreasoning animals, they understand,	
12d	ἐν τῇ φθορᾷ αὐτῶν καὶ φθαρήσονται	ἐν τούτοις φθείρονται.	10d
	in their destruction they will also be destroyed	in these things they are destroyed.	

The texts found in 2 Pet 2:12 and Jude 10 are grammatically related through a transformation of verbal form between the participle βλασφημοῦντες ("blaspheming") in 12c and the indicative verb βλασφημοῦσιν ("they blaspheme") in 10b, as well as a transformation of tense between φθαρήσονται ("they will be destroyed") in 12d and φθείρονται ("they are destroyed") in 10d. There is also an adjectival-adverbial transformation of a common root between φυσικὰ ("instinctive") in 12b and φυσικῶς ("instinctively") in 10c. In addition, the parallel texts display a similar use of prepositional phrases (12d ‖ 10d) and relative clauses (12c ‖ 10b).

Another example of grammatical equivalence is found in the early Christian teaching of the *Didache*. Of particular interest is an intriguing two-line parallel between *Did.* 16:1 and Luke 12:35.

v.	Did. 16:1	Luke 12:35	v.
1a	οἱ λύχνοι ὑμῶν μὴ σβεσθήτωσαν	Ἔστωσαν ὑμῶν αἱ ὀσφύες περιεζωσμέναι	35a
	let your lamps not be extinguished	Let your loins be girded	
1b	καὶ αἱ ὀσφύες ὑμῶν μὴ ἐκλυέσθωσαν	καὶ οἱ λύχνοι καιόμενοι·	35b
	and your loins not be loose	and your lamps burning;	

This parallel exhibits grammatical transformations in two key ways. First, the stand-alone imperatives found in *Didache*, σβεσθήτωσαν ("let . . . be extinguished") and ἐκλυέσθωσαν ("let . . . be loose"), are expressed in the parallel lines of Luke as an imperative,Ἔστωσαν ("Let . . . be"), plus the participles περιεζωσμέναι ("girded") and καιόμενοι ("burning"). Second, there is a positive-negative transformation — what is expressed positively in Luke appears in *Didache* as a negative expression.[56]

Correspondence of Structural Arrangement

The structural arrangement of parallels concerns how the basic units are combined together to create a whole. Assessment of correspondence in this aspect primarily involves comparing the structural organization and relative order of the basic units. Other distinguishing formal features of the parallel material, however, might also be assessed, such as literary linking devices or lexical-grammatical patterns that appear in the material. Again, parallel elements can be identical or related in some way. If the overall structure or order of the constituent parts is essentially the same for both parallel elements, then the elements are considered *identical*. This represents the highest degree of structural correspondence. Parallels that exhibit a recognizable transformation between their respective structural arrangements demonstrate a lesser degree of correspondence. These kinds of parallels are considered *related* by their organizational patterns.

The most common examples of parallels that are structurally *related* are those that exhibit a reversal in the order of parallel words, lines, pairs of lines, or even in the order of entire paragraphs. The reversal phenomenon

56. Crossan attributes this parallel to independent "actualizations of a common oral matrix" (*Birth of Christianity*, 104).

is not uncommon in the NT and other early Christian writings. It appears in several of the examples given earlier. The three-fold parallel involving Matt 24:7, Mark 13:8, and Luke 21:11 exhibits a reversal of clauses. In the parallel between *1 Clem.* 17:3 and Job 1:1, the order of the first three adjectives, δίκαιος ("righteous"), ἄμεμπτος ("blameless"), and ἀληθινός ("true"), is reversed. For *Did.* 16:1 and Luke 12:35, the order of the lines is reversed. Finally, with 2 Pet 2:12 and Jude 10, there is a reversal of line-pairs between 12b–12c and 10b–10c.

The scoring scheme for correspondence of structural arrangement is fairly straightforward. Parallels with essentially identical structures receive the highest score of two. Parallels that exhibit a recognizable transformation in their organizational patterns receive a lower score of one. Zero points are given for parallels whose respective organizational structures appear to be only loosely related.

Correspondence of Meaning

Assessment of correspondence of meaning is somewhat subjective in that it requires interpretation of the parallel material. Since no two NT books are exactly the same, it must be assumed that the occasion and purpose were different for the writing of each document. Hence it is unreasonable to expect intertextual parallel material to reflect precise semantic identity. For this reason, the context must be considered when assessing semantic correspondence of parallel texts. In the present methodology, this means interpreting the parallels in light of their respective literary contexts. The task, therefore, requires evaluating the semantic relationship between the context-sensitive meanings of the parallel elements.

For the sake of simplicity, parallels are assessed according to three types of semantic relationships: (1) comparable, (2) sequential, and (3) dissimilar. A comparable relationship is indicated when the thoughts conveyed by the parallel elements are similar enough to seem analogous in their respective literary contexts. Comparable semantic relationships can take two different forms. The most common form is evident when both parallel elements convey the same basic idea or concept. An alternative form is evident when the parallel elements convey ideas or concepts that are in contrast to or opposite of one another. Parallels that exhibit either of these two forms are considered semantically comparable. A sequential relationship is indicated when the thoughts of the two parallel elements may be perceived as conceptually related in a temporal or logical sequence.

For the purpose of assessing semantic correspondence, the direction of the sequence of ideas is irrelevant. Therefore, no assumptions are made about whether a sequence indicates progression from element_A to element_B, or digression from element_B to element_A. It is sufficient to note that the concepts expressed in the parallel elements reflect a sequential relationship. Since this type of relationship reflects a lesser degree of correspondence, semantically sequential parallels are considered weaker evidence of directness. A good example of a sequential semantic relationship is found in the previously discussed NT || OT parallel between 1 Pet 2:10 and Hos 2:25 LXX (2:23 English), where the expression in 1 Peter suggests completion or fulfillment of what is stated in Hosea. Finally, if the thoughts expressed by the parallel elements are neither comparable nor sequential, then the semantic relationship is considered dissimilar and the parallel receives zero points for correspondence of meaning.

Parallels between NT documents are generally comparable in the sense that they convey common points or ideas. However, there are cases that exhibit sequential semantic relationships. In the Synoptic Gospels, such a case is evident in the story about the healing of the hemorrhaging woman. In Luke 9:47 readers are told that the woman declared the reason why she touched Jesus, but the reason itself is only revealed in the parallel accounts in Matt 9:21 and Mark 5:28. This suggests a sequential cause-effect relationship. The woman believed she would be healed if she touched Jesus' garment. This is the cause, which is found in Matthew and Mark. Luke records only the effect — she touched his garment and was healed.

Correspondence of Function

Correspondence of function is assessed by observing how the parallel elements are used by the authors for their intended purposes. Specifically, this involves evaluating the pragmatic purpose of one parallel element and comparing with the pragmatic purpose of the other parallel element. For the reason noted above, this needs to be done in light of the literary context of each parallel element.

The strongest evidence of directness is indicated when the function of the parallel material in both documents is contextually equivalent. That is, they serve essentially the same purpose in their respective contexts. For example, in both contexts the parallel material might be used as a basis for theological claims, a behavioral example, or a reminder of important truths.

Weaker evidence of directness is indicated when the function of the parallel material is contextually modified. A modified functional relationship may be evident when the function is similar in both cases, but the range of application within the respective contexts is noticeably different or the specific approach is different. An example would be a case where common material is used to exhort readers, where in one document there are no restrictions on application, but in the other document application is restricted to certain people. Another example would be if parallel material is used positively in one document and negatively in the other to achieve a similar outcome. If the pragmatic purposes of the parallel elements are dissimilar, then the score is zero.

Member of Higher-Order Parallel

In the vertical dimension, correspondence is assessed by evaluating the higher-order memberships held by each of the two parallel elements. For this methodology, a higher-order parallel is defined as a particular grouping of three or more lower-order parallels that occurs in both documents. The parallels that form the group are referred to as "members" of the higher-order parallel. Parallels that are not members of any higher-order parallel are classified as "orphans."

Assignment of scores is done according to the possible combinations of different types of memberships. The strongest evidence of directness is indicated when both elements are members of the same higher-order parallel, and the higher-order parallel exhibits essentially identical arrangement of members in both documents. The second strongest evidence is indicated when the elements are members of the same higher-order parallel, but the arrangement of members differs. Weaker evidence is shown when both elements are members of different higher-order parallels. Weaker still is the case where only one of the elements has membership in a higher-order parallel and the other element is an orphan. The weakest case is when both elements are orphans. Parallels are awarded a score of 0, 1, 2, 3, or 4 according to these five possible combinations of membership. Four points are given for the combination that indicates the strongest evidence of directness, and zero points are awarded for the weakest combination.

Scores for Specific Indicators of Directness

Scores are computed for each of the seven indicators of directness based on the criteria delineated above for stronger and weaker strength of the evidence. Research conducted for this project shows no strong indication of relative strength between the seven indicators. Hence the two major categories of scoring, rarity and correspondence, are given equal value.[57] The scoring scale is set so that the rarity of occurrence indicator (#1) and the combined intertextual correspondence indicators (#2–6) are weighted equally, with 10 maximum points for each. Moreover, the five intertextual correspondence indicators also are all weighted equally. The indicator for membership in a higher-order parallel (#7) is given a relatively lower weight with a maximum of 4 points because the cumulative effect of low-order parallels is already accounted for in the probability analysis. Scoring of this indicator is intended to give extra credit to account for the arrangement of parallels in clusters.

As shown in table 1.9, the maximum possible total score is 24. Since $DI = (\Sigma \text{ scores}) \times EM$, and $EM = \#units \div \#units_{max}$, the maximum possible value for DI occurs when $\#units = \#units_{max}$, which is set at 112.[58] Therefore, DI_{max} also is equal to 24:

$$
\begin{aligned}
DI_{max} &= 24\,(\#units/\#units_{max}) \\
&= 24\,(112/112) \\
&= 24
\end{aligned}
$$

Using the scoring scheme described above, data can be extracted from individual parallels in a form that can be used in the probability analysis.

---

57. The default position established for this methodology is that all things are valued equally unless there is a compelling reason to do otherwise.

58. See the earlier discussion on "Extent Multiplier" for derivation of the value assigned to $\#units_{max}$ (pp. 29–33).

TABLE 1.9. Points awarded for specific indicators of directness

No.	Indicator	Criterion / Formula	Points
1	Rarity of Occurrence	weighted Σ rarity_body	10 max 0 min
2	Correspondence of Basic Units	(2 (#identical units) + 1 (#related units)) ÷ (#total units in the longest of the two parallel elements)	2 max 0 min
3	Correspondence of Grammatical Constructs	(2 (#identical constructs) + 1 (#equivalent constructs)) ÷ (#total constructs in the longest of the two parallel elements)	2 max 0 min
4	Correspondence of Structural Arrangement	identical related patterns no pattern	2 1 0
5	Correspondence of Meaning	comparable sequential dissimilar	2 1 0
6	Correspondence of Function	equivalent modified dissimilar	2 1 0
7	Member of Higher-Order Parallel	same higher-order parallel (same order) same higher-order parallel (different order) different higher-order parallel one orphan both orphans	4 3 2 1 0
		Maximum Total Score (DI_{max}) =	24

This completes the first stage of the methodology for determining the probability of intertextual borrowing between NT books. As explained in the preceding pages, the methodology is developed within the objective framework of probability theory and focuses on cumulative evidence of directness observed in the intertextual parallels. Relevant evidence of directness is identified as rarity of occurrence in the relevant bodies of literature and the degree of correspondence between the parallel elements. The result is a collective probability of directness which represents the probability that *at least one* of the parallels derives from a direct literary connection. The CP_{dir} number makes no claims about the likelihood of a direct connection between individual parallels, only about the likelihood that not all of them are non-direct. A high likelihood of at least one direct-connect parallel is sufficient to demonstrate a direct literary connection between the documents. In the event of such an outcome, assessment of the probability of intertextual borrowing may proceed to stage 2 of the methodology, which addresses the question of who is most likely to have borrowed from whom.

CHAPTER 2

Direction of Borrowing
Assessment Methodology

The literary dependence assessment method presented in the previous chapter establishes a basis from which to proceed to the next stage of the methodology. Given that a direct relationship of literary dependence has been established as highly probable between a pair of NT documents, the obvious question that follows is: Who borrowed from whom? Or conversely, which document came first and thereby claims relative priority? The nature of the question is quite different than the question of literary dependence and therefore requires a fresh look at the objective, alternative approaches, and relevant evidence. Although the general approach is similar to that used in the case of literary dependence, there are significant differences in the methodological details. The conceptual framework underlying the methodology is similar to that described in chapter 1. The task involves establishing a preferred approach, identifying appropriate criteria for a borrowing relationship, discovering what constitutes relevant evidence, and selecting appropriate analysis tools and methods. Once the conceptual framework is defined, the methodology takes shape through development of the analysis method ("Probability of Borrowing") and by specifying how the necessary data is derived from intertextual parallels ("Scoring Scheme").

Conceptual Framework

General Approach

Assessment of directionality between two documents that are literarily interdependent follows the same basic approach that is used to discern the probability of literary dependence. Here too, the assessment is based on measurable features of the text; however, the particular features are different. For the question of literary dependence, the main interest is in the relational possibilities of parallels, and in particular, the need to show a direct genealogical relationship in order to claim literary dependence. Hence the methodology in chapter 1 is focused on evidence of *directness* in the intertextual relationship. The method for assessing directionality or relative priority also involves relational possibilities. However, in this case, the question concerns the *directional* possibilities of the relationship.

Assuming that the likelihood of literary dependence between two documents has already been established according to the method described in chapter 1, the directional possibilities are quite simple. Either the parallel material flows from document_A to document_B, or the material flows from document_B to document_A. Direct literary dependence also does not preclude the possibility that material might flow in one direction for some parallels and in the other direction for other parallels. Such a phenomenon might indicate a special case of literary dependence, namely, co-development. In the case of co-development, multiple authors work together, sharing their work with one another. In order to ascertain the most likely direction of borrowing between two interdependent documents, the likelihood of borrowing by each of the two authors must first be determined. Hence the methodology presented here in chapter 2 is focused on evidence of *borrowing* in the intertextual relationship.

The direction of borrowing is approached in a manner similar to that of literary dependence. In both cases, the minimum criterion is easily identified. For the question of literary dependence, a direct literary relationship between two documents can be established with just one indisputable direct-connect parallel. So too, an author's position as a literary borrower can be established with just one indisputable instance of borrowing from the other document. Moreover, since the primary interest of the present methodology is the intertextual relationship at the whole document level, it is not necessary to determine a direction of borrowing for each individual parallel. Rather, the whole-document perspective requires weighing the cumulative effect and seeing if the weight of evidence is well balanced or if it points to one document or the other as most likely to contain borrowed parallel material. Therefore, just as the likelihood of literary dependence is based on cumulative evidence that at least one of the parallels derives from a direct literary connection, the likelihood of borrowing for each directional scenario is based on cumulative evidence that at least one of the parallels is borrowed. The task of methodology development, then, is focused on two key questions: (1) What constitutes evidence of borrowing? and (2) How can the overall probability of borrowing be determined from such evidence? Again, the process begins with the question of evidence.

Evidence of Borrowing

Identification of relevant and available evidence of borrowing is not as straightforward as many scholarly studies seem to indicate. In order to evaluate the options, it is helpful first to consider different ways in which the question has been approached. The research conducted for this project suggests that the major types of assessment methods can be distinguished according to the same two general parameters that are used in chapter 1 to distinguish the major types of parallel relationships, namely, mode and directness. The first parameter, mode of assessment, concerns whether directionality is discerned from logical or temporal indicators. A temporal approach determines directionality based on relative temporal positioning of the two documents. A logical approach, on the other hand, determines directionality based on the logical relationship between parallel elements. The second parameter, directness of assessment, concerns whether the approach is direct or indirect. A direct approach assesses directionality from the parallels themselves. An indirect approach utilizes intermediate or surrogate means by which to obtain an assessment of directionality. The possible permutations of these two parameters define the major approaches to assessing the direction of a dependent literary relationship. As shown in figure 2.1, this results in four major types of approaches, one of which is dominated by two different methods.

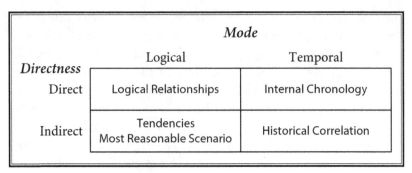

FIGURE 2.1. Major approaches to assessing directionality

The Direct-Temporal Approach

The direct-temporal approach, referred to here as the "Internal Chronology" approach, determines directionality from common temporal markers that are contained in the texts. Directionality of the intertextual relationship is based on the position of each document relative to the common temporal marker. Temporal markers of this type might include references to the reign of a particular ruler, the passing of certain laws or edicts, specific battles, or other recorded events. Since conclusive evidence of this type is quite rare in the NT, the internal chronology approach is of little use for assessing directionality of interdependent NT documents. Even the direct reference to "our beloved brother Paul" and his letters in 2 Pet 3:15–16 is insufficient for establishing relative priority between 2 Peter and any letters that claim Paul as author because the author of 2 Peter does not specify which of Paul's letters are included in the reference. Similarly, the stated description of 2 Peter as "the second letter I am writing to you" (2 Pet 3:1) is of little help for relative dating of the document because the first letter is not specifically identified by the author.

The Indirect-Temporal Approach

The indirect-temporal approach to assessing directionality attempts to show temporal correlation of the writing of each document with a historical marker of some kind. The relative dating of each document then is determined by the relative dating of the associated historical markers. This is the "Historical Correlation" approach. With this approach, the document that is associated with the earlier historical marker is considered the prior document. Many examples of historical correlations appear in studies of NT writings. Some of the more prominent cases include correlation of the occasion for writing with a particular period of persecution,[1] correlation of the grammar of the writing with an earlier or later dialect of Greek,[2] correlation of the theological ideas conveyed in the writing with the presence of popular philosophical teachings,[3] and correlation of the instructions given to readers with major periods of development of the early Christian movement, as recorded in the book of Acts and other accounts of early Christian faith communities.[4] The historical correlation approach, however, is unsuitable for this methodology because it relies on evidence external to the documents of interest, much of which is disputable. Moreover, the task of accurately correlating internal evidence with external evidence is fraught with difficulty as both are subject to interpretation. A clear example of the difficulty involved in correlating internal and external evidence is

1. For example, the situation reflected in 1 Peter has led scholars to correlate the writing of the book to periods of Christian persecution during the reigns of Nero (54–68 C.E.), Domitian (81–96 C.E.), and Trajan (98–117 C.E.). See, e.g., Heinrich Julius Holtzmann, *Einleitung in das Neue Testament* (Freiburg: Mohr [Siebeck], 1886), 522–24.

2. David Daube, for instance, argues that use of the imperatival participle reflects an earlier stage of Greek language development than does the use of finite imperatives. Hence passages that are marked by an imperatival participle must be borrowed from earlier sources (e.g., Rom 12:9–19; Eph 4:2; Col 3:16–17; Heb 13:5; 1 Pet 2:18; 3:1, 7–9; 4:7–10) ("Appended Note: Participle and Imperative in 1 Peter," in *The First Epistle of St. Peter: The Greek Text with Introduction, Notes and Essays*, ed. Edward Gordon Selwyn [London: Macmillan & Co. Ltd., 1955], 467–88).

3. The situation reflected in the letter to the Colossians, for example, has led to correlations with the presence of Jewish forms of Gnosticism as well as Greco-Roman Cynicism. So Richard E. DeMaris, *The Colossian Controversy: Wisdom in Dispute at Colossae*, JSNTSup 96 (Sheffield: Sheffield Academic, 1994); Jarl Fossum, "Colossians 1.15–18a in the Light of Jewish Mysticism and Gnosticism," *NTS* 35, no. 2 (April 1989): 183–201; Troy W. Martin, *By Philosophy and Empty Deceit: Colossians as Response to a Cynic Critique*, JSNTSup 118 (Sheffield: Sheffield Academic, 1996).

4. For example, Bernard Orchard and Harold Riley correlate each of the three Synoptic Gospels as a response to successive phases or crises which the pre-70 Christian communities faced, as evidenced in Acts and writings of the early Fathers. Thus they assign priority to Matthew, with Luke second and Mark third (*The Order of the Synoptics: Why Three Synoptic Gospels?* [Macon, GA: Mercer University Press, 1987], 275–77).

found in the plethora of scholarly hypotheses regarding the occasion for writing Colossians.[5] Given the difficulty involved in correlating internal and external evidence, the historical correlation method is not a reliable means of establishing the relative priority of two interdependent documents.

The Indirect-Logical Approach

Indirect-logical approaches establish directionality by evaluating parallels according to some externally derived logical criteria. The sources consulted for this study show that the indirect-logical category is dominated by two particular methods, which are referred to here as "Tendencies" and "Most Reasonable Scenario."

Tendencies

The tendencies method evaluates parallels according to the tendencies or practices exhibited by scribes or authors when transmitting or utilizing another work in their own writing. For example, if one parallel element is longer in length than the other, then the shorter element is considered prior due to the tendency for length to increase with repeated transmission and use. While application of observed tendencies is most common in analyses of the Synoptic Problem,[6] it also shows up in studies of other NT intertextual relationships. In particular, it is not unusual to find references to the commonly acknowledged tendencies of increasing length,[7] increasing clarification and correction,[8] and even better Greek grammar

---

5. Good summaries of the major hypotheses can be found in Douglas J. Moo, *The Letters to the Colossians and to Philemon*, The Pillar New Testament Commentary (Grand Rapids, MI: Eerdmans, 2008), 46–60; Peter T. O'Brien, *Colossians and Philemon*, WBC 44 (Nashville, TN: Thomas Nelson, Inc., 2000), xxx–xxxviii.

6. See, e.g., Robert H. Stein, *The Synoptic Problem: An Introduction* (Grand Rapids, MI: Baker Books, 1987), 48–84.

7. Increasing length has been noted for 2 Pet 2:1–3 || Jude 4; 2 Pet 2:4 || Jude 6; 2 Pet 2:15 || Jude 11 by J. N. D. Kelly, *A Commentary on the Epistles of Peter and of Jude*, BNTC (London: Adam & Charles Black, 1969), 226.

8. The apparent chronological correction in 2 Pet 2:4ff of the OT events mentioned in Jude 5–7 is often noted by scholars as an indicator that 2 Peter borrowed from Jude. So Johannes Kahmann, "The Second Letter of Peter and the Letter of Jude: Their Mutual Relationship," in *The New Testament in Early Christianity: La*

and writing style.[9] References to the commonly acknowledged tendency of increasing detail between parallel texts also are fairly common,[10] as well as the tendency of increasing theological development.[11]

The tendencies method of assessing directionality seems like a good approach since it appears to deal directly with parallel elements in the texts and it is easy to evaluate. However, there are two major problems with this approach that render its usefulness for this project doubtful. First, many of the presumed tendencies have been leveraged from the field of NT textual criticism. In fact, all of the tendencies mentioned above have roots in textual criticism.[12] In the interest of reconstructing the transmission process in the manuscript tradition, text critics have postulated that variant readings may be due to scribal tendencies to make certain kinds of intentional or unintentional changes when copying manuscripts. Intentional changes have been attributed to scribal tendencies to improve spelling and grammar, harmonize parallel accounts, add complementary and amplifying phrases, clarify historical and geographical references, conflate different readings, emphasize theological interests, and insert miscellaneous details.[13] Such "tendencies" then give rise to general rules or guidelines for determining

---

réception des écrits néotestamentaires dans le christianisme primitif, ed. Jean-Marie Sevrin, BETL 86 (Leuven: Peeters & Leuven University Press, 1989), 106; Kelly, *Peter and Jude*, 227; Werner Georg Kümmel, *Introduction to the New Testament*, rev. ed., trans. Howard Clark Kee (Nashville, TN: Abingdon, 1975), 431.

9. Daube assumes a tendency toward better Greek in his evaluation of parallels between Peter and Paul, where 1 Peter exhibits imperatival participles and Paul utilizes imperatives (1 Pet 3:1 || Eph 5:22 || Col 3:18; and 1 Pet 2:18 || Eph 6:5 || Col 3:22). Daube suggests that "given the good Greek of 1 Peter, it is unlikely that 1 Peter would have replaced Paul's clear imperatives with imperative participles" ("Participle and Imperative," 488).

10. For example, increasing detail is noted for the parallel between Jude 11 and 2 Pet 2:15–16 by Kahmann, "Second Peter and Jude," 109; and for the parallel between *1 Clem.* 17:1 and Heb 11:37, 32 by Donald Alfred Hagner, *The Use of the Old and New Testaments in Clement of Rome*, NovTSup 34 (Leiden, The Netherlands: E. J. Brill, 1973), 187.

11. Kümmel draws attention to perceived theological development between Ephesians and Colossians as evidence for priority of Colossians (Col 1:26 || Eph 3:5; Col 2:2 || Eph 3:4; Col 1:20 || Eph 2:16; Col 2:7 || Eph 2:20f) (*Introduction*, 360). So also, C. Leslie Mitton, *The Epistle to the Ephesians: Its Authorship, Origin and Purpose* (Oxford: Clarendon, 1951), 68–71.

12. See Bruce M. Metzger, *The Text of the New Testament: Its Transmission, Corruption, and Restoration*, 3rd ed. (New York: Oxford University Press, 1992), 195–206.

13. Metzger, *Text of the New Testament*, 195–206.

which variant reading of the text is more likely to reflect the original text.[14] For example, two of the basic rules of textual criticism are to prefer the more difficult reading and to prefer the shorter reading, both of which are based on observed tendencies.[15] Application of rules derived from scribal tendencies is a commonly accepted practice in modern textual criticism. Transference of this practice, along with the specific tendencies, to the field of NT intertextual studies, however, is questionable. Scribal tendencies in the manuscript transmission process do not necessarily apply in the case of one author borrowing material from an existing document in the crafting of a new document. Since the purpose of a scribe in the transmission process is not the same as the purpose of an original author who chooses to make use of other documents, it should not be assumed that their work would be characterized by the same practices and tendencies. For this reason, the presence of such "tendencies" in NT intertextual parallels may be more reflective of the manuscript transmission process or the creative purpose of the author rather than relative priority of the documents.

Legitimate applicability of tendencies to NT intertextuality is further challenged by a second problem with this method. An important study published by E. P. Sanders in 1969 has convincingly shown that perceived tendencies in early Christian writings might be more imagined than real.[16] With the goal of validating whether and how tendencies might serve as criteria for assessing relative dating, Sanders engages in an extensive investigation of how the tradition about Jesus developed in the early Christian community of faith.[17] His study focuses on the three Synoptic Gospels as well as certain post-canonical sources that contain sufficient reference to the synoptic tradition to permit evaluation of developmental tendencies. Specifically, these include the textual tradition, the early church Fathers and Apologists (2 Clement, Did. 1:3 — 2:1, and Justin Martyr), as well as the Apocryphal Gospels, excluding the Gospel of Thomas. Within these selected

---

14. See, e.g., Kurt Aland and Barbara Aland, The Text of the New Testament: An Introduction to the Critical Editions and to the Theory and Practice of Modern Textual Criticism, 3rd ed., trans. Erroll F. Rhodes (Grand Rapids, MI: Eerdmans, 1989), 280–82; Metzger, Text of the New Testament, 207–46.

15. See Aland and Aland, Text of the New Testament, 281; Metzger, Text of the New Testament, 209–10.

16. E. P. Sanders, The Tendencies of the Synoptic Tradition (Cambridge: Cambridge University Press, 1969).

17. Sanders, Tendencies, 2.

writings, Sanders investigates the commonly acknowledged tendencies of increasing length, increasing detail, diminishing Semitisms, and the preference for direct discourse over indirect discourse.[18] These types of tendencies all had been employed by scholars to evaluate relative dating of synoptic material prior to Sanders's investigation. The results indicate that, for the purpose of relative dating, tendencies should be applied only with extreme caution. In the final chapter, Sanders summarizes the results as follows:

> There are no hard and fast laws of the development of the Synoptic tradition. On all counts the tradition developed in opposite directions. It became both longer and shorter, both more and less detailed, and both more and less Semitic. Even the tendency to use direct discourse for indirect, which was uniform in the postcanonical material which we studied, was not uniform in the Synoptics themselves. For this reason, *dogmatic statements that a certain characteristic proves a certain passage to be earlier than another are never justified.*[19]

Although the Synoptic tradition is shown to have developed in both directions on all counts, Sanders does find evidence of a general tendency of later transmitters to add detail and to prefer direct discourse over indirect discourse. However, since the data is mixed, even these tendencies are only weak indicators, and then only if the tendencies are consistent throughout the entire document.[20] Based on Sanders's study, it is prudent to be wary of evaluating priority of different facets of the Synoptic tradition based on presumed tendencies.[21] Since there is no evidence to suggest that tendencies are more trustworthy in regard to other NT writings such as the epistles, it is best to avoid introducing the uncertainty of tendencies into an analysis of NT intertextuality.

---

18. Sanders also investigates the use of conflation as an indicator of priority, which is discussed later in this chapter.

19. Sanders, *Tendencies*, 272.

20. Sanders, *Tendencies*, 273–74.

21. Juha Pakkala's study of variant and parallel passages in the manuscript tradition of the Hebrew scriptures also challenges the axiom that later editors tended to expand the older texts (*God's Word Omitted: Omissions in the Translation of the Hebrew Bible*, FRLANT 251 [Göttingen: Vandenhoeck & Ruprecht, 2013]).

Most Reasonable Scenario

The second particular method that dominates the indirect-logical approach to directionality is the "Most Reasonable Scenario" method (henceforth MRS). This method follows along the lines of the basic maxim of textual criticism, which is to "choose the reading which best explains the origin of the others."[22] More specifically, the MRS method establishes priority by evaluating which of the possible directionality scenarios offers the best explanation of both the similarities and the differences between the two documents. Attention is focused on explaining the redactional practices of both authors, assuming that each author leveraged the work of the other author, and then determining which scenario seems most reasonable in the eyes of the person doing the evaluation.[23] Explanations may involve matters of form, arrangement, meaning, or function, and although the MRS approach usually entails lower-order individual parallels, it has also been applied to entire documents.

The best examples of the MRS method applied to whole documents involve the relationship between the Synoptic Gospels (a.k.a. the Synoptic Problem) and the relationship between 2 Peter and Jude. In the case of the Synoptic Problem, an MRS method is usually employed to explain the pattern of agreement and disagreement regarding the narrative sequence or the order of pericopes in the Synoptic Gospels.[24] For 2 Peter and Jude, an MRS argument is generally invoked to claim that Jude must be prior

22. Metzger, *Text of the New Testament*, 207.

23. Examples of scholarly works that utilize some kind of MRS approach to directionality include: John Dominic Crossan, *The Birth of Christianity: Discovering What Happened in the Years Immediately after the Execution of Jesus* (New York: HarperSanFrancisco, 1998), 107; Mark S. Goodacre, *The Synoptic Problem: A Way Through the Maze* (New York: T&T Clark International, 2001), 81–82; Peter M. Head, *Christology and the Synoptic Problem: An Argument for Markan Priority*, SNTSMS 94 (Cambridge: Cambridge University Press, 1997), 44–48; Wolf-Dietrich Köhler, *Die Rezeption des Matthäusevangeliums in der Zeit vor Irenäus*, WUNT 2.24 (Tübingen: Mohr [Siebeck], 1987), 13. See also Duane Frederick Watson's work, which reflects a MRS approach based on rhetorical criticism (*Invention, Arrangement, and Style: Rhetorical Criticism of Jude and 2 Peter*, SBLDS 104 [Atlanta, GA: Scholars Press, 1988], 163–87).

24. See, e.g., David J. Neville, *Arguments from Order in Synoptic Source Criticism: A History and Critique*, New Gospel Studies 7 (Macon, GA: Mercer University Press, 1994); David J. Neville, *Mark's Gospel—Prior or Posterior? A Reappraisal of the Phenomenon of Order*, JSNTSup 222 (London: Sheffield Academic, 2002).

because there would have been no need to write the letter if 2 Peter were already available.[25] The method has also been applied at the whole document level to Ephesians and Colossians in order to determine their relative priority. Andrew T. Lincoln, for instance, argues against the hypothesis that the author of Colossians abbreviated sections from Ephesians that seem to contain important content (e.g., Eph 2:11–22 || Col 1:21–23; Eph 5:21–33 || Col 3:18–19). According to Lincoln, "[t]he far more obvious hypothesis is that Colossians served as the basis for Ephesians, which omits the interaction with a specific false teaching and the greetings from and to particular individuals and expands the rest of the material to make it more general and to adapt it to its own purposes."[26]

The MRS approach is appealing in that it seems to offer a rational way to discern the most likely direction of dependence. The main problem with the approach, however, is that plausible explanations can always be found for dependence in both directions, and discernment of which is more reasonable is highly subjective. Ernest Best draws attention to this problem repeatedly in his evaluation of parallels between Ephesians and Colossians. One example highlighted by Best involves the parallel between Eph 6:21–22 and Col 4:7–8, and in particular, the awkwardness of the first five words that appear in Eph 6:21 but not in Col 4:7, ῞Ινα δὲ εἰδῆτε καὶ ὑμεῖς ("So that you also may know"). Best shows how the presence of this ῞ινα clause can be explained both ways. First, since the style of Ephesians is not normally so "clumsy," the ῞ινα clause may have come from Col 4:8 and therefore marks an intrusion of foreign material into the letter. In that case, Colossians would be prior. On the other hand, the author of Colossians may have recognized the difficulty posed by the ῞ινα clause in Ephesians and omitted it in order to make the passage read more clearly, in which

25. So, e.g., Peter H. Davids, *The Letters of 2 Peter and Jude*, The Pillar New Testament Commentary (Grand Rapids, MI: Eerdmans, 2006), 141–42; Kelly, *Peter and Jude*, 226; Michael J. Gilmour, *The Significance of Parallels between 2 Peter and Other Early Christian Literature*, AcBib 10 (Leiden, The Netherlands: Brill Academic, 2002), 83–86; James Moffatt, *An Introduction to the Literature of the New Testament*, The International Theological Library (New York: Charles Scribner's Sons, 1911, reprinted 1929), 351; John A. T. Robinson, *Redating the New Testament* (London: SCM Press Ltd., 1976), 192; Thomas R. Schreiner, *1, 2 Peter, Jude*, NAC 37 (Nashville, TN: Broadman & Holman, 2003), 419.

26. Andrew T. Lincoln, *Ephesians*, WBC 42 (Dallas, TX: Word Books, 1990), l–li.

case, Ephesians would be prior.[27] Another example offered by Best involves
the parallel between Eph 5:15–16 and Col 4:5. One possible explanation is
that the author of Ephesians expanded and explained the thought of Col
4:5 and omitted the reference to behavior toward non-Christians in accordance with his emphasis on conduct internal to the community of faith.
Another possible explanation is that the author of Colossians abbreviated
Eph 5:15–16 and removed an ethical theme that might not have suited the
specific purpose of his letter.[28]

The problematic subjective nature of the MRS approach is also raised
by Michael Green in his comments on the relationship between 2 Peter
and Jude. Two prominent examples exemplify Green's concern. The first
example involves parallels between 2 Peter and Jude, where Jude alone
draws material from the Apocryphal books of *1 Enoch* and the *Testament
(Assumption) of Moses*. On the one hand, scholars have suggested that the
author of 2 Peter may have held a stricter view of Scripture and therefore
was reluctant to include Jude's apocryphal material.[29] However, according
to Green, this difference may also be explained as Jude's sharpening of
Peter's allusions by adding familiar apocryphal references.[30] The second
example involves the amount of parallel material in Jude. Since only about
a half-dozen verses in Jude do not find parallels in 2 Peter, many scholars
argue that 2 Peter must have used Jude because it makes no sense for Jude
to have written a letter in which he contributes so little of his own thinking.[31]
Green, however, points out that the alternative scenario is also plausible.
Since Jude informs his readers that he had to change his plan for the letter
in order to address an imminent danger threatening the faithful assembly
(Jude 3), it is not hard to imagine that he hastily wrote the main tenets for
countering false teaching using materials that were available and adding

---

27. Ernest Best, "Who Used Whom? The Relationship of Ephesians and Colossians," *NTS* 43, no. 1 (January 1997): 77–79.

28. Best, "Who Used Whom?" 83–84.

29. So, e.g., Kelly, *Peter and Jude*, 227; Kümmel, *Introduction*, 431.

30. Michael Green, *The Second Epistle General of Peter and the General
Epistle of Jude: An Introduction and Commentary* (Grand Rapids, MI: Eerdmans,
1968), 52–53.

31. So Gilmour, *Significance of Parallels*, 83–86; Kelly, *Peter and Jude*, 226;
Davids, *2 Peter and Jude*, 141–42; Moffatt, *Introduction*, 351; Robinson, *Redating*, 192;
Schreiner, *1, 2 Peter, Jude*, 419.

very little of his own, with the understanding that he might follow this up later with another letter as originally planned.[32]

The problem highlighted by Best and Green regarding the bipolar nature of MRS arguments is abundantly evident in published NT studies. There are numerous cases where the same basic parallel characteristics are understood by different scholars as indicating directionality in opposite directions. Whereas one scholar sees movement from specific to general,[33] another scholar sees movement from general to specific;[34] while one scholar sees movement from ambiguous to unambiguous,[35] another scholar sees movement from self-explanatory to hermeneutically dependent;[36] while one scholar sees movement from an incorrect to a correct chronological or logical sequence of parallel elements,[37] another scholar might see movement to a more context-sensitive order of parallel elements.[38] As illustrated by these perplexing examples, the subjective bipolar nature of the MRS approach makes it generally unreliable as a means of establishing relative priority or the direction of borrowing between two literarily dependent documents. The results are too dependent on an uncontrollable external factor, namely, the subjective reasoning of those performing the assessment.

32. Michael Green, *Second Peter and Jude*, 55.

33. For example, Kahmann, "Second Peter and Jude," 108.

34. For example, Hagner, *Use of the Old and New Testaments*, 187; Kahmann, "Second Peter and Jude," 109.

35. So Kahmann, "Second Peter and Jude," 107.

36. So Peter H. Davids, "The Pseudepigrapha in the Catholic Epistles," in *The Pseudepigrapha and Early Biblical Interpretation*, ed. James H. Charlesworth and Craig A. Evans, JSPSup 14 (Sheffield: Sheffield Academic, 1993), 230–33; Hagner, *Use of the Old and New Testaments*, 200; Kümmel, *Introduction*, 431; Jeffery M. Leonard, "Identifying Inner-Biblical Allusions: Psalm 78 as a Test Case," *JBL* 127, no. 2 (Summer 2008): 261–62; Moffatt, *Introduction*, 351.

37. So Kahmann, "Second Peter and Jude," 106; Kelly, *Peter and Jude*, 227; Kümmel, *Introduction*, 431.

38. Mark S. Goodacre applies this reasoning to explain the different narrative sequences in the Synoptic Gospels (*The Case Against Q: Studies in Markan Priority and the Synoptic Problem* [Harrisburg, PN: Trinity Press International, 2002], 86).

The Direct-Logical Approach

The fourth major approach to assessing directionality is the direct-logical approach. Methods that fall in this category seek to establish directionality directly from the logical relationships observed in the parallels and their host documents, without resorting to external factors such as historical events, perceived tendencies of development, or the subjective reasoning of individual researchers. This is called the "Logical Relationships" approach.

For the purpose of assessing directionality between two documents that are literarily dependent, logical relationships are considered in three dimensions. The first dimension is intra-documentary in that it involves the relationship between the parallel material and the larger discourse of its host document. The second dimension is inter-documentary in that it involves the relationship between parallel elements that are observed in the two interdependent documents. The third dimension is extra-documentary as it extends beyond the two documents of interest and considers potential relationships with other more likely source documents.

Intra-Documentary Relationship

In the intra-documentary dimension, the primary question pertaining to borrowing concerns whether or not the author of one document knew and used parallel material from another document. In order to answer this question, investigation focuses on how the parallel material is integrated into the whole document. Of particular interest is evidence that the parallel material has been inserted from an outside source. This suggests two different types of evidence. The first type of integration evidence is that which marks the parallel material as foreign to the host document. Such evidence might appear as various kinds of disturbances in the flow of the discourse, including foreign language, unusual writing style, uncharacteristic concepts, or a particular function that is unparalleled in the rest of the document.[39]

---

39. Examples of works that consider various kinds of disturbances as evidence of directionality (or conversely, intra-document cohesion) include: John Coutts, "The Relationship of Ephesians and Colossians," *NTS* 4 (1958): 201; Crossan, *Birth of Christianity*, 105–6; Paul Ellingworth, "Hebrews and 1 Clement: Literary Dependence or Common Tradition?" *BZ* ns 23, no. 2 (1979): 262–69; Gilmour, *Significance of Parallels*, 53–54; Goodacre, *Case Against Q*, 40–43; Dietrich-Alex Koch, *Die Schrift als Zeuge des Evangeliums: Untersuchungen zur Verwendung und zum Verständnis der Schrift bei Paulus*, BHT 69 (Tübingen: Mohr [Siebeck], 1986), 13–14; William L.

This is where the concept of "fingerprinting" mentioned in chapter 1 might be useful (pp. 19–21). Although inadequate for demonstrating a direct literary connection between two documents, the presence of foreign literary characteristics or "fingerprints" in one of two interdependent documents does help establish the direction of borrowing. Research conducted for this project indicates that evidence of literary disturbance is readily available in the NT and other early Christian writings.

The second type of integration evidence is that which indicates the author actually borrowed the parallel material from another source. Such evidence may be detected by considering the borrowing practices of the author and evaluating whether or not the use of parallel material fits the author's pattern of borrowing.[40] Since a legitimate borrowing pattern can be established only on known cases of borrowing, evaluations of this type for NT ‖ NT parallels typically look for indications that the author's use of NT parallel material fits a pattern of OT usage. Such usage patterns may involve matters of language, form, interpretation, or function. This kind of integration evidence also is generally available in the NT and other early Christian writings. The primary indicators of directionality in the intra-documentary dimension, then, are disturbance in the flow of the discourse and consistency with the author's observed borrowing habits.

Inter-Documentary Relationship

In the inter-documentary dimension, the primary question pertaining to borrowing concerns whether or not the observed parallels indicate some kind of movement from one document to the other. In other words, do

---

Lane, *Hebrews 1–8*, WBC 47A (Nashville, TN: Thomas Nelson, 1991), cli; Andreas Lindemann, *Paulus im ältesten Christentum*, BHT 58 (Tübingen: Mohr [Siebeck], 1979), 18; John Howard Bertram Masterman, *The First Epistle of S. Peter: Greek Text, with Introduction and Notes* (London: MacMillan & Co., Ltd., 1900), 39; Robert J. Miller, "Is There Independent Attestation for the Transfiguration in 2 Peter?" *NTS* 42 (1996): 624; Michael Thompson, *Clothed with Christ: The Example and Teaching of Jesus in Romans 12.1–15.13*, JSNTSup 59 (Sheffield: Sheffield Academic, 1991), 31–37.

40. The following published works stress the need to evaluate consistency with the author's borrowing practices (a.k.a. redactional practices) when assessing literary dependence and relative priority: Goodacre, *Case Against Q*, 86–94; Leonard, "Identifying Allusions," 262; Charles E. Hill, *The Johannine Corpus in the Early Church* (Oxford: Oxford University Press, 2004), 70; Miller, "Independent Attestation," 623; Sanders, *Tendencies*, 146, 259.

the parallel elements give evidence of logical progression between the two documents? Semantically, the phenomenon might appear as a continuation of events or circumstances conveyed by the parallel thoughts from one element to the other.[41] Formally, logical progression might be evidenced by dispersion of parallel elements to a higher level of discourse for further elaboration.[42] Logical progression of parallel elements might also involve the lexical-grammatical features of the texts or even the particular functions of the parallel materials in the greater discourses of their host documents. The logical-progression type of evidence is only rarely cited in studies of NT ‖ NT intertextuality, perhaps because parallels of this kind are most often viewed as evidence against literary dependence or against common authorship rather than as evidence of directionality. Nevertheless, if logical progression is evident in parallels between two documents for which a high probability of literary dependence has already been demonstrated, then the phenomenon would constitute evidence of directionality. Thus the primary indicators of directionality in the inter-documentary dimension involve logical progression between parallel elements of two documents.

Extra-Documentary Relationship

Other sources beyond the two documents of interest are considered in the extra-documentary dimension. If another source can be identified with high confidence for just one of two parallel elements, then the probability of having borrowed from the other parallel document diminishes. Hence the document with the identified source is more likely to be the supplier rather than the borrower in the NT ‖ NT intertextual relationship. In effect, a likely external source for one of two parallel elements helps identify the NT ‖ NT borrower by the process of elimination.

---

41. Hagner's work is rare among published studies in that he recognizes continuation of thought associated with borrowed material; e.g., Hagner, *Use of the Old and New Testaments*, 218. So also, Harold W. Attridge, *The Epistle to the Hebrews: A Commentary on the Epistle to the Hebrews*, Hermeneia (Philadelphia, PN: Fortress, 1989), 7.

42. Examples of published works that advocate dispersion as an indicator of relative temporal priority include: Gail R. O'Day, "Jeremiah 9.22–23 and 1 Corinthians 1.26–31: A Study in Intertextuality," *JBL* 109 (1990): 265; Kahmann, "Second Peter and Jude," 106.

The logic of the external source indicator of borrowing is illustrated in figure 2.2. For the sake of illustration, this particular case of borrowing involves a NT || NT parallel and an external LXX source.

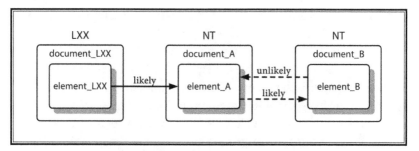

FIGURE 2.2. Logic of the external source indicator

The case illustrated in figure 2.2 involves a parallel between element_A of NT document_A and element_B of NT document_B. Element_A finds a likely source in an identifiable element of a LXX document. Since the LXX predates the NT, it is reasonable to assume that the parallel material moved from element_LXX to element_A. The possibility that element_A is borrowed from *both* element_LXX *and* element_B is highly improbable. Hence it is unlikely that element_A derives from element_B. This means that element_B is unlikely to be the supplier in the intertextual relationship between element_A and element_B. If element_B is not the supplier, then by process of elimination element_B is more likely to be the borrower.[43] However, if element_B also finds a likely source in an identifiable element of the LXX, then the effect cancels out and the likely direction of borrowing between element_A and element_B is inconclusive. Therefore, the primary indicator of borrowing in the extra-documentary dimension is a clearly identified external source for just one of the parallel elements.

The logical relationships approach is the most promising approach for assessing the most likely direction of borrowing based on intertextual parallels. Although not found in published works as frequently as the use

43. C. Leslie Mitton uses this method with 1 Peter || Ephesians parallels and another NT source to argue for the priority of Ephesians over 1 Peter. According to Mitton, the Ephesians material derived from Colossians and therefore cannot also have derived from 1 Peter. Hence the 1 Peter material must have derived from Ephesians (*Ephesians: Its Authorship, Origin and Purpose*, 186–87).

of historical correlations, tendencies, and various MRS methods, the use of logical relationships is inherently more reliable because assessments do not rely on disputable historical information, unverifiable development practices, or uncontrollable subjective reasoning on the part of individuals performing the evaluation. The logical relationships approach permits consistent results based on measurable features of the texts, regardless of who performs the assessment. Furthermore, relevant evidence of logical relationships is readily available in literary parallels. Therefore, the logical relationships approach is adopted for this methodology.

With the logical relationships approach, the necessary evidence of directionality is found in evidence of borrowing, which involves disturbance in the host document, consistency of borrowing practices, logical progression between parallel elements, and identification of a likely external source for one of the parallel elements. It is important, however, to keep in mind that none of these indicators is decisive in and of themselves. A skilled author could have incorporated external material seamlessly into the discourse without any disturbance, chosen to diverge from a normal pattern of LXX usage, incorporated an illogical progression, or even disguised the use of an external source. Indeed, an author's creative purpose might defy direct-logical evaluation at any given point. That is why the probability of borrowing for this methodology is based on cumulative evidence of all indicators across entire documents rather than solitary indicators of direction or selected individual parallels. The methodology to establish the probability of literary dependence, as defined in chapter 1, further prohibits limiting this follow-up analysis to certain selected parallels.[44] Having now established the direct-logical type of evidence as most appropriate, the next question concerns how the overall likelihood of borrowing can be determined from such evidence.

---

44. The present methodology for assessing the direction of borrowing assumes that the likelihood of literary dependence between two documents has already been demonstrated using the probability analysis method prescribed in chapter 1. This means that there is a high probability that *at least one* of the parallels derives from a direct literary connection. However, due to the non-deterministic nature of probability, the identity of the direct-connect parallel(s) cannot be determined. Hence there is no legitimate basis for determining which parallels are most significant for a follow-up analysis of directionality. For this reason, it is invalid to base the methodology in chapter 2 on only a selected set of parallels that might look more significant than others.

Probability of Borrowing

As in the case of literary dependence, the methodology for assessing the direction of borrowing takes shape by structuring the task as a probability analysis. Since an author's position as borrower can be established with just one parallel that is certainly borrowed, *the objective of the methodology is to determine for each directional scenario the overall probability that at least one of the parallels is borrowed based on evidence of borrowing found in the collection of parallels.* As explained above, evidence of borrowing is indicated by disturbance in the host document, consistency of borrowing practices, logical progression between parallel elements, and identification of a likely external source for one of the parallel elements.

The Basic Probability Calculation

The probability of a particular directional scenario is represented by the overall probability that one of the authors borrowed parallel material. Since the basic calculation is similar to the calculation for literary dependence, the data flow from evidence of borrowing exhibited by individual parallels to the probability of borrowing at the whole document level, as shown in figure 2.3, should look familiar. The only difference is that an extent multiplier is not required for any of the direct-logical indicators of borrowing.

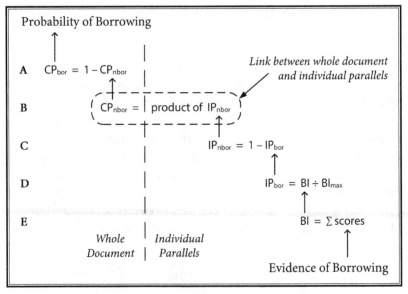

FIGURE 2.3. Calculation of the probability of borrowing

Since an author's position as a borrower can be established with just one clearly borrowed parallel, the ultimate parameter of interest is the overall probability that at least one of the parallels is borrowed. This collective probability of borrowing is denoted as CP_{bor},[45] which is shown on line A at the top of the diagram in figure 2.3. The term CP_{bor} is a number between zero and one that represents the probability of borrowing over the entire collection of parallels. The event that at least one of the parallels is borrowed is the same as the event that *not all* of the parallels are not-borrowed. The complement is the event that *all* of the parallels are not-borrowed. This is denoted as CP_{nbor}, the collective probability of not-borrowed. Moreover, since the probability of an event is equal to one minus the probability of its complement, it follows that $CP_{bor} = 1 - CP_{nbor}$ (line A).[46] The term IP_{nbor} denotes the probability that an individual parallel is not-borrowed. The probability that *all* of the parallels are not-borrowed is equal to the product

45. Parameter nomenclature: "CP" = Collective Probability; "IP" = Individual Probability; "BI" = Borrowing Index; and the subscript indicates the event of interest (bor = borrowed; nbor = not borrowed; max = maximum).

46. The probability rule of subtraction for complements states that the probability that a certain event *will* occur is equal to one minus the probability that the same event *will not* occur.

of IP_{nbor} for all the parallels (line B).[47] As in the computation of the probability of directness, the link here between the probability calculation at the whole document level and the probability calculations for individual parallels is made through the complement *not-borrowed* probabilities. In order to link this to the probability of borrowing exhibited by individual parallels, the complement relationship is reapplied in the reverse direction. The event that a parallel is not-borrowed is the same as the event that it is *not* borrowed, the complement of which is that it *is* borrowed. Therefore, $IP_{nbor} = 1 - IP_{bor}$, where IP_{bor} denotes the probability that an individual parallel *is* borrowed (line C).

The link to evidence observed in the parallels is made by defining IP_{bor} as a function of the scores associated with the indicators of borrowing. This is done through the use of a "Borrowing Index," denoted BI, which represents the degree to which parallel material looks like it is borrowed. The number is computed first by assigning scores for disturbance in the host document, consistency of borrowing practices, progression between parallel elements, and identification of a likely external source, according to the criteria established in the section entitled "Scoring Scheme," which is presented later in this chapter. The BI is equal to the sum of all scores for that particular parallel (line E). This is converted to a representative probability value between zero and one by dividing by the maximum possible value, BI_{max} (line D). The resulting value, IP_{bor}, represents the probability that an individual parallel element is borrowed.

The methodology described above is similar to that of chapter 1 in that the overall probability of the event of interest, either literary dependence or borrowing, can be computed directly from evidence exhibited in the parallel texts. In this case, the probability that an author borrowed is represented by CP_{bor} over the entire set of intertextual parallels, each of which has a BI value based on observed evidence. Determining the probability that an individual author borrowed material, however, is not the final step of the assessment process because each author of two interdependent documents is a potential borrower of the other's work.

---

47. The probability rule of multiplication for independent events states that the probability that events A and B both occur is equal to the probability that event A occurs times the probability that event B occurs.

Evaluation of Alternative Scenarios

In order to determine the most likely direction of a dependent intertextual relationship, it is necessary to evaluate both directional scenarios because both authors are potential borrowers. Specifically, the assessment process must consider which, if any, directional scenario is more likely, that the author of document_A borrowed from document_B, or that the author of document_B borrowed from document_A. Accordingly, a comparison is made between the probability that the author of document_A is the borrower and the probability that the author of document_B is the borrower. The procedure is relatively straightforward. First, the collective probability of borrowing (CP_{bor}) is calculated for each document. Then the respective probabilities are evaluated to determine which scenario, if any, is more likely. Final assessment of directionality, or relative priority, depends on the combination of the two results. The four possibilities are shown in figure 2.4.

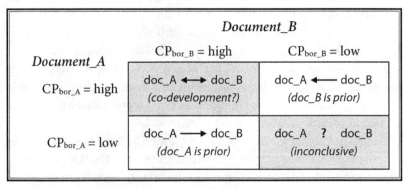

FIGURE 2.4. Significance of borrowing probabilities

As indicated in figure 2.4, the direction of borrowing between the two documents may be established when CP_{bor} is high for one document and low for the other document. For the two cases where this occurs, the document with the high CP_{bor} value is the borrower and the other document is prior. The other two cases shown in figure 2.4 are inconclusive for discerning relative priority. In the case where both of the CP_{bor} values are low, the evidence is insufficient to conclude borrowing on the part of either author. In the case where both of the CP_{bor} values are high, both documents are shown to contain material that looks like it is borrowed, in which case the possibility of co-development or mutual sharing between the authors must be considered.

An Illustrative Example

The assessment method described above may be illustrated using the same two hypothetical documents that appeared in the illustrative example of chapter 1. Again, for the purpose of illustrating the basic approach, the indicator scores for each parallel are provided in appendix B rather than in the following discussion. Here it is sufficient simply to observe the BI and the probability calculations. The scores for all the parallels are produced by the scoring scheme that is described in the next section.

Intermediate Calculations

$$BI \quad = (\Sigma \text{ scores})$$

$$IP_{bor} \quad = BI \div BI_{max}$$

$$IP_{nbor} \quad = 1 - IP_{bor}$$

$$CP_{nbor} = \text{product of } IP_{nbor}$$

$$CP_{bor} \quad = 1 - CP_{nbor}$$

In the first document to be considered, document_A, the parallel material exhibits different types of disturbances in nine of the fourteen parallels observed between document_A and document_B. Three of the parallels reflect distinctive practices that are consistent with the author's treatment of LXX material. For seven of the parallels, there is evidence of various types of progression from document_B to document_A. Finally, three of the parallels exhibit evidence of borrowing in that a likely LXX source is identified for the parallel elements in document_B. When all of these factors are taken into consideration, the collective probability of borrowing for document_A is 0.88, as shown in table 2.1.

TABLE 2.1. Probability of borrowing (document_A)

No.	Parallel	Individual			Collective	
		BI	IP_{bor}	IP_{nbor}	CP_{nbor}	CP_{bor}
					1	0
1	word 1	0	0.00	1.00	1.00	0.00
2	word 2	1	0.08	0.92	0.92	0.08
3	word 3	1	0.08	0.92	0.85	0.15
4	phrase 1	2	0.15	0.85	0.72	0.28
5	phrase 2	2	0.15	0.85	0.61	0.39
6	phrase 3	3	0.23	0.77	0.47	0.53
7	clause 1	3	0.23	0.77	0.36	0.64
8	clause 2	1	0.08	0.92	0.33	0.67
9	clause 3	3	0.23	0.77	0.26	0.74
10	comp-clause 1	3	0.23	0.77	0.20	0.80
11	comp-clause 2	3	0.23	0.77	0.15	0.85
12	comp-clause 3	2	0.15	0.85	0.13	0.87
13	cluster 1	0	0.00	1.00	0.13	0.87
14	cluster 2	1	0.08	0.92	0.12	0.88

The second document, document_B, exhibits much less evidence of having borrowed material. Two parallels show evidence of disturbance and two parallels reflect logical progression from document_A. None of the parallels reflect a distinctive practice that is consistent with the author's treatment of LXX material, and none exhibit evidence of borrowing in that the element in document_A finds a likely source in the LXX. As a result, the collective probability of borrowing for document_B is only 0.28, as shown in table 2.2.

TABLE 2.2. Probability of borrowing (document_B)

No.	Parallel	Individual			Collective	
		BI	IP_{bor}	IP_{nbor}	CP_{nbor}	CP_{bor}
					1	0
1	word 1	1	0.08	0.92	0.92	0.08
2	word 2	2	0.15	0.85	0.78	0.22
3	word 3	0	0.00	1.00	0.78	0.22
4	phrase 1	0	0.00	1.00	0.78	0.22
5	phrase 2	0	0.00	1.00	0.78	0.22
6	phrase 3	0	0.00	1.00	0.78	0.22
7	clause 1	0	0.00	1.00	0.78	0.22
8	clause 2	0	0.00	1.00	0.78	0.22
9	clause 3	0	0.00	1.00	0.78	0.22
10	comp-clause 1	0	0.00	1.00	0.78	0.22
11	comp-clause 2	0	0.00	1.00	0.78	0.22
12	comp-clause 3	1	0.08	0.92	0.72	0.28
13	cluster 1	0	0.00	1.00	0.72	0.28
14	cluster 2	0	0.00	1.00	0.72	0.28

Since CP_{bor_A} is relatively high (0.88) and CP_{bor_B} is relatively low (0.28), this hypothetical case falls in the upper-right quadrant of the chart in figure 2.4. Hence the author of document_A is more likely to have borrowed from document_B, and document_B is more likely to be the prior document. It is important to note that only the parallels that exhibit evidence of borrowing have an impact on the collective probability of borrowing. This is because for parallels that exhibit no such evidence, BI is equal to zero. This is the case for parallels #3, #4, #5, #6, #7, #8, #9, #10, #11, #13, and #14 in the illustrative example concerning document_B (table 2.2). If BI = 0, it follows that $IP_{bor} = 0$ and $IP_{nbor} = 1$. Hence, since $1 \times n = n$, the product of the IP_{nbor} values (CP_{nbor}) remains unchanged, and accordingly, CP_{bor} remains unchanged. Thus parallels that exhibit no evidence of borrowing indicators contribute nothing to the overall probability of borrowing. The outcome is determined by the accumulation of evidence, not the number of parallels included in the analysis.

This simple illustrative example shows how the direction of borrowing between two literarily interdependent documents can be determined by examining the parallels for key indicators of borrowing. Although the outcome may not be conclusive for all NT ‖ NT documents that are likely to be related through literary dependence, the method is reliable to the degree that the necessary data can be extracted from individual parallels in the form of scores which produce a meaningful BI (Borrowing Index).

Scoring Scheme

The data necessary for the probability analysis is derived from intertextual parallels by assigning a score for each parallel that represents the degree to which the material looks like it is borrowed. As explained above, the most reliable indicators involve direct-logical relationships and may be evidenced by disturbance in the host document, consistency of borrowing practices, logical progression between parallel elements, and identification of a likely external source for one of the parallel elements. The scoring scheme, therefore, is designed to produce a relative quantitative measure for degree of borrowing based on these types of evidences. The primary factors that contribute to scoring are the specific indicators and whether or not they are observed in the texts.

Specific Indicators of Borrowing

Disturbance in the Host Document

Intra-documentary disturbance is indicated by various types of discord between the parallel material and the whole document. In general, a disturbance may be thought of as anything that looks like an intrusion of foreign matter into the discourse. Evidence of a "disturbing" relationship may be found in multiple aspects of the relationship between the parallel element and the rest of the document. These might include matters of language, style, meaning, and function.

Disturbance of Language

A language disturbance may occur when the particular language of the parallel material is uncharacteristic of the document as a whole. This can involve key terms or phrases, unusual word forms, or even grammatical constructions that are not found elsewhere in the document. For example, the phrase τὸ κατὰ σάρκα ("according to the flesh") that appears in *1 Clem.* 32:2 and Rom 9:5, while characteristic of Pauline writings, seems foreign in *1 Clement*.[48] Grammatical examples might involve the shared use of an imperatival participle which is found only in the parallel material of a document.[49] An uncharacteristic use of prepositions also might constitute grammatical disturbance. For instance, the rare construction of εἰς followed by an accusative, εἰς ὅν ("in whom"), has been noted as a prepositional disturbance in 2 Pet 1:17.[50] Robert Miller, in fact, views the disturbance as evidence of literary dependence upon Matthew (2 Pet 1:17 || Matt 12:18, cf. Matt 3:17; Matt 17:5).[51]

Disturbance of Style

The most common aspect of disturbance found in the sources consulted for this project has to do with the particular writing style reflected in parallel elements. The phenomenon is characterized by a noticeable difference in the presentation of the parallel material as compared to the overall flow of the document. Variously described as an unusual pattern of writing, awkward editing, syntactical or stylistic tension, and even editorial fatigue, this type of disturbance can take many different forms.

Specific characteristics of style disturbances are illuminated by certain cases where literary dependence is commonly acknowledged, such as NT use of the OT. Indeed, the Pauline epistles are especially revealing in this regard. For example, syntactical tension involving OT references may be

---

48. So Oxford Society of Historical Theology, *The New Testament in the Apostolic Fathers* (Oxford: Clarendon, 1905), 39.

49. Daube, for example, views unusual use of the imperatival participle as an indicator of borrowed material ("Participle and Imperative," 467–88).

50. Richard J. Bauckham, *Jude, 2 Peter*, WBC 50 (Nashville, TN: Thomas Nelson, 1983), 209–10; Miller, "Independent Attestation," 623–24.

51. Miller, "Independent Attestation," 623–24.

observed in Rom 9:7b; 10:18; and Gal 3:6, 12b.[52] Stylistic tension has been observed in Rom 10:18; 11:34; 12:20; 1 Cor 10:26; 15:32b, 33; and 2 Cor 9:10.[53] Cases of "awkward editing" have also been identified in parallels between Ephesians and Colossians. Werner Georg Kümmel, for instance, claims that the author of Ephesians "clumsily appends the relative clause" of Col 3:7 after the phrase "in the sons of disobedience" in Eph 2:2–3, thereby betraying his dependence on Colossians.[54] Similarly, in regard to a parallel between Eph 6:21–22 and Col 4:7–8, Margaret MacDonald notes that "the author of Ephesians maintains the change in number from 'news about me, what I am doing' (v. 21) to 'how we are' (v. 22)" and concludes that "the shift seems out of place in Ephesians, which concentrates so deliberately on the authority of the apostle alone (e.g., Eph 1:1; 3:1–4)."[55]

Similar signs of awkward editing involving parallels between 2 Peter and Jude also have been noted. Johannes Kahmann, for instance, claims that "Jude 10 is a clearly understood sentence in which revilement and the following of natural instincts like animals are denounced. . . . In comparison, the construction of 2 Pet 2,12 is cumbersome and artificial."[56] Kahmann goes on to note that "in 2 Pet 2,17 the imagery of Jude 12.13 is recognizable in ἄνυδροι, which 2 Pet somewhat clumsily connects with πηγαὶ in place of νεφέλαι in the mists being driven by the wind, and especially in the conclusion of 2,17"; furthermore, "the relative οἷς, which Jude joins directly to ἀστέρες πλανῆται, hangs somewhat in the air in 2 Pet 2,17."[57]

Stylistic disturbance is also evident in the Synoptic Gospels in the form of editorial fatigue, which Mark Goodacre claims is "the most decisive indicator of Markan priority."[58] An example is found in Matt 8:1–4 || Mark 1:40–45 || Luke 5:12–16, where, according to Goodacre, Matthew and Luke initially make characteristic edits, only to lapse into the wording of Mark later in the pericope.[59]

52. Koch, *Die Schrift als Zeuge*, 13.

53. Koch, *Die Schrift als Zeuge*, 14.

54. Kümmel, *Introduction*, 359.

55. Margaret Y. MacDonald, *Colossians and Ephesians*, SP 17 (Collegeville, MN: The Liturgical Press, 2000), 353.

56. Kahmann, "Second Peter and Jude," 108–9.

57. Kahmann, "Second Peter and Jude," 109–10.

58. Goodacre, *Synoptic Problem*, 82.

59. Goodacre, *Case Against Q*, 41–42. See also Mark 6:14–29 || Matt 14:1–12.

One final example involves the quotations of Pss 2:7–8 and 109:1 LXX (110:1 English) that appear in both *1 Clem.* 36:4–5 and Heb 1:5, 13. While the practice of introducing an OT quotation as a direct address by God is characteristic of Hebrews, the use of such an introductory formula is found only here in *1 Clement.*[60] As such, it constitutes a disturbance in the normal style of *1 Clement.*

Disturbance of Meaning or Concept

Evidence of borrowing within a document might be indicated by unusual meanings or conceptual singularities. This is indicated by the presence of terminology that seems to have a different nuance of meaning when compared to other uses of the same terminology in the same document. The presence of a single localized concept that seems foreign or removed from the central themes of the document might also indicate borrowing. Good examples may be found in published studies of the intertextual relationship between 1 Peter and Hebrews, especially the studies done by H. H. B. Ayles and J. H. B. Masterman, who assume that the striking parallels between these documents derive from literary dependence. Noting that many of the concepts that are found in both 1 Peter and Hebrews seem more foreign in the former than the latter, Ayles and Masterman use this criterion to claim priority of Hebrews.[61] Duane Watson applies the same basic principle in his rhetorical-critical approach to the relationship between 2 Peter and Jude. If parallel propositions or topics which are central to one document "appear for the first time in the other work in the parallel section, possibly never to appear again," then, according to Watson, the book in which the topic or proposition is central is likely to be primary.[62]

---

60. Lane, *Hebrews 1–8*, cli.

61. H. H. B. Ayles, *Destination, Date, and Authorship of the Epistle to the Hebrews* (London: C. J. Clay & Sons, 1899), 66; Masterman, *First Peter*, 39. The particular examples cited by Ayles, however, suggest that the greater degree of perceived "foreignness" of parallel concepts in 1 Peter is probably better explained by the subordinate structure of the christological mini-expositions in the greater discourse of 1 Peter rather than borrowing of foreign material. See the discussion of parallel #CC2 in chapter 1 of Elizabeth A. Myers, *Intertextual Borrowing between 1 Peter and Hebrews: Probability of Literary Dependence and the Most Likely Direction of Borrowing* (Cody, WY: Pistos Ktistes Publishing LLC, 2020), 155–57.

62. Watson, *Invention*, 172.

Disturbance of Function

Although no specific examples were found in the research conducted for this project, it is also possible to find a disturbance of function associated with parallel material within the document. This would be evident by a particular use of literary concepts or devices associated with the parallel material that deviates from a normal pattern of usage found in the rest of the document. An example might involve two documents, both of which make similar use of a parallel list of virtues for instructing readers on proper behavior. If the use of attribute-lists in this way is unusual in one of the documents, then it may be considered a disturbance of function in that particular document. Another example might involve the function of LXX citations. If LXX citations normally are used to explicate christological truths in a particular document, then the appearance of a parallel LXX citation in an exhortation might constitute a disturbance of function in the greater discourse of the document.

Consistency of Borrowing Practices

The second type of intra-documentary evidence that helps to establish directionality is a corollary to the first type. Rather than looking for discord between a parallel element and its host document, the investigation looks for harmony with the author's demonstrated borrowing practices. Since regular or distinctive practices can be established only on known instances of borrowing, for NT authors the reference for comparison is best limited to use of the OT where references are reasonably certain. Harmony between a parallel element and the author's borrowing practices may be considered with respect to language, structure, interpretation, and function of the borrowed material in the author's discourse.

Consistency of Language

Consistency of language is evident in cases where parallel NT elements exhibit lexical-grammatical patterns or practices that fit the author's lexical-grammatical practices pertaining to borrowed OT material. For example, the author might have a habit of substituting nouns for pronouns, inserting verbs into verbless clauses, replacing imperatival participles with finite imperative verbs, or changing certain words like "soul" to "heart," "mind," or "life." Accurate assessments of language consistency, however, may prove difficult. NT writings generally contain a collection of verbatim quotations, similarly-worded allusions, and even echoes or motifs that show little or no verbal correspondence with the presumed OT sources. While specific sources may be identified for references that exhibit a high degree of verbal correspondence, identification of clear sources for allusions and echoes is less certain. Thus it is not always clear which set of apparent references should be used to establish the author's borrowing practices. Text critical issues associated with the LXX introduce another source of uncertainty. Ellingworth draws attention to this problem by highlighting the fact that "recent developments in the study of the LXX text have probably made the question of the text-type underlying the OT of the author of Hebrews more difficult rather than easier to answer."[63] While Ellingworth's comment is made in regard to Hebrews, it also applies to other NT documents that contain LXX references. Uncertainty about the source text underlying OT references can significantly impact what might be considered a regular or distinctive pattern of borrowing. In light of these issues, it may be difficult to discern the author's lexical-grammatical OT borrowing practices with enough distinction and confidence to use as a key indicator of borrowing for NT || NT parallels. Nevertheless, if specific patterns or distinctive practices can be shown to exist, independent of potential variations in the texts, then such patterns and practices are valid references for comparison and can be used to assess consistency in the treatment of language between NT || OT and NT || NT parallels.

Consistency of Interpretation

Consistency of interpretation is evident when parallel NT elements reflect the same methods of interpretation that the author employs with borrowed OT material. This might include a wide variety of interpretive approaches that were employed in first-century Judaism, which generally fall into the broad categories described as literalist, midrashic, pesher, and allegorical. Assessing parallel NT material according to consistency of interpretation, however, may not be very fruitful. The NT writers surely understood both the LXX and the Hebrew Bible as sacred scripture and referenced these

---

63. Paul Ellingworth, *The Epistle to the Hebrews: A Commentary on the Greek Text*, NIGTC (Grand Rapids, MI: Eerdmans, 1993), 37. The main complicating factors are summarized by Ellingworth on pages 37–38.

texts accordingly in their writings. It should not be assumed that the use of other contemporary writings in NT documents would reflect the same interpretive practices as references to Scripture. For this reason, consistency with OT borrowing practices concerning matters of interpretation might be rare indeed. Still, if parallel NT material reflects methods of interpretation that are consistent with how the author interprets OT material, then such consistency is a reasonable indicator of borrowing.

Consistency of Function

Consistency of function is assessed by comparing the pragmatic purpose of parallel NT elements with that of borrowed OT material. Consistency is evident when parallel NT elements serve essentially the same purpose as borrowed OT material. For example, borrowed material might be used as a basis for theological claims, as an example for readers, or to remind readers of important truths. Since the NT writers likely understood both the LXX and the Hebrew Bible as sacred scripture and referenced these texts accordingly in their writings, it is reasonable to expect that the use of contemporary writings in NT documents might not reflect the same purposes as references to sacred scripture. For this reason, consistency with OT borrowing practices also might be rare for NT || NT parallels. Nonetheless, if parallel NT material serves essentially the same purpose as borrowed OT material, then such consistency is an indicator of borrowing.

Consistency of Structure

Consistency of form or structural arrangement is assessed by noting the formal characteristics and structural arrangement of the parallel element, and comparing with the author's treatment of OT material. Does the NT author generally retain formal features such as parallelism, syntax, order of components, and transition devices? If not, is there a discernible pattern of transformation? Does the NT parallel of interest fit a general borrowing pattern or exhibit a distinctive form or arrangement that is also evident in the author's use of OT material? If so, such consistency suggests that the author may have also borrowed the NT parallel element.

A special case of borrowing that involves the structural arrangement of parallel elements is the phenomenon commonly known as "conflation." Conflation is the co-location or joining together of parallel elements from multiple sources, or from distributed locations in one source. The very definition of the term implies that the conflator is the borrower and the conflated material is prior. Although frequently noted by scholars as an indicator of relative priority,[64] this line of reasoning is questionable. In the case of NT use of the OT, conflation is a potentially reliable indicator because the conflated OT material is already known to have been written before the NT document was written. This is not necessarily so in the case of NT || NT intertextuality. For parallels between NT documents, or any other documents where relative priority is not already known, arguments based on conflation are problematic. The nature of the problem is clearly exposed by Sanders in *The Tendencies of the Synoptic Tradition*. In this influential work, Sanders evaluates the use of conflation as an indicator of priority. Since only one case of certain conflation is needed to establish that the conflator's work came after the conflated materials, this appears to be a simple and sure indicator of priority. However, as demonstrated by Sanders, using conflation as a criterion for determining relative priority is more complicated than it first appears because not all perceived conflations are true conflations. Sanders explains:

> The difficulty [to prove conflation] may be easily illustrated. If one document has 'A', another 'B', and another 'AB', the explanation comes readily to mind that the third conflated the first two. But it is also conceivable that the first and second used the third, each one copying a portion. The difficulty, then, is how to distinguish between apparent conflation and true conflation.[65]

Sanders wisely suggests that in order for a hypothesis of conflation to be valid, it should reflect a consistent pattern throughout the document and be evaluated relative to each possible scenario of conflation.

The fallacy of assessing relative priority on an isolated hypothesis of conflation is echoed by John Coutts, who illustrates how several parallels between Ephesians and Colossians can be viewed as multiple conflation

---

64. Examples of works that advocate conflation of texts as an indicator of relative priority include: Michael W. Holmes, "Paul and Polycarp," in *Paul and the Second Century*, ed. Michael F. Bird and Joseph R. Dodson (New York: T&T Clark International, 2011), 62; Lincoln, *Ephesians*, li–lii; Andrew T. Lincoln and A. J. M. Wedderburn, *The Theology of the Later Pauline Letters*, New Testament Theology (Cambridge: Cambridge University Press, 1993), 86–90; C. Leslie Mitton, *Ephesians*, NCB (London: Oliphants, 1976), 12; Mitton, *Ephesians: Its Authorship, Origin and Purpose*, 55–81; Thompson, *Clothed with Christ*, 35.

65. Sanders, *Tendencies*, 264.

scenarios in both directions. One example highlighted by Coutts involves three expressions in Ephesians, denoted "X," "Y," and "Z" (Eph 2:20–22 [X]; 3:17 [Y]; 4:15b–16 [Z]) and four expressions in Colossians, denoted "A," "B," "C," and "D" (Col 1:23a [A]; 2:7 [B], 19 [C], 2 [D]). Coutts explains that if Ephesians is dependent on Colossians, then X could be a conflation of A, B, and C; Y could be a conflation of A, B, and D; and Z could be a conflation of mostly C, but also B and D. However, if Colossians is dependent on Ephesians, then A might derive from Y; B could be a conflation of Y and X; and C and D both might derive from Z.[66] These kinds of conflation arguments, in effect, reflect another form of the MRS (Most Reasonable Scenario) approach to directionality. For this reason, the present methodology treats conflation as an indicator of relative priority only in relation to the author's pattern of borrowing. If the author shows a propensity for conflating OT material, then perceived conflation of NT elements might also suggest borrowed material.

Progression of Parallel Elements

The inter-documentary horizontal dimension focuses on the relationship between parallel elements and seeks evidence of logical progression from one element to the other. Although specific references to logical progression among parallels are rare in the published works consulted for this study, specific indicators may be found in multiple aspects of the horizontal parallel relationship.

Progression of Language

Progression of language is evidenced primarily by a difference in verbal tense between the parallel elements where the tenses may be understood to indicate a relative time frame and not just the aspect of the action that is in view. If the literary contexts support temporal understandings of the tense forms that appear in both elements, then differences might suggest that the authors stand at different viewpoints relative to the parallel verbal action. Their relative frames of reference, then, may be determined by the nature of the differences. Logical progression is indicated if author_A writes from a

---

66. Coutts, "Relationship," 201–2. Coutts argues for the priority of Ephesians based primarily on evidence of intra-documentary disturbance in Colossians.

position that is antecedent to the verbal action (future tense) and author_B writes from a position that is contemporaneous with or subsequent to the verbal action (present or past tense); or if author_A writes from a position that is contemporaneous with the verbal action (present tense) and author_B from a position that is subsequent to the verbal action (past tense). In either case, the difference in verbal tense suggests that author_A wrote before author_B.

Language progressions of this type are not uncommon in references to the OT made by NT writers (e.g., Rom 11:4 citing 3 Kgdms 19:18 LXX [1 Kgs 19:18 English]; John 12:40 citing Isa 6:10; 1 Pet 2:8 citing Isa 8:14). The phenomenon is also present in parallels between NT books. An example is found in 2 Pet 2:1 || Jude 4. Whereas 2 Peter announces that "there will be false teachers among you, who will sneak in destructive heresies, even denying the Master who bought them," Jude claims that "certain men have sneaked in, ..., who pervert the grace of our God into licentiousness, even denying our only master and Lord, Jesus Christ." The difference in tense observed here suggests that 2 Peter predates Jude. Scores for progression indicated by verbal tense may be offset by scores for other indicators of borrowing; nevertheless, it is still important to note the logical progression of the language between the parallel elements.

Progression of Structure

Progression of structure or arrangement is indicated by some kind of logical development in the particular formal or structural characteristics of parallel elements. The phenomenon is best explained by two particular types that appear in the research data. The first type, referred to as "dispersion," occurs when multiple parallel elements are clustered together in one document and are dispersed over a wider range of material in the other document. At first glance, this might look like conflation, only in the reverse direction. However, there is an important difference between dispersion and conflation. Conflation involves the physical location of parallel elements within a document, where distributed elements from one document (or documents) are joined together, or co-located, in another document. The phenomenon of conflation is *flat* in the sense that conflated elements, in both source and host documents, occupy a position at the same low level of discourse. Conflation is simply a matter of convergence of the common elements within the base level of the discourse. While dispersion reflects discourse development, no discourse development is associated with conflation.

For the purpose of the present methodology, dispersion is defined as the expansion of clustered elements, generally in the same order, to a higher level of discourse with evidence of content development. In effect, the clustered elements in one document appear in the other document as higher-level components of the discourse outline, key points of which receive further elaboration. In other words, the clustered group serves as a concise outline which is expanded and developed more fully in the second document. A good example is the reference to Jer 9:22–23 Hebrew (9:23–24 English) in 1 Cor 1:26–31. Gail R. O'Day explains the nature of dispersion in this case:

> The parallels between Jer 9:22 and 1 Cor 1:26–29 can be pursued in yet another direction. All three terms in the opening triad of v. 26 and its expansion in vv. 27–28 reflect particular issues that threaten to divide and disrupt the Corinthians. The first term in the triad, wisdom, and its counterpoint, foolishness, together are the central topic of chaps. 1–4. Wisdom is indeed one of the central causes of boasting in the community (e.g., 4:6). The second set, strong/weak, constitutes the heart of Paul's argument in chaps. 8–10, where the growing breach between strong and weak Christians threatens the unity of the church. Finally, the third element, noble/lowly birth, receives its full embodiment in the controversy over the Lord's Supper in chap. 11. The celebration of the Eucharist is marred in Corinth by economic and class divisions.[67]

This example illustrates how parallel elements in a source document are not only expanded in the host parallel (1 Cor 1:26–31) but also dispersed to a higher level of discourse for further elaboration. Another example of dispersion occurs between 2 Peter and Jude, where elements of Jude are dispersed throughout 2 Peter, where they receive further development.[68]

The second type of formal or structural progression has to do with the *portability* of the parallel elements. The present methodology uses the term "portable" to refer to written or oral material that is, by virtue of its formal characteristics (e.g., structure, syntax), believed to be formulated for widespread ease of use in liturgical or catechetical settings. This generally applies to material that is perceived as "hymnic" or "creedal" in nature. Such

---

67. O'Day, "Jeremiah 9.22–23 and 1 Corinthians 1.26–31," 265.

68. Kahmann calls attention to the dispersion of material between 2 Peter and Jude as evidence for the priority of Jude ("Second Peter and Jude," 106).

material is identified by the presence of certain features such as strophic arrangement, relative clauses, participial construction, and various types of parallelism, including repetition, antithesis, chiastic arrangement, and rhythm.[69] Formulating material in this way presumably makes it easier to remember and recite across a broad spectrum of situations and peoples, thereby facilitating its portability throughout early Christian communities. The presence of portable features in NT passages has typically prompted scholars to surmise that the material was borrowed, in its portable form, from some hypothetical tradition that predates the NT writing.[70] The basic premise underlying these claims is that *portable material is meant to be ported*, and that is how it comes to be known by many people and ends up in NT writings.

This same premise is fundamental for detecting progression of formal structure involving portable parallels. Before explaining how progression is detected, however, it is important to reiterate the relationship between literary dependence and direction of borrowing in the present methodology. Literary dependence is established on cumulative evidence of rarity of occurrence and degree of correspondence, as stipulated in chapter 1. The result of the analysis is a number that represents the collective probability that *at least one* of the parallels derives from a direct literary connection. The identity of the direct-connect parallel(s), however, is unknown due to the non-deterministic nature of probability. Hence the identities of the non-direct parallel(s) also are unknown. The methodology for assessing directionality assumes that a high probability of literary dependence has already been established in this way. Since a direct relationship of literary dependence is already deemed highly probable, and since the identities of

---

69. For fuller discussions of formal features associated with portable material see Markus Barth, "Traditions in Ephesians," *NTS* 30 (1984): 10; Hulitt W. Gloer, "Homologies and Hymns in the New Testament: Form, Content and Criteria for Identification," *PRSt* 11, no. 2 (Summer 1984): 124–29; Kazuhito Shimada, "The Formulary Material in First Peter: A Study According to the Method of Traditionsgeschichte" (Ann Arbor, MI: Xerox University Microfilms, 1966), 102–4 (reproduced in Sharon Clark Pearson, *The Christological and Rhetorical Properties of 1 Peter* [Lewiston, NY: Edwin Mellen, 2001], 227–28).

70. Attribution of portable material to independent use of common hypothetical traditions is quite common in published studies. See, e.g., Barth, "Traditions," 3–27; Gloer, "Homologies and Hymns," 115–32; Pearson, *Christological and Rhetorical Properties*; also many commentaries on "hymnic" passages such as Phil 2:6–11; Col 1:15–20; 1 Tim 3:16.

both the direct and the non-direct parallels are unknown, at this point in the process there is no legitimate role for speculation about hypothetical traditions as sources for individual parallels. Rather, the probability analysis is focused solely on assessing directionality at the whole document level over the entire set of parallels.

The prerequisite relationship between literary dependence and the direction of borrowing is important for the detection of progression of formal structure in NT || NT parallels because it allows for singular focus on directionality. Given that a direct relationship of literary dependence has already been established as highly probable, the most likely direction of movement between the parallel elements can be discerned by noting which of the elements appears to be more portable. If the parallel element in document_A exhibits a high degree of portability and the corresponding element in document_B does not, then the portability premise points to document_A as being prior because *portable material is meant to be ported*, and therefore is more likely to have been ported than the parallel which has a low degree of portability.

The fact that the parallel element in document_B appears to be less portable does not diminish the likelihood that it derives from the portable parallel element in document_A. There are at least two reasons why this is true. First, the use of portable material in early Christian writings often results in significant differences and loss of portable features. The parallel between *1 Clem.* 36:2–6 and Heb 1:3–13 is a good example of a parallel that exhibits movement from more to less portable and is still attributed to literary dependence.[71] Second, arguments which claim that intertextual parallels derive from hypothetical portable tradition sources are themselves predicated on the presence of significant textual differences. This is evident in the major points of such arguments which generally proceed as follows: (1) The similarities are too striking to be coincidental; (2) the differences preclude the possibility of literary dependence; (3) therefore, both parallel elements must derive from a common traditional source.[72] Now, if both

---

71. So Attridge, *Hebrews*, 6–7.

72. Cases where differences between parallels lead scholars to attribute the parallels to hypothetical portable source traditions rather than to literary dependence abound in published works. For example, Attridge, *Hebrews*, 28–31; Paul J. Achtemeier, *1 Peter: A Commentary on First Peter*, Hermeneia (Minneapolis, MN: Fortress, 1996), 12–23; John H. Elliott, *1 Peter*, AB 37в (New Haven: Yale University Press, 2001), 20–40; Leonhard Goppelt, *A Commentary on 1 Peter*, ed. Ferdinand Hahn, trans. John E. Alsup (Grand Rapids, MI: Eerdmans, 1993), 26–37; Erich

parallel elements derive from the same traditional source, then the fact that they are not identical means that one, if not both, of the parallel elements reflects some kind of transformation of the underlying portable source material. Even if the parallels draw upon different versions of a common tradition, the different versions themselves would constitute evidence of divergence from an earlier common source. Hence the given arguments for hypothetical source traditions inherently acknowledge that particular use of portable material can result in noticeable transformations. The only significant difference between literary dependence and hypothetical source hypotheses is whether the portable material is found in hypothetical or extant sources. Therefore, if a high probability of literary dependence has already been established between documents, then progression of formal structure may be evidenced by parallels that exhibit a significant difference in portability, with the direction moving from more to less portable.

Progression of Thought

Logical progression of thought may be identified by evidence of a sequential relationship where the thoughts conveyed by the two parallel elements reflect a continuation or progression of events or circumstances from the perspective of the two authors. Progression of thought frequently exhibits a stimulus-response relationship in which one document includes a stimulus, to which the other document provides evidence of a response. For example, document_A might raise a question, either explicitly or implicitly, which then is answered in document_B. Donald Hagner draws attention to this phenomenon in the parallel between 1 Clem. 50:6–7 and Rom 4:7–9. The parallel elements both begin with nearly identical quotations of Ps 31:1–2 LXX (32:1–2 English), which is immediately followed in 1 Clement by the statement, οὗτος ὁ μακαρισμὸς ἐγένετο ἐπὶ τοὺς ἐκλελεγμένους ὑπὸ τοῦ θεοῦ διὰ Ἰησοῦ Χριστοῦ τοῦ κυρίου ἡμῶν ("This blessing came upon those

---

Grässer, "Der Hebräerbrief, 1938–63," *TRu* ns 30, no. 2 (1964): 195–97; L. D. Hurst, *The Epistle to the Hebrews: Its Background of Thought*, SNTSMS 65 (Cambridge: Cambridge University Press, 1990), 130; Michael Mees, "Die Hohepriester-Theologie des Hebräerbriefes im Vergleich mit dem Ersten Clemensbrief," *BZ* ns 22, no. 1 (1978): 115–24; Edward Gordon Selwyn, "Essay II: Bearing of Evidence on the Supposed Dependence of 1 Peter on Other Epistles," in *The First Epistle of St. Peter: The Greek Text with Introduction, Notes and Essays* (London: Macmillan & Co. Ltd., 1955), 365–466; Ceslas Spicq, "La Iᵃ Petri et le témoignage évangélique de Saint Pierre," *ST* 20 (1966): 37.

who have been chosen by God through Jesus Christ our Lord"). As Hagner observes, "It is almost as though Clement were answering the question Paul asks immediately following the same citation (Rom 4.9): Ὁ μακαρισμὸς οὖν οὗτος ἐπὶ τὴν περιτομὴν ἢ καὶ ἐπὶ τὴν ἀκροβυστίαν;" ("Is this blessing then on the circumcised, or on the uncircumcised also?").[73] Harold Attridge draws attention to another question-answer relationship between *1 Clem.* 36:2–6 and Heb 1:5–13, where "1 Clement explicitly asks, then answers an obvious question — Who are the enemies? — posed by the catena in its form in Hebrews."[74] A similar stimulus-response relationship occurs when a particular concern is raised in document_A and then addressed in document_B. This phenomenon is evident in the prayer of *1 Clem.* 61:1–2, where "Clement is fulfilling the urgent request expressed in 1 Tim 2.1–2."[75]

Stimulus-response relationships may also be indicated when observed parallels between two documents reflect different levels of authority, such as between rulers and subjects, or between parents and children. For example, document_A might issue a specific directive, to which document_B gives evidence of compliance. Thought-progression between parallel elements might also be reflected a sequence of chronological events. In that case, document_A would convey the beginning of a chronological sequence of events, and document_B would follow with evidence of continuing or finishing the sequence.[76]

Progression of Function

Published studies reveal that logical progression of the functional aspect of parallels is recognized even less frequently than progression of thought. Watson's rhetorical-critical evaluation of the relationship between 2 Peter and Jude, however, suggests that relevant evidence in early Christian letters might be found in the rhetorical function of parallel texts. Presupposing that 2 Peter and Jude reflect typical conventions of Greco-Roman epistolary rhetoric, Watson shows how the different rhetorical functions of parallel elements might reveal the direction of dependence. Since a rhetor

---

73. Hagner, *Use of the Old and New Testaments*, 218.

74. Attridge, *Hebrews*, 7.

75. Hagner, *Use of the Old and New Testaments*, 232.

76. Examples of parallels exhibiting a progression of a chronological sequence of events were not found in the sources consulted for this study. However, this does not mean that such parallels do not exist.

must invent, support, and arrange arguments that will be persuasive for a specific audience and exigence, Watson stresses the extreme unlikelihood that "a document can be used with the basic argumentation intact and still be very persuasive to another audience facing a different or even similar exigence."[77] The sequential correspondence of parallels between 2 Peter and Jude, then, is most perplexing, unless there is a shift in the rhetorical pattern between the letters. This is, in fact, what emerges from Watson's rhetorical-critical evaluation of the parallels. Summarizing his observations, Watson explains the conundrum:

> The material shared by Jude and 2 Peter is found in the *narratio* (v 4), *probatio* (vv 5–14, 16), and *peroratio* (vv 17–18) of Jude, and the *probatio* (2:1–10a; 3:1–3), and *digressio* (2:10b–18) of 2 Peter. Since the *narratio* and *peroratio* are by nature highly individual and situation specific, it is improbable that a rhetor would borrow material to compose them. The content of the *narratio* is supplied by the facts of the case, and contains the propositions needing proof to support the case. The content of the *peroratio* is conditioned by the same propositions in recapitulation, and by an appeal to the emotions deemed useful in eliciting the desired response from the audience. Jude's *narratio* (v 4) and part of the *peroratio* (vv 17–18) have counterparts in 2 Pet 2:1–3 and 3:1–3 respectively. Jude's borrowing from 2 Peter is unlikely on the grounds of invention, and the nature of the *narratio* and *peroratio*."[78]

Since the shift in the rhetorical pattern fits rhetorical conventions if the author of 2 Peter borrowed from Jude, but not if Jude borrowed from 2 Peter, Watson concludes that Jude is the prior document. Although there might be objections to the MRS (Most Reasonable Scenario) nature of Watson's argument and his presupposition that NT letter writers employed standard conventions of Greco-Roman epistolary rhetoric, the attention that he brings to the rhetorical function of parallel elements is indeed helpful for discerning relative priority and the direction of borrowing. For behind the presumed rhetorical conventions is the underlying reality that the basis of persuasion *logically* precedes both the need for persuasion and the act of persuasion, regardless of the chronological order in which these respective

---

77. Watson, *Invention*, 169.
78. Watson, *Invention*, 170.

elements appear in a discourse. Since the basis of persuasion in NT letters is generally found in expositional material, and the need for and the act of persuasion is generally found in exhortational material, logical progression between parallel elements might be evidenced by a shift in rhetorical function between exposition and exhortation. In other words, if an element in document_A serves an expositional function and the parallel element in document_B serves an exhortational function, then the logical relationship between them suggests that document_A precedes document_B.

External Source

The final indicator of borrowing potential is based on whether the parallel material in either document has a more likely external source. Although C. Leslie Mitton utilizes this type of indicator with a perceived external NT source,[79] previous scholarly efforts to assess the likelihood of literary dependence between NT letters may have lacked the rigor that has been established with the present methodology. Therefore, possible external sources are restricted to earlier documents that would have been available to the NT authors, and where a specific reference can be identified with a high degree of confidence. For example, if element_A finds a likely source in the LXX and parallel element_B does not, then it is reasonable to conclude that element_A probably is borrowed from the LXX source and not from element_B. Thus document_A would have to be the supplier rather than the borrower in the relationship with document_B. If document_A is the

---

79. C. Leslie Mitton uses this type of indicator with a NT source (Colossians) to argue for the priority of Ephesians over 1 Peter. In the case of 1 Pet 1:10–12 || Eph 3:2–6 || Col 1:26–27, he suggests that if indeed Ephesians derived from Colossians, "then Ephesians here cannot be derived from 1 Peter, and so it must be that 1 Peter is derived from Ephesians" (*Ephesians: Its Authorship, Origin and Purpose*, 186). Mitton further notes that "though the passage in 1 Peter includes some words which are common to both Ephesians and Colossians, several others have their equivalent only in the passage in Ephesians" (p. 186). So too in the case of 1 Pet 2:2–6 || Eph 2:18–22 || Rom 5:2 + 1 Cor 3:12 + Col 2:19 + Col 2:7, where Mitton claims that since Ephesians derived from Colossians, it cannot be said that Ephesians also derived from 1 Peter for the same parallel elements. Moreover, in regard to the other elements, "we cannot accuse [Paul] of dependence upon 1 Peter for the use of words and phrases which he has already shown to be part of his own vocabulary by his use of them in earlier letters" (p. 187).

supplier, then it follows that document_B is most likely to have borrowed the parallel material from document_A.

Identification of a likely source for a parallel element must be based on more than just the degree of verbal resemblance. As demonstrated in chapter 1, literarily dependent relationships can vary widely in the degree of correspondence. While some writers copy the material verbatim, others might choose to paraphrase or modify the material in various ways to better fit the purpose and style of the discourse. Text critical issues involving the Greek NT and the source documents also might account for variations in the parallel material. Consequently, the present methodology recognizes a source for a parallel element only if the literary context of the parallel material also gives reason to believe that the connection was intended by the author. This might appear in the form of an introductory formula or some other indicator that the NT author had the particular source in view. The external source indicator, then, does not require identification of a specific underlying text tradition, or an approach to NT textual criticism beyond what is specified in the procedure sections of chapters 3 and 4 of this book, where the methodology for assessing the likelihood of literary dependence is applied to two different pairs of NT documents.

Scores for Specific Indicators of Borrowing

Assigning point scores for each of the borrowing indicators is quite simple. None of the indicators involves varying degrees for strength of evidence. The only criterion is whether or not an indicator is observed in the parallel text. For this methodology, the thirteen indicators are all valued equally.[80] If an indicator is observed, one point is awarded for that indicator. If the indicator is not observed, zero points are awarded. Since $BI = \Sigma$ scores, the maximum possible score for an individual parallel, BI_{max}, is equal to 13, as shown in table 2.3.

---

80. The default position established for this methodology is that all things are valued equally unless there is a compelling reason to do otherwise. Research conducted for this project gives no reason to believe that certain indicators constitute stronger evidence of borrowing and therefore should be weighted more heavily in the scoring scheme. Hence the default position is retained, and all indicators receive the same score.

TABLE 2.3. Points awarded for specific indicators of borrowing

No.	Indicator	Criterion	Points
1	Disturbance of Language	observed	1
		not observed	0
2	Disturbance of Style	observed	1
		not observed	0
3	Disturbance of Meaning	observed	1
		not observed	0
4	Disturbance of Function	observed	1
		not observed	0
5	Consistency of Language	observed	1
		not observed	0
6	Consistency of Structure	observed	1
		not observed	0
7	Consistency of Interpretation	observed	1
		not observed	0
8	Consistency of Function	observed	1
		not observed	0
9	Progression of Language	observed	1
		not observed	0
10	Progression of Structure	observed	1
		not observed	0
11	Progression of Thought	observed	1
		not observed	0
12	Progression of Function	observed	1
		not observed	0
13	External Source	observed	1
		not observed	0
		Maximum Total Score (BI_{max}) =	13

Using this scoring scheme, relevant data can be extracted from individual parallels in a form that can be used in the probability analyses for each of the two documents of interest. The most likely direction of borrowing can then be determined by comparing the collective probability of borrowing (CP_{bor}) for each document and seeing which, if any, directional scenario yields a conclusive result.

As shown in the preceding pages, stage 2 of the methodology, which assesses the most likely direction of borrowing, is very similar to stage 1, which assesses the likelihood of literary dependence. Both stages employ an analytical approach that is designed to assess the likelihood of an event of interest based on specific evidence of distinguishing characteristics of the particular event. For literary dependence, the relevant indicators pertain to relational directness as evidenced by rarity of occurrence and degree of correspondence. For direction of borrowing, the relevant indicators involve direct-logical relationships related to the notion of borrowing, as evidenced by disturbance in the host document, consistency of borrowing practices, logical progression between parallel elements, and identification of a likely external source for one of the parallel elements. Here too the assessment methodology considers collective probability at the whole document level. Since each stage of the methodology addresses a specific question that arises from the phenomena of intertextual parallels, both stages are needed for a meaningful investigation. A determination of literary dependence is insufficient for the question of intertextual borrowing without also addressing the direction of borrowing, and a determination of borrowing direction is invalid without first establishing the probability of literary dependence. The practical significance of each stage of the methodology comes to light in part 2, where usage and reliability is demonstrated via application to two different pairs of NT documents.

Demonstration of the Methodology

CHAPTER 3

Negative Test Case:
Literary Dependence
between James and Philippians

The assessment methodology presented in part 1 provides a disciplined analytical approach to evaluating parallels between NT books for the likelihood of intertextual borrowing. Its usefulness for NT scholarship, however, requires that it can be applied in a consistent manner and that it is capable of producing credible results. The best way to demonstrate such usefulness is to apply the methodology to selected pairs of NT documents where the likelihood of intertextual borrowing is already fairly certain. These cases occur at the two extremes of the probability scale, where the result is either strongly negative or strongly positive.

As explained in chapter 1, a negative result for the question of literary dependence occurs when the computed collective probability of directness, CP_{dir}, is low. A positive result occurs when CP_{dir} is high. Credibility at the low end may be demonstrated by showing that when the methodology is applied to two documents which bear little resemblance to one another, the analysis produces an expected negative result indicating that intertextual borrowing is highly unlikely. In that case, the result might be verified both by common sense and by the absence of scholarly works that posit a direct connection between the two documents. Similarly, credibility at the high end may be demonstrated by showing that for two documents that are strikingly similar, application of the methodology produces an expected positive result. Here too, the outcome might be verified as it coheres, not only with common sense, but also with scholarly consensus that intertextual borrowing is highly likely. The low-end negative test case is addressed in the present chapter with an analysis of the parallels between James and Philippians. The high-end positive test case, which involves Jude and 2 Peter, follows in chapters 4 and 5.

Expected Outcome

The letters of James and Philippians present an excellent negative test case for the methodology. A comparison of the two documents gives little reason to believe that one of the authors borrowed material from the other document. Indeed, the letters have very little in common. The letter of James claims to be written by "James" (Jas 1:1), which may correspond to multiple different references to persons of that name in the NT. The absence of any further identification suggests that the author would have been well known to the early community of faith. This effectively limits the likely candidates to James, the son of Zebedee, who was one of Jesus' twelve disciples (Matt 4:21; 10:2; 17:1; Mark 1:19, 29; 3:17; 5:37; 9:2; 10:35, 41; 13:3; 14:33; Luke 5:10; 6:15; 8:51; 9:28, 54; Acts 1:13; 12:2) or James the Just, who became the leader of the Jerusalem assembly and is identified as the half-brother of Jesus (Gal 1:19) and possibly a brother of Jude (Matt 13:55; Mark 6:3; Acts 12:17; 15:13; 21:18; 1 Cor 15:7; Gal 1:19; 2:9, 12; Jude 1). It is also possible that the letter was written pseudonymously using the name of James. However, it seems unlikely that a pseudonymous author would claim the authority of "James" without further identifying "James" as a person of authority.[1] As noted by Karen Jobes, the concerns addressed in the letter lead most scholars to believe that it could not have been written before 44 C.E., the year James, son of Zebedee, reportedly was killed at the hands of Herod Agrippa I (Acts 12:2). More likely is that the letter was written by James the

---

1.   Karen H. Jobes, *Letters to the Church: A Survey of Hebrews and the General Epistles* (Grand Rapids, MI: Zondervan, 2011), 155.

Just, who, according to Josephus, was stoned to death sometime around 62 C.E. (*Antiquities* 20:9:1).[2]

The exact identity of the recipients of James is even more elusive than that of the letter's author. The correspondence is addressed to a broadly dispersed community, namely, "the twelve tribes in the Diaspora" (Jas 1:1). Given the Jewish-Christian nature of James, this is generally understood to refer to Jewish Christians scattered throughout the eastern Mediterranean world, perhaps as a result of the persecution that took place in Jerusalem, as reported in Acts 8:1.[3]

Despite uncertainty about the identity of "James" and the absence of more specific information about the recipients, the purpose of the letter is not difficult to discern. The content and the author's frequent use of moral imperatives reveal a concern for covenant faithfulness in the face of daily trials. The purpose of the letter for the original Jewish Christian recipients apparently was to instruct them how to live faithfully in obedience to "the perfect law of liberty" (Jas 1:25) within the framework of their Jewish heritage.[4] This includes instructions involving testing and trials (1:2–4, 12), poverty and oppression (1:9–11; 2:1–13; 5:1–6), partiality (2:1–13), speech (1:20, 26; 3:1–12; 4:11–12; 5:12), faith and good deeds (1:6–8; 2:14–26; 5:14), and the law (1:24; 2:8–13; 4:11–12). The letter does not contain anything of a personal nature concerning either the author or his intended recipients. The organizational structure of the letter is difficult to discern as the various topics appear and reappear with little or no indication of a logical flow to the discourse. Although numerous attempts have been made to discover an underlying structure, a clear winner has yet to be proposed and the question of structure remains unresolved in NT scholarship.

In regard to language and style of writing, the letter of James exhibits several noteworthy characteristics. With only a few exceptions (i.e., 2:2–4; 3:15–16; 4:13–15), the sentences are relatively short. The author makes use of rhetorical devices such as alliteration (e.g., the initial δ in 1:1, 6, 21; 2:16;

---

2. For fuller treatments of the authorship of James, see Peter H. Davids, *The Epistle of James: A Commentary on the Greek Text*, NIGTC (Grand Rapids, MI: Eerdmans, 1982), 2–22; Jobes, *Letters to the Church*, 150–58; Luke Timothy Johnson, *The Letter of James*, The Anchor Yale Bible 37A (London: Yale University Press, 1995), 89–124; Douglas J. Moo, *The Letter of James*, The Pillar New Testament Commentary (Grand Rapids, MI: Eerdmans, 2000), 9–22.

3. Jobes, *Letters to the Church*, 164.

4. Jobes, *Letters to the Church*, 166.

3:8), parechesis (1:24), paronomasia (1:1–2), and word play (2:13). James also employs exemplification in that the letter presents a positive example intended to motivate desirable behavior on the part of the recipients (i.e., the prophets in Jas 5:10). The letter is further characterized by a distinctive use of Greco-Roman style diatribe, which appears in several different forms. These include direct address to the readers and the use of second-person verbs (e.g., 1:2, 16; 2:5; 3:1), question and answer sequences (e.g., 3:13; 4:14; 5:13–14), and comparisons (e.g., 1:6; 3:5–6).[5] Finally, the letter of James contains many allusions to the OT.

The letter to the Philippians is quite different. The author's claim to be the apostle Paul has been widely accepted, thereby marking the document as authentically Pauline.[6] The letter is addressed to "all the saints in Christ Jesus who are in Philippi" (Phil 1:1), a city in the province of Macedonia. According to Acts 16, Paul himself founded this community of faith. The letter to the Philippians was written while Paul was in prison, probably sometime in the late 50s or early 60s C.E. Apparently, the Philippian emissary Epaphroditus had recently delivered a monetary gift to Paul from the faithful assembly in Philippi (Phil 4:10–20; cf. 2:25–30). The letter includes news and instructions concerning specific persons who were known to both Paul and the Philippian community of faith (Phil 2:19–24, 25–30; 4:2, 3, 18). It also reveals detailed information concerning Paul and his circumstances and therefore is considered one of the most personal of all the Pauline letters.

The various sections of the letter suggest that Paul had multiple purposes in mind as he composed this warm and affectionate correspondence to the Philippians. These are succinctly summarized by Peter O'Brien as:

> to express his gratitude to his Philippian friends for their generosity, to explain why he decided to send Epaphroditus back so quickly, to inform his readers of his present circumstances and how his imprisonment has served to advance the gospel, to indicate his possible future plans including the visit of Timothy and his hopes of visiting them himself, to warn the Philippians of the dangers

5. See Johnson, *Letter of James*, 7–10.

6. So, e.g., Peter T. O'Brien, *The Epistle to the Philippians: A Commentary on the Greek Text*, NIGTC (Grand Rapids, MI: Eerdmans, 1991), 9–10; G. F. Hawthorne, "Philippians, Letter to the," in *DPL*, ed. Gerald F. Hawthorne, Ralph P. Martin, and Daniel G. Reid (Downers Grove, IL: InterVarsity Press, 1993), 707–13; Moisés Silva, *Philippians*, 2nd ed., BECNT (Grand Rapids, MI: Baker Academic, 2005), 1–2.

posed by the Judaizing opponents from outside the congregation, and especially to urge his Christian friends to stand firm for the gospel and to be united in Christian love.[7]

Despite the personal nature of the correspondence and the diversity of topics covered, Paul's letter to the Philippians appears to have been carefully constructed, even though the precise structure is still a matter of debate.[8] In his comprehensive rhetorical analysis of the book, Duane Watson suggests that Philippians was "organized and written according to the principles of Greco-Roman rhetoric."[9] Regardless of the exact organizational structure of the letter, scholars generally concur that it is not just an unorganized collection of thoughts. Rather, the letter reflects a well-conceived train of thought designed to achieve the author's purpose.[10]

Although Philippians exhibits some of the same characteristics of language and style that are found in James, the general style of writing is very different. As in James, Paul employs rhetorical or poetic devices. For example, the hymn of Phil 2:6–11 exhibits alliteration, assonance, and rhythm.[11] The exhortation found in Phil 4:8–9 reflects anaphora, asyndeton, repetition, and parallelism,[12] and the explanation of Paul's radical change of values gives further evidence of parallelism and word plays (Phil 3:7–11).[13] The letter to the Philippians also employs exemplification in that the author presents positive examples for the audience to follow, namely, Christ (Phil 2:5) and Paul himself (Phil 3:17). However, unlike James, the letter to the

---

7. O'Brien, *Epistle to the Philippians*, 38.

8. The question of structure is often influenced by a related question concerning the integrity or unity of the text. For the present purpose, unity of the letter is assumed because the assessment methodology is intended to be applied to whole documents, regardless of their potentially fragmented development.

9. Duane Frederick Watson, "A Rhetorical Analysis of Philippians and Its Implications for the Unity Question," *NovT* 30 (1988): 57.

10. For example, Richard R. Melick, *Philippians, Colossians, Philemon*, NAC 32 (Nashville: Broadman & Holman, 1991), 42–44; O'Brien, *Epistle to the Philippians*, 38–39; Silva, *Philippians*, 14–15; Watson, "Rhetorical Analysis," 57–88; Ben Witherington, III, *Paul's Letter to the Philippians: A Socio-Rhetorical Commentary* (Grand Rapids, MI: Eerdmans, 2011), 21–30.

11. Witherington, *Paul's Letter to the Philippians*, 135.

12. Gordon D. Fee, *Paul's Letter to the Philippians*, NICNT (Grand Rapids, MI: Eerdmans, 1995), 16; Witherington, *Paul's Letter to the Philippians*, 254.

13. Fee, *Philippians*, 16; O'Brien, *Epistle to the Philippians*, 381–415.

Philippians reveals the author's fondness of long complex sentences (e.g., Phil 1:12–14; 2:1–4, 5–8; 3:8–11). The average length of the sentences in this Pauline letter is significantly longer than the average sentence in James. The style of Philippians is further distinguished from that of James by a paucity of allusions or echoes to Scripture,[14] as well as the absence of the style of diatribe that is so characteristic of James.

Despite the obvious differences between James and Philippians, the two NT books do exhibit some *conceptual* similarities. For example, both authors indicate that there is a relationship between "work" and "perfection" (Jas 1:4; 2:22; Phil 1:6), both instruct their audiences to focus on the things of God rather than the things of earth (Jas 1:5; 3:13–18; Phil 3:19), both encourage single-mindedness and unity (Jas 1:8; 4:8; Phil 1:27; 2:2), and both warn against grumbling and complaining (Jas 4:11–12; 5:9; Phil 2:14). However, significant *verbal* parallels are missing. The 1,742 Greek words that comprise the letter of James include multiple occurrences of 554 unique words that appear in various forms throughout the letter. The 1,629 Greek words of Philippians include 440 unique words that occur in various forms. Of the 164 unique words that are shared by both books, most reflect vocabulary that is common in the NT and other contemporary literature. Other than some instances of rare terminology and a few short phrases, obvious verbal parallels are not found.

Given the high degree of dissimilarity between James and Philippians, it comes as no surprise that nowhere in the research conducted for this study is it suggested that one of these authors borrowed material from the other document. This is not to say that comparisons between James and the Pauline letters have not occurred. On the contrary, much has been written about the authors' seemingly contradictory views of justification, salvation, faith, law, and works. The comparisons, however, primarily involve Romans and Galatians. Paul's letter to the Philippians is not a factor in those discussions. Thus James and Philippians present an excellent test case for the assessment methodology presented in part 1. When the documents are analyzed for the likelihood of literary dependence, we should expect a negative result indicating that a direct literary connection is unlikely. Analysis of the literary parallels between these two books should produce a very low value for CP_{dir}.

---

14. For an explanation, see Witherington, *Paul's Letter to the Philippians*, 27–28.

Procedure

Before applying the methodology to any pair of documents, a database of parallels to be included in the analysis must be established. Selection of parallels requires careful thought. If the list were to be stacked with shared common words such as articles, pronouns, conjunctions, and prepositions, or common nouns such as "God" or "Jesus," or common verbs such as "is" or "say," or loosely related concepts, the analysis might be inappropriately skewed in favor of literary dependence simply due to the high number of "parallels." For this reason, it is important to limit the list to parallels that are significant for the analysis. This is done by selecting parallels according to specific criteria. Although the qualifying criteria may be different for different genres or bodies of literature, for the present study of NT letters, the qualifying condition is defined as follows: To be included in the study a parallel must meet at least two of the following three criteria: (1) The score for rarity of occurrence is at least 2.00; (2) Either the parallel itself is a higher-order parallel or both of its constituent elements are members of a higher-order parallel, although not necessarily the same higher-order parallel; (3) The combined score for correspondence of basic units and correspondence of grammatical constructs is at least 0.50.[15] Application of these qualifying criteria effectively weeds out "parallels" that might skew the outcome simply due to quantity rather than quality of evidence.

Given the textual history of the NT and the importance of lexical-grammatical features for establishing correspondence, selection of parallel texts must go hand-in-hand with an evaluation of alternative readings. The present study adopts a straightforward approach to textual criticism that favors conservative judgments in regard to intertextual correspondence. The NA[27] Greek text is assumed as the default NT text. Evaluation of variant readings is focused on the readings that are discussed in Bruce Metzger's *A Textual Commentary on the Greek New Testament*.[16] For every entry in

---

15. The qualifying condition was determined through an iterative process of analyzing approximately 250 parallels between NT books (Philippians, Hebrews, James, 1 Peter, 2 Peter, and Jude) according to different criteria for the various indicators and seeing which combinations produced a manageable set of parallels that appeared significant for the question of literary dependence.

16. Bruce M. Metzger, *A Textual Commentary on the Greek New Testament*, 2nd ed. (Stuttgart: Deutsche Bibelgesellschaft, 1994).

Metzger's *Textual Commentary* that involves a parallel between the two documents, readings are selected according to the following criteria: (1) If the alternative reading has no impact on scoring or if the alternative is not well attested in early witnesses, then the default text is retained; (2) If the alternative reading does impact scoring and the alternative is well attested in early witnesses, then the reading that yields the lower correspondence score is selected. For the purpose of establishing the parallel texts, qualification of alternative readings is based solely on external evidence of the textual witnesses because determination of intrinsic and transcriptional probabilities might be impacted by the outcome of the study.[17] Text that is shown in square brackets in NA[27] is not included unless it is noted in the *Textual Commentary* and meets the criteria delineated above.

Six other procedural points that pertain to scoring of the selected parallels should be noted. First, for multi-word parallels, the extent of a parallel element is defined as the shortest string of consecutive words that is needed to convey the thought of the parallel element. The entire string is included in correspondence assessments. Second, the extent of a cluster is equal to the number of lower-order parallels that form the cluster. Third, rarity evaluations are limited to accessible, electronically-searchable Greek texts.[18] Fourth, since exhaustive morphological and syntactical searches of

17. In the practice of NT textual criticism, transcriptional probabilities are based on the habits of the scribes in the transmission process (e.g., corrections, clarifications, duplications, omissions); intrinsic probabilities are based on the habits of the author (e.g., style, vocabulary, thought). See David Alan Black, *New Testament Textual Criticism: A Concise Guide* (Grand Rapids, MI: Baker Books, 1994), 35–36; Bruce M. Metzger, *The Text of the New Testament: Its Transmission, Corruption, and Restoration*, 3rd ed. (New York: Oxford University Press, 1992), 209–210.

18. The Greek documents and databases used for the analysis include: Kurt Aland et al., eds., *Novum Testamentum Graece (BNT)*, 27th ed. (Stuttgart: Deutsche Bibelgesellschaft, 2001), BibleWorks, v. 10; *BibleWorks Greek Apostolic Fathers Morphology (APM)* (Norfolk: BibleWorks, LLC., 2012), BibleWorks, v. 10; *BibleWorks Greek New Testament Morphology (BNM)* (Norfolk: BibleWorks, LLC., 2001), BibleWorks, v. 10; *BibleWorks LXX/OG Morphology and Lemma Database (BLM)* (Norfolk: BibleWorks, LLC., 2001), BibleWorks, v. 10; Peder Borgen, Kåre Fuglseth, and Roald Skarsten, *The Philo Concordance Database in Greek (PHI)* (n.p.: n.p., 2005), BibleWorks, v. 10; Peder Borgen, Kåre Fuglseth, and Roald Skarsten, *The Philo Concordance Database in Greek with Lemmatization and Morphological Tagging with Corrections (PHM)*, ed. Jean-Noel Aletti and Andrzej Gieniusz (n.p.: n.p., 2007), BibleWorks, v. 10; Craig A. Evans, *The Greek Pseudepigrapha (OPG)* (n.p.: OakTree Software, 2008), BibleWorks, v. 10; *Greek New Testament and LXX Database (BGT)* (Norfolk: BibleWorks, LLC., 1999), BibleWorks, v. 10; *Greek New Testament*

Greco-Roman literature can be rather cumbersome at this point in time, the best-case scenario and the worst-case scenario for rarity of occurrence in the Greco-Roman body of literature are used in order to establish the upper and lower limits for the rarity of occurrence scores. If the entire range of values for the resulting CP_{dir} is either very high or very low, the result is conclusive and there is no need to measure the actual number of instances in Greco-Roman literature. However, if the range of values for CP_{dir} spans the mid-point of the probability scale between zero and one, then a precise count of occurrences in Greco-Roman literature will be required in order to reach a conclusive outcome. Fifth, the rarity score of a cluster is equal to the score of its rarest member. Sixth, since a higher-order parallel, by definition, presumes the presence of common lower-order parallels that are assessed individually for correspondence, higher-order clusters are assessed only for correspondence of meaning, correspondence of function, correspondence of structural arrangement (e.g., the order of the member parallels), and membership in other higher-order clusters. In accordance with the procedure defined above, the negative test case involving James and Philippians begins with selection of an appropriate set of parallels to include in the study.

---

and LXX Morphological Database (BGM) (Norfolk: BibleWorks, LLC., 1999), Bible-Works, v. 10; Flavius Josephus, Flavii Josephi opera edidit et apparatu critico instruxit Benedictus Niese (JOS), trans. Benedictus Niese, 6 vols. (Berlin: Weidmann, 1887), BibleWorks, v. 10; Flavius Josephus, Flavii Josephi opera edidit et apparatu critico instruxit Benedictus Niese: Greek Morphology (JOM) (Norfolk: BibleWorks, LLC., 2003), BibleWorks, v. 10; Rex A. Koivisto, The Greek Pseudepigrapha Morphologically-tagged Text (OPM) (n.p.: OakTree Software, 2008), BibleWorks, v. 10; J. B. Lightfoot, The Apostolic Fathers (APF), ed. J. R. Harmer, 2nd ed. (London: Macmillan, 1898), BibleWorks, v. 10; Alfred Rahlfs, Septuaginta: Id est Vetus Testamentum iuxta LXX interpretes edidit Alfred Rahlfs (LXT) (Stuttgart: Deutsche Bibelgesellschaft, 1935), BibleWorks, v. 10; Perseus Digital Library, ed. Gregory R. Crane (Medford, MA: Tufts University), www.perseus.tufts.edu; Thesaurus Linguae Graecae: A Digital Library of Greek Literature (Irvine, CA: University of California, 2014), www.tlg.uci.edu.

Selection of Parallels

The pool of potential parallels includes all single words and multi-word expressions that bear resemblance to one another between the two books. This collection, however, contains many parallels that are not significant for the question of literary dependence. They simply reflect the vocabulary and ideology of a common milieu. Application of the qualifying criteria defined above narrows the list to twenty parallels. This smaller collection of parallels serves as the primary database for assessing the likelihood of literary dependence between James and Philippians. For convenience, each selected parallel is assigned a descriptive reference label. Nonetheless, the parallels are selected based on the rarity and correspondence scores derived from particular features of the parallel texts, not the label descriptions. The complete list can be found in appendix C.

Arrangement of the parallels is illustrated in figure 3.1, in the order in which they occur in each document. Each element is shown with the reference where the text is found, the descriptive label, and the assigned parallel number. From the disorderly arrangement, it is easy to see that none of the parallels are clustered closely together in groups of three or more to form higher-order parallel clusters. Hence the analysis does not include any clusters, only individual first-order parallels consisting of single words (#1–14) and groups of words (#15–20).

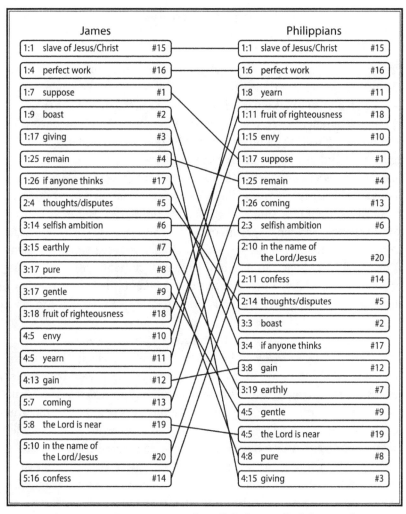

FIGURE 3.1. Arrangement of parallels (James || Philippians)

Probability Analysis

Presentation of the probability analysis is organized according to the two distinct categories of parallels that are evident in the database of parallels between James and Philippians. The first category, the single-word parallel, involves a parallel between a single word in James and a single word in Philippians. This is the simplest type of literary parallel. The second category, the word-group parallel, represents a higher degree of complexity in that it involves a parallel between groups of words that express a particular thought. This category may include, for example, parallels of word-pairs, prepositional phrases, simple clauses, compound clauses, full sentences, and even paragraph-length groups of words. These two categories represent lower-order one-to-one parallels where a single instance in one document is matched by a single instance in the other document, with perhaps an occasional duplicate in either document. As mentioned above, none of the lower-order parallels between James and Philippians combine to form higher-order parallel clusters.

Evaluation of the parallels by category is presented in the following pages, proceeding from lowest to highest order of complexity. Discussion of each parallel begins by citing the relevant Greek texts, with the parallel expressions enclosed within curly brackets ("{ ... }"). For ease of comparison, the corresponding English translations maintain the grammatical features of the Greek texts as much as possible. Each word-group parallel is also accompanied by a diagram that illustrates verbal correspondence of the parallel expressions, with the constituent parts of each expression shown in the order in which they appear in the text of each document.[19] The block structure shows the grammatical constructs that are used to determine correspondence scores. Equivalent constructs are connected with a dashed line; identical constructs are connected with a solid line. In the discussion of each parallel, the constructs of James and Philippians are referred to as Jn or Pn, respectively, where the variable "n" is the construct number. See appendix I for an explanation of the abbreviations.

At the end of each group of parallels, the contribution of the group to the probability of literary dependence is shown in a table that includes the Directness Index (DI), the Probability of Directness (IP$_{dir}$), and the

---

19. The only exceptions are postpositive conjunctions (e.g., δέ, γάρ, οὖν), which may be shown first, and embedded constructs, which are indicated with ellipses.

Probability of Non-Directness (IP_{ndir}) for each individual parallel, as well as the collective probability calculations based on all the parallels presented up to that point in the analysis (CP_{ndir}, CP_{dir}). Since the overall probability of literary dependence is represented by CP_{dir}, the effect of each additional parallel on the overall assessment can be seen in the changes that occur in the rightmost column of each table. The tables presented in this chapter reflect the best-case rarity scores for Greco-Roman literature because the best-case value for the final CP_{dir} is most critical for a negative test case. Calculations for rarity of occurrence scores and verbal correspondence scores are provided in appendices D and E, respectively. Indicator scores and probability calculations for all the parallels are provided in appendices F (best case), G (worse case), and H (worst case). Finally, all of the parallels within each group are presented in the order in which they occur in James.

Single-Word Parallels

Fourteen of the parallels that meet the qualifying condition for this study are single-word parallels (#1–14). Although some of these parallel words have duplicate occurrences in either James or Philippians, only one parallel for each word is included in the probability analysis, usually the pair that exhibits the strongest correspondence. The task of scoring single-word parallels is relatively straightforward. The extent multipliers are all equal to 0.009 since all are just one word.[20] The scores for correspondence of basic units and correspondence of structural arrangement are all zero because these two indicators are applicable only to multi-word parallels. The scores for correspondence of grammatical constructs are either 1.00 (#1–4, #7–9, #11, #12, #14) or 2.00 (#5, #6, #10, #13), depending on whether the parallel words match in root only or also in form. Thus for single-word parallels, the combined scores for correspondence of basic units and correspondence of grammatical constructs always meet the third qualifying criterion. All fourteen of the single-word parallels meet the first criterion with best-case rarity scores that range from 6.10 to 9.41. At the single-word level, correspondence of function reflects how the word is applied in its immediate context. For nearly all the single-word parallels, the parallel concepts are

---

20. The extent multiplier (EM) = $1 \div 112 = 0.009$. For a detailed explanation, see chapter 1, pp. 29–33.

semantically comparable in that they convey the same basic idea. The only
exception is parallel #5. Although most of the single-word parallels are
semantically comparable, only one exhibits functional equivalence (#7).
The rest reflect either dissimilar (#1, #3–5, #10–14) or modified (#2, #6, #8,
#9) functions in their respective documents.

Parallel #1:   Suppose (οἴομαι)
                                                   (Jas 1:7 || Phil 1:17)

Jas 1:7	Phil 1:17
μὴ γὰρ {οἰέσθω} ὁ ἄνθρωπος ἐκεῖνος ὅτι λήμψεταί τι παρὰ τοῦ κυρίου,	οἱ δὲ ἐξ ἐριθείας τὸν Χριστὸν καταγγέλλουσιν, οὐχ ἁγνῶς, {οἰόμενοι} θλῖψιν ἐγείρειν τοῖς δεσμοῖς μου.
For that man must not {suppose} that he will receive anything from the Lord,	the former proclaim Christ out of selfish ambition, not sincerely, {supposing} to stir up affliction to my chains.

The verb οἴομαι is rare in the NT. In addition to these two texts, the
verb appears only in John 21:25. Additional instances are found in all other
examined bodies of literature, including the LXX, the works of Philo and
Josephus, the Pseudepigrapha, and the writings of the Apostolic Fathers.
The instances in this parallel appear with different morphological forms,
but both convey the same basic thought of "suppose," "think," or "expect."
In Jas 1:7 the term is used to describe a consequence of doubting one's faith
when asking for wisdom from God. In Phil 1:17 it is used to describe the
motivation of those who proclaim Christ out of selfish ambition. Thus
while the thoughts are comparable, the respective functions are dissimilar.

Parallel #2:   Boast (καυχάομαι)
                                                (Jas 1:9 || Phil 3:3)

Jas 1:9	Phil 3:3
{Καυχάσθω} δὲ ὁ ἀδελφὸς ὁ ταπεινὸς ἐν τῷ ὕψει αὐτοῦ,	ἡμεῖς γάρ ἐσμεν ἡ περιτομή, οἱ πνεύματι θεοῦ λατρεύοντες καὶ {καυχώμενοι} ἐν Χριστῷ Ἰησοῦ καὶ οὐκ ἐν σαρκὶ πεποιθότες,
But the lowly brother {shall boast} in his high position,	For we are the circumcision, who worship in the Spirit of God and {boast} in Christ Jesus and put no confidence in the flesh,

The verb καυχάομαι ("boast") appears nearly three dozen times in the NT, including an additional instance in James (Jas 4:16). Although it is not found in the works of Philo and appears only once in the works of Josephus (*Ant.* 8:372), there are multiple instances in each of the other examined bodies of literature. While the instances involved in this parallel exhibit different morphological forms, they convey similar thoughts, namely, the idea of glorifying or taking pride in oneself. The terms, then, are considered semantically comparable. Their respective functions, however, are best understood as modified. Although both indicate reasons for boasting, in Jas 1:9 the term is part of an exhortation, and in Phil 3:3 it is the basis of an exhortation (Phil 3:2).

Parallel #3:   Giving (δόσις)
                                                (Jas 1:17 || Phil 4:15)

Jas 1:17	Phil 4:15
πᾶσα {δόσις} ἀγαθὴ καὶ πᾶν δώρημα τέλειον ἄνωθέν ἐστιν καταβαῖνον ἀπὸ τοῦ πατρὸς τῶν φώτων, παρ᾽ ᾧ οὐκ ἔνι παραλλαγὴ ἢ τροπῆς ἀποσκίασμα.	οἴδατε δὲ καὶ ὑμεῖς, Φιλιππήσιοι, ὅτι ἐν ἀρχῇ τοῦ εὐαγγελίου, ὅτε ἐξῆλθον ἀπὸ Μακεδονίας, οὐδεμία μοι ἐκκλησία ἐκοινώνησεν εἰς λόγον {δόσεως} καὶ λήμψεως εἰ μὴ ὑμεῖς μόνοι,

Jas 1:17	Phil 4:15
Every good {act of giving} and every perfect gift is from above, coming down from the Father of lights, with whom there is no variation or shadow of change.	And you yourselves know, Philippians, that in the beginning of the gospel, when I left Macedonia, no assembly shared with me in the matter of {giving} and receiving except you alone,

The noun δόσις ("giving") is rare in the NT, occurring only in the texts that form this parallel. The writings of the Apostolic Fathers contain only one instance (*Herm. Mand.* 5:2:2), but multiple instances are found in all other examined bodies of literature. These two NT instances appear in morphologically different forms. Nevertheless, they are semantically comparable in that each expresses the same basic notion, namely, a free act of transferring something of value from one party to another. Functional correspondence is best understood as dissimilar. Whereas, the term in Jas 1:17 is used to identify something that is important for readers to know in order to avoid being deceived, the parallel term in Phil 4:15 is used to describe something about the author's past situation.

Parallel #4:   Remain (παραμένω)
                                          (Jas 1:25 || Phil 1:25)

Jas 1:25	Phil 1:25
ὁ δὲ παρακύψας εἰς νόμον τέλειον τὸν τῆς ἐλευθερίας καὶ {παραμείνας} οὐκ ἀκροατὴς ἐπιλησμονῆς γενόμενος ἀλλὰ ποιητὴς ἔργου, οὗτος μακάριος ἐν τῇ ποιήσει αὐτοῦ ἔσται.	καὶ τοῦτο πεποιθὼς οἶδα ὅτι μενῶ καὶ {παραμενῶ} πᾶσιν ὑμῖν εἰς τὴν ὑμῶν προκοπὴν καὶ χαρὰν τῆς πίστεως,
But he who peers into the perfect law of liberty and {remains}, not having become a forgetful hearer but a working doer, this man will be blessed in his doing.	And convinced of this, I know that I will abide and {remain} with you all for your progress and joy of faith,

The verb παραμένω ("remain") appears only two other times in the NT (1 Cor 16:6; Heb 7:23). It also occurs twice in the OT Pseudepigrapha

(*1 En.* 97:10; *T. Job* 20:9), as well as multiple times in the other examined bodies of literature. The two instances that appear in James and Philippians exhibit different morphological forms. Nevertheless, they are semantically comparable in that each instance expresses the idea of "remain," "abide," or "continue." Moreover, like the previous parallel, the respective functions are dissimilar. The instance in Jas 1:25 is used to indicate obedience to a law, but the parallel instance in Phil 1:25 is used to indicate continuance of the author's earthly life.

Parallel #5:   Thoughts/Disputes (διαλογισμός)
                                 (Jas 2:4 ‖ Phil 2:14)

Jas 2:4	Phil 2:14
οὐ διεκρίθητε ἐν ἑαυτοῖς καὶ ἐγένεσθε κριταὶ {διαλογισμῶν} πονηρῶν;	Πάντα ποιεῖτε χωρὶς γογγυσμῶν καὶ {διαλογισμῶν},
have you not made distinctions among yourselves, and become judges with evil {thoughts}?	Do all things without complaints and {disputes}.

The two terms that form this parallel exhibit identical morphological forms. The masculine plural genitive form of the noun διαλογισμός, as it appears here, is found elsewhere only in Rom 14:1, *Pr. Levi* 1:7, and *1 Clem.* 21:3. Other forms of the noun may be found in the NT, the LXX, the OT Pseudepigrapha, and the works of Josephus. Despite the identical forms, however, the parallel nouns in James and Philippians convey thoughts that are semantically dissimilar. In Jas 2:4 διαλογισμῶν conveys the idea of "thoughts" or "motives"; however, in Phil 2:14 it is better understood as meaning "disputes" or "arguments."[21] Given the semantic dissimilarity, it comes as no surprise that the respective functions also are dissimilar. While in Jas 2:4 the term is used to indicate a mindset or attitude of the readers that the author condemns, in Phil 2:14 it is used in an exhortation to indicate undesirable behavior.

21. See, e.g., Davids, *Epistle of James*, 110; Johnson, *Letter of James*, 223–24 ("designs"); Moo, *Letter of James*, 104–5; O'Brien, *Epistle to the Philippians*, 290–92; Silva, *Philippians*, 123–28; Witherington, *Paul's Letter to the Philippians*, 161–62.

Parallel #6:   Selfish Ambition (ἐριθεία)
                                                (Jas 3:14 || Phil 2:3)

Jas 3:14	Phil 2:3
εἰ δὲ ζῆλον πικρὸν ἔχετε καὶ {ἐριθείαν} ἐν τῇ καρδίᾳ ὑμῶν, μὴ κατακαυχᾶσθε καὶ ψεύδεσθε κατὰ τῆς ἀληθείας.	μηδὲν κατ᾽ {ἐριθείαν} μηδὲ κατὰ κενοδοξίαν ἀλλὰ τῇ ταπεινοφροσύνῃ ἀλλήλους ἡγούμενοι ὑπερέχοντας ἑαυτῶν,
But if you have bitter jealousy and {selfish ambition} in your heart, do not brag and lie against the truth.	not according to {selfish ambition} and not according to deceit, but in humility regard one another higher than yourselves,

This is the rarest of the single-word parallels. Beyond these two NT books, various forms of the noun ἐριθεία ("selfish ambition") are found only in the NT (Rom 2:8; 2 Cor 12:20; Gal 5:20) and the Apostolic Fathers (Ign. *Phld.* 8:2). The two instances that form this parallel exhibit identical morphological forms (feminine singular accusative) and convey the same basic idea, namely an attitude of "selfish ambition." Hence, the parallel is considered semantically comparable. Functional correspondence, however, is best understood as modified. Although in both cases the terms describe similar undesirable attitudes, the term in James is used rhetorically to indict readers for inappropriate behavior, and the term in Philippians is used in an exhortation to discourage inappropriate behavior.

Parallel #7:   Earthly (ἐπίγειος)
                                                (Jas 3:15 || Phil 3:19)

Jas 3:15	Phil 3:19
οὐκ ἔστιν αὕτη ἡ σοφία ἄνωθεν κατερχομένη ἀλλὰ {ἐπίγειος}, ψυχική, δαιμονιώδης.	ὧν τὸ τέλος ἀπώλεια, ὧν ὁ θεὸς ἡ κοιλία καὶ ἡ δόξα ἐν τῇ αἰσχύνῃ αὐτῶν, οἱ τὰ {ἐπίγεια} φρονοῦντες.
This is not the wisdom that comes down from above, but is {earthly}, natural, demonic.	whose end is destruction, whose god is the belly, and whose glory is in their shame, who set their mind on {earthly things}.

The adjective ἐπίγειος ("earthly") is found in all examined bodies of literature except the LXX. An additional instance is also found in Phil 2:10. The instances that form this parallel display different morphological forms. Semantically, the parallel terms are comparable in that they both express the idea of existing on or belonging to the earth, as opposed to heaven. This is the only single-word parallel between James and Philippians that reflects functional equivalence between the parallel terms. In both cases, the terms serve as bases for preceding exhortations (Jas 3:13; Phil 3:17) and are applied to that which drives ungodly behavior (i.e., wisdom, Jas 3:15; mindset, Phil 3:19).

| Parallel #8: | Pure (ἁγνός)
(Jas 3:17 ǀǀ Phil 4:8) |

Jas 3:17	Phil 4:8
ἡ δὲ ἄνωθεν σοφία πρῶτον μὲν {ἁγνή} ἐστιν, ἔπειτα εἰρηνική, ἐπιεικής, εὐπειθής, μεστὴ ἐλέους καὶ καρπῶν ἀγαθῶν, ἀδιάκριτος, ἀνυπόκριτος.	Τὸ λοιπόν, ἀδελφοί, ὅσα ἐστὶν ἀληθῆ, ὅσα σεμνά, ὅσα δίκαια, ὅσα {ἀγνά}, ὅσα προσφιλῆ, ὅσα εὔφημα, εἴ τις ἀρετὴ καὶ εἴ τις ἔπαινος, ταῦτα λογίζεσθε·
But the wisdom from above is first {pure}, then peaceable, gentle, obedient, full of mercy and good fruits, impartial, without hypocrisy.	Finally, brothers, whatever is true, whatever is honorable, whatever is just, whatever is {pure}, whatever is lovely, whatever is commendable, if anything exhibits virtue and if anything merits praise, think about these things.

Various forms of the adjective ἁγνός ("pure") appear in all the bodies of literature that were examined for this project. Although the two instances that comprise this parallel exhibit different morphological forms, the terms convey similar thoughts, namely, the notion of being pure, unadulterated, or holy. Thus the semantic correspondence is classified as comparable. In both cases, the adjective is used to indicate something to which readers should turn their focus. However, since the instance in Jas 3:17 is applied to something that serves as a basis for a preceding exhortation (i.e., wisdom, Jas 3:13), and the instance in Phil 4:8 is applied to something that is directly part of an exhortation, functional correspondence of this parallel is best understood as modified.

Parallel #9:   Gentle (ἐπιεικής)
                                                      (Jas 3:17 || Phil 4:5)

Jas 3:17	Phil 4:5
ἡ δὲ ἄνωθεν σοφία πρῶτον μὲν ἁγνή ἐστιν, ἔπειτα εἰρηνική, {ἐπιεικής}, εὐπειθής, μεστὴ ἐλέους καὶ καρπῶν ἀγαθῶν, ἀδιάκριτος, ἀνυπόκριτος.	τὸ {ἐπιεικὲς} ὑμῶν γνωσθήτω πᾶσιν ἀνθρώποις. ὁ κύριος ἐγγύς.
But the wisdom from above is first pure, then peaceable, {gentle}, obedient, full of mercy and good fruits, impartial, without hypocrisy.	Let your {gentleness} be known to all men. The Lord [is] near.

In addition to the instances found in Jas 3:17 and Phil 4:5, various forms of the adjective ἐπιεικής ("gentle") appear three times in the NT (1 Tim 3:3; Titus 3:2; 1 Pet 2:18) and four times in the LXX (Esth 3:13; 8:12; Ps 85:5; Song 5:12). Multiple instances also are found in the writings of Philo and Josephus, as well as the Pseudepigrapha and the Apostolic Fathers. The adjectives that form this parallel differ in morphological form, but they still express comparable thoughts as each conveys the same general idea of being gentle or kind. Functional correspondence of this parallel is similar to that of parallel #8. Here too both instances of the adjective are applied to something to which the readers should aspire. However, since the instance in Jas 3:17 is applied to something that serves as a basis for a preceding exhortation (i.e., wisdom, Jas 3:13), and the instance in Phil 4:5 is applied to something that is directly part of an exhortation, functional correspondence of this parallel is best understood as modified.

Parallel #10:   Envy (φθόνος)
                                                    (Jas 4:5 || Phil 1:15)

Jas 4:5	Phil 1:15
ἢ δοκεῖτε ὅτι κενῶς ἡ γραφὴ λέγει· πρὸς {φθόνον} ἐπιποθεῖ τὸ πνεῦμα ὃ κατῴκισεν ἐν ἡμῖν,	τινὲς μὲν καὶ διὰ {φθόνον} καὶ ἔριν, τινὲς δὲ καὶ δι᾽ εὐδοκίαν τὸν Χριστὸν κηρύσσουσιν·
Or do you think that the scripture vainly says, "To the point of {envy}, the spirit that he caused to dwell in us yearns"?	Some indeed are preaching Christ from {envy} and strife, but also some from goodwill;

The noun φθόνος ("envy") is found in its various forms multiple times in all the examined bodies of literature. These include the NT (Matt 27:18; Mark 15:10; Rom 1:29; Gal 5:21; 1 Tim 6:4; Titus 3:3; 1 Pet 2:1), the LXX (1 Macc 8:16; 3 Macc 6:7; Wis 2:24; 6:23), and the Apostolic Fathers (*1 Clem.* 3:2; 4:7, 13; 5:2). The instances that constitute this parallel exhibit the same morphological form (masculine singular accusative) and convey comparable thoughts in the notion of "envy," or "jealousy." In Phil 1:15 the noun is used to indicate a negative factor that motivates some who preach Christ. Variant readings of the Greek text and the ambiguous grammar of Jas 4:5, however, make it difficult to discern the function of the parallel noun with any certainty. It is not clear to whom or what the noun applies, and what is meant by the alleged scriptural reference.[22] For this reason, functional correspondence of this parallel is best classified as dissimilar.

Parallel #11:   Yearn (ἐπιποθέω)
                                                    (Jas 4:5 || Phil 1:8)

Jas 4:5	Phil 1:8
ἢ δοκεῖτε ὅτι κενῶς ἡ γραφὴ λέγει· πρὸς φθόνον {ἐπιποθεῖ} τὸ πνεῦμα ὃ κατῴκισεν ἐν ἡμῖν,	μάρτυς γάρ μου ὁ θεὸς ὡς {ἐπιποθῶ} πάντας ὑμᾶς ἐν σπλάγχνοις Χριστοῦ Ἰησοῦ.

22. For a good explanation of the textual and grammatical difficulties, see Johnson, *Letter of James*, 280–82.

Jas 4:5	Phil 1:8
Or do you think that the scripture vainly says, "To the point of envy, the spirit that he caused to dwell in us {yearns}"?	For God is my witness, how {I yearn} for all of you with the affection of Christ Jesus.

The verb ἐπιποθέω ("yearn") is found multiple times in the LXX, the works of Philo, and the NT, including an additional instance in Philippians (Phil 2:26). However, no instances are found in the Pseudepigrapha, the writings of Josephus, or the writings of the Apostolic Fathers. Despite the different morphological forms exhibited by the instances that form this parallel, semantic correspondence is comparable. Both instances express the same basic notion of yearning, longing, or having a strong desire for something or someone. In Phil 1:8 the verb is used to indicate an attitude or feeling of the author in his present situation. Discerning the function of the verb in James, however, is problematic. Since this parallel involves the same ambiguous text in James as that of parallel #10 above, functional correspondence here also is best classified as dissimilar for the same reason as that given for parallel #10.

Parallel #12:   Gain (κερδαίνω)
                                                            (Jas 4:13 || Phil 3:8)

Jas 4:13	Phil 3:8
Ἄγε νῦν οἱ λέγοντες· σήμερον ἢ αὔριον πορευσόμεθα εἰς τήνδε τὴν πόλιν καὶ ποιήσομεν ἐκεῖ ἐνιαυτὸν καὶ ἐμπορευσόμεθα καὶ {κερδήσομεν}·	ἀλλὰ μενοῦνγε καὶ ἡγοῦμαι πάντα ζημίαν εἶναι διὰ τὸ ὑπερέχον τῆς γνώσεως Χριστοῦ Ἰησοῦ τοῦ κυρίου μου, δι᾽ ὃν τὰ πάντα ἐζημιώθην, καὶ ἡγοῦμαι σκύβαλα, ἵνα Χριστὸν {κερδήσω}
Come now, you who say, "Today or tomorrow we will go to this or that city and spend a year there and engage in business and {gain}";	But even more, I regard all things as loss because of the surpassing knowledge of Christ Jesus my Lord, on account of whom I have suffered the loss of all things, and I regard them as dung, so that {I might gain} Christ

The verb κερδαίνω ("gain") makes multiple appearances in the NT, the works of Philo, and the writings of Josephus. Only two instances are found in the Pseudepigrapha (*Sib. Or. Pro.* 1:6; Aris. Ex. 1:270), and only one instance is found in the writings of the Apostolic Fathers (*2 Clem.* 6:2). Zero instances are found in the LXX. The two instances in James and Philippians appear in different morphological forms. They convey kindred thoughts in that each expresses the idea of making a profit or gaining value. Their respective functions, however, are different. While the term in Jas 4:13 is used to expose the faulty thinking of ignorant readers, the parallel term in Phil 3:8 is used to describe the new radical thinking of the author. Thus the verbs that constitute this parallel are considered semantically comparable and functionally dissimilar.

Parallel #13:   Coming (παρουσία)
                                                        (Jas 5:7 || Phil 1:26)

Jas 5:7	Phil 1:26
Μακροθυμήσατε οὖν, ἀδελφοί, ἕως τῆς {παρουσίας} τοῦ κυρίου. ἰδοὺ ὁ γεωργὸς ἐκδέχεται τὸν τίμιον καρπὸν τῆς γῆς μακροθυμῶν ἐπ᾽ αὐτῷ, ἕως λάβῃ πρόϊμον καὶ ὄψιμον.	ἵνα τὸ καύχημα ὑμῶν περισσεύῃ ἐν Χριστῷ Ἰησοῦ ἐν ἐμοὶ διὰ τῆς ἐμῆς {παρουσίας} πάλιν πρὸς ὑμᾶς.
Therefore, be patient, brothers, until the {coming} of the Lord. Behold! The farmer awaits the precious fruit of the earth, being patient about it until it receives early and late rain.	so that your boasting in me might abound in Christ Jesus through my {coming} again to you.

In addition to four instances that are found in James and Philippians (Jas 5:7, 8; Phil 1:26; 2:12), the NT contains twenty instances of the noun παρουσία ("coming"). Multiple occurrences are found in each of the other examined bodies of literature. The two instances selected for this parallel display identical morphological forms (feminine singular genitive). Both also convey the same basic idea of "coming," "appearance," or "arrival." The respective functions, however, are dissimilar. On the one hand, the instance in Jas 5:7 is applied to the Lord and indicates a goal in an exhortation to be patient. On the other hand, the instance in Phil 1:26 is applied to the author and indicates his own anticipated travels.

Parallel #14:   Confess (ἐξομολογέω)
                                                   (Jas 5:16 || Phil 2:11)

Jas 5:16	Phil 2:11
{ἐξομολογεῖσθε} οὖν ἀλλήλοις τὰς ἁμαρτίας καὶ εὔχεσθε ὑπὲρ ἀλλήλων ὅπως ἰαθῆτε. Πολὺ ἰσχύει δέησις δικαίου ἐνεργουμένη.	καὶ πᾶσα γλῶσσα {ἐξομολογήσηται} ὅτι κύριος Ἰησοῦς Χριστὸς εἰς δόξαν θεοῦ πατρός.
Therefore, {confess} your sins to one another, and pray for one another, so that you might be healed. The prayer of a righteous man is able to accomplish much.	and every tongue {confess} that Jesus Christ is Lord, to the glory of God the Father.

This is the most common of all the parallels between Philippians and James that meet the qualifying criteria. Although the verb ἐξομολογέω ("confess") is found only once in James and once in Philippians, there are eight other occurrences elsewhere in the NT. The number of occurrences in the works of Philo, Josephus, the Pseudepigrapha, and the Apostolic Fathers ranges from seven to fifteen, and the LXX contains 136 instances. The two instances found in James and Philippians exhibit different morphological forms.[23] They are semantically comparable in that each conveys the same basic notion, namely, to confess, acknowledge, or admit something. The instance of the verb found in Jas 5:16 serves as an imperative for the readers, the object of which is their own sin. The instance found in Phil 2:11, on the other hand, is part of an exposition about why God exalted Jesus. In this context, the verb is applied to all people, its object is Jesus Christ, and it indicates an anticipated result. Thus the two verbs that form this parallel are functionally dissimilar.

23. Parallel #14, "confess" (ἐξομολογέω), involves a variant reading in Phil 2:11. The NA²⁷ text has the subjunctive ἐξομολογήσηται, which is well attested in early manuscripts. The alternative indicative ἐξομολογήσεται also is well supported by early witnesses. Since the parallel in Jas 5:16 is the imperative ἐξομολογεῖσθε, the alternate reading has no impact on the correspondence scores. In both cases, the parallel terms reflect morphological differences of the same lexical root. Hence the NA²⁷ text is retained for the analysis. See Metzger, *Textual Commentary*, 546. The subjunctive is also retained in the newer edition, NA²⁸.

This completes the group of single-word parallels included in the probability analysis. The best-case probability of literary dependence based only on these fourteen single-word parallels is provided in table 3.1.

TABLE 3.1. Probability of directness (Jas || Phil, single words, best case)

No.	Description	Reference		Individual			Collective	
		Jas	Phil	DI	IP_{dir}	IP_{ndir}	CP_{ndir}	CP_{dir}
							1	0
1	suppose (οἴομαι)	1:7	1:17	0.082	0.003	0.997	0.997	0.003
2	boast (καυχάομαι)	1:9	3:3	0.095	0.004	0.996	0.993	0.007
3	giving (δόσις)	1:17	4:15	0.091	0.004	0.996	0.989	0.011
4	remain (παραμένω)	1:25	1:25	0.087	0.004	0.996	0.985	0.015
5	thoughts/ disputes (διαλογισμός)	2:4	2:14	0.081	0.003	0.997	0.982	0.018
6	selfish ambition (ἐριθεία)	3:14	2:3	0.129	0.005	0.995	0.977	0.023
7	earthly (ἐπίγειος)	3:15	3:19	0.108	0.005	0.995	0.972	0.028
8	pure (ἁγνός)	3:17	4:8	0.091	0.004	0.996	0.969	0.031
9	gentle (ἐπιεικής)	3:17	4:5	0.095	0.004	0.996	0.965	0.035
10	envy (φθόνος)	4:5	1:15	0.092	0.004	0.996	0.961	0.039
11	yearn (ἐπιποθέω)	4:5	1:8	0.099	0.004	0.996	0.957	0.043
12	gain (κερδαίνω)	4:13	3:8	0.098	0.004	0.996	0.953	0.047
13	coming (παρουσία)	5:7	1:26	0.093	0.004	0.996	0.950	0.050
14	confess (ἐξομολογέω)	5:16	2:11	0.081	0.003	0.997	0.946	0.054

As shown in table 3.1, the parallels in this category contribute very little to the overall probability of literary dependence, as the CP_{dir} value rises from zero to only 0.054. This is due mainly to the fact that the rarity and correspondence scores are multiplied by the extent multiplier (EM), which for single-word parallels falls at the bottom of the scale.

Word-Group Parallels

In addition to the single-word parallels, examination of the texts reveals six multi-word parallels that meet the qualifying condition (#15–20). All of these word-group parallels are relatively short, the longest of which has an extent of only six words. Each is discussed in detail below.

Parallel #15:   Slave of Jesus Christ
(Jas 1:1 || Phil 1:1)

Jas 1:1	Phil 1:1
Ἰάκωβος θεοῦ καὶ κυρίου {Ἰησοῦ Χριστοῦ δοῦλος} ταῖς δώδεκα φυλαῖς ταῖς ἐν τῇ διασπορᾷ χαίρειν.	Παῦλος καὶ Τιμόθεος {δοῦλοι Χριστοῦ Ἰησοῦ} πᾶσιν τοῖς ἁγίοις ἐν Χριστῷ Ἰησοῦ τοῖς οὖσιν ἐν Φιλίπποις σὺν ἐπισκόποις καὶ διακόνοις,
James, a {slave} of God and {of} the Lord {Jesus Christ}, to the twelve tribes in the Diaspora: Greetings!	Paul and Timothy, {slaves of Christ Jesus}, to all the saints in Christ Jesus who are in Philippi, with the overseers and deacons.

Parallel #15, "slave of Jesus Christ" (Jas 1:1 || Phil 1:1), involves the authors' self-identification as a slave of Jesus Christ. Similar author identifications using a form of δοῦλος ("slave") with the genitive Ἰησοῦ Χριστου ("of Jesus Christ") are found in four other NT writings (Rom 1:1; Titus 1:1; 2 Pet 1:1; Jude 1) but not in any other examined bodies of literature.

Verbal correspondence is easily seen in figure 3.2. All three pairs of parallel terms share the same lexical roots and therefore are counted as identical basic units. Viewing each individual word as a separate construct reveals two pairs of identical grammatical constructs (J1 || P3, J2 || P2). In addition, constructs J3 and P1 are considered grammatically equivalent because, although the two words derive from the same root and serve the same syntactical function in their respective sentences, they do so in a way that reflects a singular-plural morphological transformation.

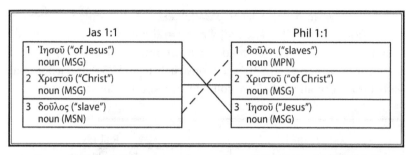

FIGURE 3.2. Verbal correspondence of parallel #15 (Jas 1:1 || Phil 1:1)

Figure 3.2 further shows that this word-group parallel exhibits a recognizable structural pattern in that the order of the parallel terms is reversed. Each expression conveys the same basic idea and is used similarly in the salutation of each document to describe the author. Thus the parallel is considered semantically comparable and functionally equivalent.

Parallel #16:   Perfect Work
                                                                    (Jas 1:4 || Phil 1:6)

Jas 1:4	Phil 1:6
{ἡ δὲ ὑπομονὴ ἔργον τέλειον ἐχέτω}, ἵνα ἦτε τέλειοι καὶ ὁλόκληροι ἐν μηδενὶ λειπόμενοι.	πεποιθὼς αὐτὸ τοῦτο, ὅτι {ὁ ἐναρξάμενος ἐν ὑμῖν ἔργον ἀγαθὸν ἐπιτελέσει} ἄχρι ἡμέρας Χριστοῦ Ἰησοῦ·
{And let endurance have [its] perfect work}, so that you might be perfect and complete, lacking in nothing.	being confident of this very thing, that {he who began in you [a] good work will perfect [it]} until the day of Christ Jesus.

Parallel #16, "perfect work" (Jas 1:4 || Phil 1:6), involves expressions that associate the adjective τέλειον ("perfect") or a form of the verb τελέω ("perfect"), which may include a prefixed preposition, with the noun ἔργον ("work") to convey the idea that work can be perfect or perfected. While the concept expressed using these terms is found only here in the NT, similar expressions are found in all other examined bodies of literature.

As shown in figure 3.3, the parallel texts contain only two pairs of same-root words (ἡ || ὁ, ἔργον || ἔργον) and one pair of related words (τέλειον || ἐπιτελέσει). Grammatical correspondence includes one pair of identical constructs (J3 || P3). Since constructs J4 and P5 reflect a nominal-verbal transformation, they are counted as grammatically equivalent.

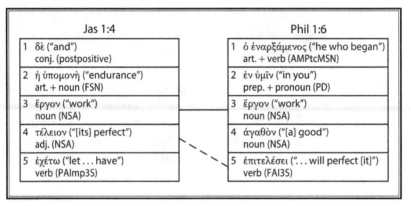

FIGURE 3.3. Verbal correspondence of parallel #16 (Jas 1:4 || Phil 1:6)

The thoughts conveyed by the parallel expressions are neither comparable nor sequential. In Jas 1:4, the expression conveys the idea that "perfect work" is the full effect or the ultimate result of practicing endurance through trials of faith. It is an outcome of the recipients' response to trials.[24] On the other hand, the expression in Phil 1:6 conveys the idea that God will "perfect" or bring to completion the "work" that he has begun in the Philippian community of faith. In this case, "perfect work" is an action performed by God.[25] Hence the semantic relationship of this parallel is best understood as dissimilar. The functional relationship also is dissimilar. Whereas the expression in James serves as part of a direct exhortation for readers to endure trials that test their faith, the parallel expression in Philippians is used by Paul to help explain the depth of his close relationship with the early faith community at Philippi.

24. See Johnson, *Letter of James*, 178; Moo, *Letter of James*, 55–56.
25. See O'Brien, *Epistle to the Philippians*, 63–65; Silva, *Philippians*, 45–48.

Parallel #17:   If Anyone Thinks
(Jas 1:26 || Phil 3:4)

Jas 1:26	Phil 3:4
{Εἴ τις δοκεῖ} θρησκὸς εἶναι μὴ χαλιναγωγῶν γλῶσσαν αὐτοῦ ἀλλὰ ἀπατῶν καρδίαν αὐτοῦ, τούτου μάταιος ἡ θρησκεία.	καίπερ ἐγὼ ἔχων πεποίθησιν καὶ ἐν σαρκί. {Εἴ τις δοκεῖ} ἄλλος πεποιθέναι ἐν σαρκί, ἐγὼ μᾶλλον·
{If anyone thinks} himself to be religious, [and yet] does not bridle his tongue but deceives his heart, this man's religion is worthless.	although I also [have reason] for confidence in the flesh. {If anyone} else {thinks} [he has reason] to put confidence in the flesh, I more so;

The next word-group parallel, #17, "if anyone thinks" (Jas 1:26 || Phil 3:4), involves the clause Εἴ τις δοκεῖ ("if anyone thinks"), which appears in precisely the same form in both documents. This is the rarest of all the parallels between James and Philippians. The clause appears elsewhere in the same form or with just minor differences only in 1 Cor 3:18; 8:2; 11:16; 14:37; and Gal 6:3. It is not found in any other bodies of literature that were examined for this project.

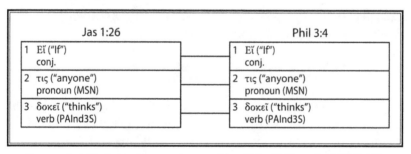

FIGURE 3.4. Verbal correspondence of parallel #17 (Jas 1:26 || Phil 3:4)

These rare parallel clauses also exhibit strong verbal correspondence, as illustrated in figure 3.4. Not surprisingly, correspondence of basic units and correspondence of grammatical constructs is perfect. All three pairs of parallel terms share the same lexical roots and exhibit the same morphological forms. Moreover, all three terms appear in the same order in both documents. Since both clauses convey the same basic thought, they are also semantically comparable. Only in function do these parallel expressions differ. In Jas 1:26 the clause is used in a passage that serves as a basis for an exhortation to be doers of the word of God and not merely hearers of the word. Specifically, the clause is used rhetorically to make the point that "religion" which is not accompanied by corresponding behavior is viewed as worthless by God.[26] In Phil 3:4 the clause also is used rhetorically to make a point which serves as a basis for an exhortation. In this case, however, the exhortation is to beware of those who seek to impose Jewish practices of the law upon members of the early Christian faith community, with the idea that even Paul considers his own history of exemplary regard for the law as irrelevant for his new life in Christ.[27] Although the expressions are used in similar ways in both James and Philippians, the intended purposes and specific points are different. For this reason, the functional relationship is best understood as modified.

Parallel #18:   Fruit of Righteousness
                                                  (Jas 3:18 || Phil 1:11)

Jas 3:18	Phil 1:11
{καρπὸς δὲ δικαιοσύνης} ἐν εἰρήνῃ σπείρεται τοῖς ποιοῦσιν εἰρήνην.	πεπληρωμένοι {καρπὸν δικαιοσύνης} τὸν διὰ Ἰησοῦ Χριστοῦ εἰς δόξαν καὶ ἔπαινον θεοῦ.
{And [the] fruit of righteousness} is sown in peace among those who make peace.	having been filled with {[the] fruit of righteousness} that comes through Jesus Christ unto the glory and praise of God.

In parallel #18, "fruit of righteousness" (Jas 3:18 || Phil 1:11), each of the authors associates the genitive noun δικαιοσύνης ("of righteousness") with a form of καρπός ("fruit"). Beyond James and Philippians, this particular association is found once in the NT (Heb 12:11), four times in the LXX (Prov 3:9; 11:30; 13:2; Amos 6:12), once in the Pseudepigrapha (*Apoc. Sedr.* 12:6), and once in the Apostolic Fathers (*Herm. Sim.* 9:19:2).

---

26. See Johnson, *Letter of James*, 205–14; Moo, *Letter of James*, 84–97.

27. See O'Brien, *Epistle to the Philippians*, 352–68; Witherington, *Paul's Letter to the Philippians*, 181–232.

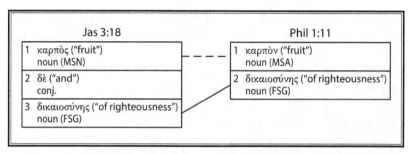

FIGURE 3.5. Verbal correspondence of parallel #18 (Jas 3:18 || Phil 1:11)

As shown in figure 3.5, the two phrases are nearly identical. With the single exception of the additional postpositive conjunction (δὲ) in Jas 3:18, the basic units share identical roots. When each word is viewed as a separate grammatical construct, figure 3.5 further shows that constructs J3 and P2 are grammatically identical. The words of constructs J1 and P1 reflect a nominative-accusative case transformation and therefore are considered grammatically equivalent. In addition, the parallel terms appear in the same order in both documents.

Although both authors apparently understand "fruit of righteousness" as an integral part of being rightly related to God/Christ, correspondence of meaning depends on how the genitive δικαιοσύνης ("of righteousness") is interpreted in each case. As noted by biblical commentators, the most likely options for these two instances are to understand the genitive as (1) a genitive of origin or source, thereby conveying the idea of fruit that comes from righteousness, or (2) a genitive of definition or apposition, thereby conveying the idea of fruit that is righteousness.[28] In both Philippians and James, the precise meanings of "righteousness" and "fruit" also are not certain. Given the uncertainty regarding interpretation of the two phrases, a semantically comparable relationship cannot be justified. Therefore, it is best to classify this parallel as semantically dissimilar.

The parallel also appears to be dissimilar in functionality as the two phrases serve different purposes in their host documents. In Jas 3:18 the phrase appears in a passage where the author exhorts his readers to let their claims of godly wisdom be evidenced by corresponding deeds (Jas 3:13–18). The phrase is used to describe the nature of such evidence. In

28. See, e.g., Davids, *Epistle of James*, 155; Johnson, *Letter of James*, 275; Melick, *Philippians, Colossians, Philemon*, 66–67; Moo, *Letter of James*, 177–78; O'Brien, *Epistle to the Philippians*, 79–83.

particular, deeds that evidence godly wisdom are described as "fruit," the product and production of which reflects wisdom from above, namely, righteousness and peace.[29] Usage in Phil 1:11 is quite different. In this case, the phrase appears in the author's opening remarks and is used to help explain the deep affection and concern that he has for his audience, thereby setting the stage for the rest of the letter. In this context, Paul presents the phrase as evidence of the audience's status as fellow saints in Christ Jesus and partakers of God's grace, namely, they have been filled with the "fruit of righteousness" which flows from their relationship with Jesus Christ.[30] Given the different purposes served by the parallel phrases in James and Philippians, the functional relationship is considered dissimilar.

Parallel #19:   The Lord Is Near
                                              (Jas 5:8 || Phil 4:5)

Jas 5:8	Phil 4:5
μακροθυμήσατε καὶ ὑμεῖς, στηρίξατε τὰς καρδίας ὑμῶν, ὅτι {ἡ παρουσία τοῦ κυρίου ἤγγικεν}.	τὸ ἐπιεικὲς ὑμῶν γνωσθήτω πᾶσιν ἀνθρώποις. {ὁ κύριος ἐγγύς}.
You also be patient; establish your hearts; because {the coming of the Lord is near}.	Let your gentleness be known to all men. {The Lord [is] near}.

Parallel #19, "the Lord is near" (Jas 5:8 || Phil 4:5), involves clauses that express the nearness of the Lord using a form of ὁ κύριος ("the Lord") and either the verb ἐγγίζω ("come near") or the adverb ἐγγύς ("near"). Although not found in other NT documents, similar expressions are not uncommon in the LXX, which contains thirteen instances (Deut 4:7; Pss 33:19; 118:151; 144:18; Joel 1:15; 2:1; 3:14; Obad 1:15; Zeph 1:7, 14; Isa 13:6; Jer 23:23; Ezek 30:3). Additional instances are found in Philo's works (*Migr.* 1:56), the Pseudepigrapha (*El. Mod.* 1:1), and the Apostolic Fathers (*Barn.* 21:3; *Herm. Vis.* 2:3:4).

---

29. So Davids, *Epistle of James*, 155; Moo, *Letter of James*, 177–78.
30. So O'Brien, *Epistle to the Philippians*, 79–83.

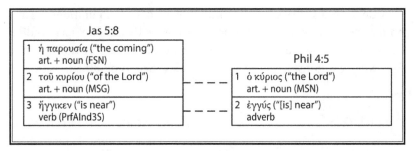

FIGURE 3.6. Verbal correspondence of parallel #19 (Jas 5:8 || Phil 4:5)

Lexical-grammatical correspondence between the two clauses is illustrated in figure 3.6. The parallel clauses have three pairs of terms that share the same roots (τοῦ || ὁ, κυρίου || κύριος, and ἤγγικεν || ἐγγύς). In addition, there are two pairs of grammatically equivalent constructs. Constructs J2 and P1 reflect a genitive-nominative case transformation, and constructs J3 and P2 reflect a verb-adverb transformation. The parallel terms also appear in the same order in each document. In regard to meaning, the parallel clauses are commonly understood to convey the same basic thought. Although "near" can be understood spatially or temporally, the association with "the coming of the Lord" in Jas 5:8 seems to indicate temporal nearness, with the return of Jesus in view.[31] The adverb in Phil 4:5 also is commonly understood as temporal nearness, indicating the second coming of Christ.[32] Thus the two clauses are semantically comparable as both convey the idea that the end of the present stage of salvation history is imminent, as indicated by the pending arrival of the Lord Jesus Christ.

The function of each clause in its respective host letter, however, is slightly different. In Jas 5:8 it provides the reason why the readers need to be patient and strong of heart, and it serves as encouragement for the early trial-tested communities of faith.[33] The parallel clause in Philippians appears in the midst of several exhortations that admonish the audience to rejoice, let their gentleness be evident to everyone, not to be anxious, and to make their requests known to God (Phil 4:4–6). Although there are no grammatical connections to these surrounding exhortations, the clause ὁ κύριος ἐγγύς ("the Lord [is] near") is generally understood to

31. So, e.g., Davids, *Epistle of James*, 184; Johnson, *Letter of James*, 315–16, 322; Moo, *Letter of James*, 223–24.

32. See O'Brien, *Epistle to the Philippians*, 488–90; Silva, *Philippians*, 193–96.

33. See Johnson, *Letter of James*, 315–16; Moo, *Letter of James*, 223–24.

provide the basis or reason for some, if not all, of the admonitions.[34] Thus both authors present the clause as a basis or motivation for surrounding exhortations. However, since the particular exhortations are different, the functional relationship of this parallel is classified as modified.

Parallel #20:   In the Name of the Lord/Jesus
                                                    (Jas 5:10 || Phil 2:10)

Jas 5:10	Phil 2:10
ὑπόδειγμα λάβετε, ἀδελφοί, τῆς κακοπαθείας καὶ τῆς μακροθυμίας τοὺς προφήτας οἳ ἐλάλησαν {ἐν τῷ ὀνόματι κυρίου}.	ἵνα {ἐν τῷ ὀνόματι Ἰησοῦ} πᾶν γόνυ κάμψῃ ἐπουρανίων καὶ ἐπιγείων καὶ καταχθονίων
As an example of suffering and patience, brothers, take the prophets, who spoke {in the name of the Lord}.	so that {in the name of Jesus} every knee should bow, in heaven and on earth and under the earth

The final parallel, #20, "in the name of the Lord/Jesus" (Jas 5:10 || Phil 2:10), is formed by two nearly identical phrases: ἐν τῷ ὀνόματι κυρίου ("in the name of the Lord," Jas 5:10) and ἐν τῷ ὀνόματι Ἰησοῦ ("in the name of Jesus," Phil 2:10). Although similar expressions appear frequently in the LXX and the NT, the same combination of ἐν τῷ ὀνόματι ("in the name") with either κυρίου ("Lord") or Ἰησοῦ ("Jesus") is quite rare. Beyond one other occurrence in Jas 5:14, this particular construction is found elsewhere only in Acts (3:6; 4:10; 10:48) and the Apostolic Fathers (Ign. *Smyrn.* 4:2).

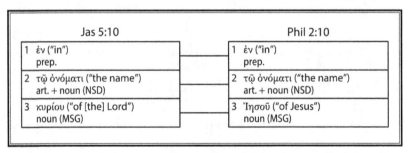

FIGURE 3.7. Verbal correspondence of parallel #20 (Jas 5:10 || Phil 2:10)

34. See O'Brien, *Epistle to the Philippians*, 489–90.

The strong verbal correspondence of the parallel is easily seen in figure 3.7. The first three words of the two parallel phrases are identical. The fourth pair, κυρίου || ᾽Ιησοῦ ("Lord" || "Jesus"), is formed by alternative terms referring to equivalent persons. Therefore, this parallel has three pairs of identical basic units and one pair of related basic units. Examination of the grammatical constructs shows that constructs J1 and P1 are grammatically identical as both are prepositions. Constructs J2 and P2 are grammatically identical as each contains a definite article plus a neuter-singular-dative noun. Since constructs J3 and P3 are both masculine-singular-genitive nouns, the third pair of constructs also are grammatically identical. Hence this parallel earns the highest possible score for correspondence of grammatical constructs. Furthermore, all the parallel terms appear in the same order in both documents.

At first glance, the parallel phrases might appear to convey the same basic thoughts, but the literary context of each suggests otherwise. The phrase in Jas 5:10 is associated with the prophets, who spoke ἐν τῷ ὀνόματι κυρίου ("in the name of the Lord"). In this context, the phrase indicates the sponsorship and authority with which they spoke. Namely, they spoke on behalf of and with the authority of the Lord.[35] On the other hand, the phrase found in Phil 2:10, ἐν τῷ ὀνόματι ᾽Ιησοῦ ("in the name of Jesus"), is associated with everyone in the world on the occasion of the Jesus' exaltation. In the context of Jesus' incarnation, death, and exaltation, the phrase seems to indicate the reason for, or object of, world-wide adoration. In other words, the adoration described in Phil 2:10–11 is in honor of the exalted Christ Jesus.[36] Given the different nuances of meaning, the parallel is best understood as semantically dissimilar.

Despite the different meanings, the function of each phrase in the discourse of its host document is remarkably similar. In Jas 5:10 it is used to describe the positive example of the prophets, who patiently endured suffering while doing God's work. The example of the prophets serves as a basis or motivation for the preceding exhortations to be patient and not to complain in the face of trials (Jas 5:8–9).[37] In Phil 2:10 the phrase also is used to describe a positive example that the audience is instructed to imitate.

<hr />

35. See Johnson, *Letter of James*, 17–19.

36. See Melick, *Philippians, Colossians, Philemon*, 107–9; O'Brien, *Epistle to the Philippians*, 239–40.

37. See Davids, *Epistle of James*, 185–86; Johnson, *Letter of James*, 17–19; Moo, *Letter of James*, 226–27.

In this case, readers are exhorted to act out of humility and concern for one another (Phil 2:3–5), following the example of Christ (Phil 2:6–11).[38] Here too, the example of Christ serves as a basis or motivation for the preceding exhortations. However, since the specific exhortations and examples are different in the two documents, the functional relationship of this parallel is classified as modified.

The effect of including all the word-group parallels in the probability analysis is shown in table 3.2. With the addition of these six word-group parallels, the best-case collective probability of directness, CP_{dir}, between James and Philippians reaches its final value of 0.153.

TABLE 3.2. Probability of directness (Jas || Phil, word groups, best case)

No.	Description	Reference		Individual			Collective	
		Jas	Phil	DI	IP_{dir}	IP_{ndir}	CP_{ndir}	CP_{dir}
15	slave of Jesus Christ	1:1	1:1	0.490	0.020	0.980	0.927	0.073
16	perfect work	1:4	1:6	0.448	0.019	0.981	0.910	0.090
17	if anyone thinks	1:26	3:4	0.500	0.021	0.979	0.891	0.109
18	fruit of righteousness	3:18	1:11	0.226	0.009	0.991	0.882	0.118
19	the Lord is near	5:8	4:5	0.394	0.016	0.984	0.868	0.132
20	in the name of the Lord/Jesus	5:10	2:10	0.580	0.024	0.976	0.847	0.153

38. See Melick, *Philippians, Colossians, Philemon*, 97–99; O'Brien, *Epistle to the Philippians*, 143–253; Silva, *Philippians*, 92–116.

The Likelihood of Literary Dependence

Before reaching a conclusion about the likelihood of literary dependence between James and Philippians, it is important to note that the result shown in table 3.2 is based on rarity of occurrence scores that include the best-case values for Greco-Roman literature. When the worst-case rarity scores are used with this same set of parallels, the final value for CP_{dir} drops to 0.094 (see appendix G). However, in the worst-case scenario for Greco-Roman literature, nine of these parallels fail to qualify for the study because the score for rarity of occurrence drops below 2.0. When the disqualified parallels are removed from the analysis, the final value for CP_{dir} drops even further to 0.074 (see appendix H). Hence the range of values for the final CP_{dir} is 0.074–0.153. Since this entire range of final values for CP_{dir} is very low, there is no need to measure the actual number of occurrences in Greco-Roman literature. The analysis is conclusive using the best-case and worst-case rarity scores for the Greco-Roman body of literature.

$$\bullet \bullet$$

Thus the probability analysis has produced the expected negative result that a direct literary connection between James and Philippians is highly unlikely. Therefore, the case of James and Philippians demonstrates credibility of the assessment methodology at the low end of the probability scale. Application of the methodology to two documents that bear little resemblance to one another does indeed yield an expected negative result. The negative result for James and Philippians also signals completion of the analysis for these two books. Since literary dependence is highly unlikely, there is no warrant for proceeding to the next stage of the methodology, which assesses the most likely direction of borrowing. Instead, we turn our attention to demonstrating credibility at the high end of the probability scale with a positive test case.

CHAPTER 4

Positive Test Case:
Literary Dependence
between Jude and 2 Peter

As explained in chapter 3, the purpose of a test case is to demonstrate that the assessment methodology presented in part 1 can be applied in a consistent manner and that it is capable of producing credible results. This is done by applying the methodology to selected pairs of NT documents where the likelihood of intertextual borrowing is already fairly certain. These cases occur at the two extremes of the probability scale, where the result is either strongly negative or strongly positive. For the methodology described in chapter 1, a negative result for the question of literary dependence occurs when the collective probability of directness, CP_{dir}, is low. A positive result occurs when CP_{dir} is high. Credibility at the low end may be demonstrated by showing that when the methodology is applied to two documents which bear little resemblance to one another, the analysis produces an expected negative result indicating that intertextual borrowing is highly unlikely. Such a demonstration is found in chapter 3 with the test case involving James and Philippians. The present chapter now demonstrates credibility at the high end by showing that for two documents which are strikingly similar, Jude and 2 Peter, application of the methodology produces an expected positive result indicating that intertextual borrowing is highly likely.

Expected Outcome

The letters of Jude and 2 Peter present an excellent positive test case for the methodology. A comparison of the two documents strongly suggests that one of the authors borrowed material from the other document. Indeed, the letters have a great deal in common, despite having different authors and intended recipients. The letter of Jude claims to have been written by someone named "Jude" who was "a brother of James" (Jude 1). The fact that no further identification is given suggests that "James" would have been well known to the intended readers. In which case, identifying himself as James's brother would have been a sufficient form of identification for the author. As explained in the previous chapter, the most likely person named "James" who was known well enough in the early Christian community to serve as a reference for identification was James the Just, who became the leader of the Jerusalem assembly and is identified as the half-brother of Jesus (Gal 1:19).[1] As a brother of James, this "Jude" also would have been a half-brother of Jesus (cf. Jude 1; Matt 13:55; Mark 6:3; Acts 12:17; 15:13; 21:18; 1 Cor 15:7; Gal 1:19; 2:9, 12). Although authorship of Jude may have been either authentic or pseudonymous, the nature of the letter suggests that it was intended for readers who were familiar with the people and events recorded in the OT and Jewish pseudepigraphal writings. For this reason, it is reasonable to conclude that the intended audience consisted of early Jewish Christians whom Jude could expect to respect his authority as a brother of James. The connection to James, the head of the assembly in Jerusalem, might also suggest a Palestinian destination.[2]

---

1. See, e.g., Richard J. Bauckham, *Jude, 2 Peter*, WBC 50 (Nashville, TN: Thomas Nelson, 1983), 14–16; Peter H. Davids, *The Letters of 2 Peter and Jude*, The Pillar New Testament Commentary (Grand Rapids, MI: Eerdmans, 2006), 8–12; Gene L. Green, *Jude and 2 Peter*, BECNT (Grand Rapids, MI: Baker Academic, 2008), 4–9; Karen H. Jobes, *Letters to the Church: A Survey of Hebrews and the General Epistles* (Grand Rapids, MI: Zondervan, 2011), 236; J. N. D. Kelly, *A Commentary on the Epistles of Peter and of Jude*, BNTC (London: Adam & Charles Black, 1969), 231–34; Thomas R. Schreiner, *1, 2 Peter, Jude*, NAC 37 (Nashville: Broadman & Holman, 2003), 404–8; R. L. Webb, "Jude," in *DLNT*, ed. Ralph P. Martin and Peter H. Davids (Downers Grove, IL: InterVarsity Press, 1997), 615–17.

2. So Davids, *Letters of 2 Peter and Jude*, 17–23; Gene Green, *Jude and 2 Peter*, 9–16; Jobes, *Letters to the Church*, 242; Kelly, *Peter and Jude*, 234.

The letter of 2 Peter claims to have been authored by "Simon Peter, a bond-slave and apostle of Jesus Christ" (2 Pet 1:1). Authentic authorship by the apostle Peter, however, has been broadly disputed for centuries. Citing arguments primarily based on the style of the Greek text, the influence of Greco-Roman concepts, relevance of the ancient testament genre, and internal references that suggest a *sitz im leben* corresponding to a time after Peter's death, the consensus of modern scholarship favors pseudepigraphal authorship of the letter.[3] Although the letter of 2 Peter is addressed to a wide audience, namely, "those who have received a faith equal to ours" (2 Pet 1:1), the author seems to be focused on those who have received earlier letters from both the claimed author and the apostle Paul, possibly somewhere in Asia Minor (2 Pet 3:1, 15). The perceived Greco-Roman character of the letter also leads scholars to believe that the intended recipients did not reside in Palestine or Syria.[4] Further identifying details remain a mystery.

Despite the different authors and intended recipients, the letters of Jude and 2 Peter exhibit remarkable similarities, one of which pertains to purpose. Jude's purpose in writing is clearly stated in verse 3: "Beloved, while making all diligence to write to you concerning our common salvation, I felt the necessity to write to you exhorting [you] to contend for the faith once handed down to the saints." Curiously, rather than an exposition about their shared salvation, as originally intended, the letter constitutes an earnest appeal for the audience to hold fast to the apostolic teachings, despite the presence of "ungodly" persons who have sneaked in among them and are misrepresenting God's grace as a license for immorality.[5] The purpose of 2 Peter, although distinct, is similar to that of Jude. Recognizing that his death was near (2 Pet 1:12–15), the author of 2 Peter writes to warn the readers about false teachers and destructive heresies that will enter the faithful assembly, and to impress upon them the need to hold fast to the truth of the apostles' teachings.[6]

---

3. So, e.g., Bauckham, *Jude, 2 Peter*, 158–62; Kelly, *Peter and Jude*, 235–37. For good summaries of the arguments, see Davids, *Letters of 2 Peter and Jude*, 123–30; Jobes, *Letters to the Church*, 356–67. Plausible arguments for authentic authorship by the apostle Peter have been advanced by Gene Green, *Jude and 2 Peter*, 144–50; Schreiner, *1, 2 Peter, Jude*, 255–76.

4. So, e.g., Jobes, *Letters to the Church*, 367–69; Davids, *Letters of 2 Peter and Jude*, 132–36; Gene Green, *Jude and 2 Peter*, 173; Kelly, *Peter and Jude*, 237.

5. Jobes, *Letters to the Church*, 242. See also Gene Green, *Jude and 2 Peter*, 18–26; Kelly, *Peter and Jude*, 227–31.

6. See Gene Green, *Jude and 2 Peter*, 153; Kelly, *Peter and Jude*, 227–31.

Verbal similarities between Jude and 2 Peter are even more remarkable. Lexically, the two documents have much in common. The 461 Greek words that comprise the letter of Jude include multiple occurrences of 297 unique words that appear in various forms throughout the letter. The 1,099 Greek words of 2 Peter include 618 unique words that occur in various forms. Of these unique words, 109 are shared by both books. In other words, more than one-third of Jude's words are also found in 2 Peter. As shown in the following analysis, most of these shared words appear in word-group parallels that are arranged together in common clusters that span much of contents of both documents. Indeed, only about a half-dozen verses in Jude do not find parallel texts in 2 Peter. Moreover, most of the parallels occur in the same order in both documents.

Given the remarkable degree of similarity between Jude and 2 Peter, even a casual read through the letters leaves little doubt that one of the authors borrowed heavily from the other document. Hence it comes as no big surprise that the strong likelihood of an intertextual relationship is frequently mentioned in commentaries and focused studies of the two letters. Although a few published works claim that the parallels are best explained by both authors having relied upon a common source,[7] direct literary dependence between Jude and 2 Peter is generally accepted in NT scholarship.[8] Thus Jude and 2 Peter present an excellent test case for the methodology presented in part 1. When the documents are analyzed for the likelihood of literary dependence, we should expect a positive result indicating that a direct literary connection is likely. Analysis of the parallels between these two books should produce a high value for CP_{dir}.

---

7. So Michael Green, *The Second Epistle General of Peter and the General Epistle of Jude: An Introduction and Commentary* (Grand Rapids, MI: Eerdmans, 1968), 50–55; B. Reicke, *The Epistles of James, Peter, and Jude*, AB 37 (Garden City: Doubleday, 1964), 189–90; Ceslas Spicq, *Les Épîtres de Saint Pierre*, SB (Paris: Gabalda, 1966), 197n1.

8. So, e.g., Bauckham, *Jude, 2 Peter*, 141–43; Davids, *Letters of 2 Peter and Jude*, 136–43; Michael J. Gilmour, *The Significance of Parallels between 2 Peter and Other Early Christian Literature*, AcBib 10 (Leiden, The Netherlands: Brill Academic, 2002), 5, 83–91; Gene Green, *Jude and 2 Peter*, 152, 159–62; David G. Horrell, *The Epistles of Peter and Jude* (London: Epworth, 1998), 140–42; Jobes, *Letters to the Church*, 258, 380–86; Kelly, *Peter and Jude*, 225–27; Jerome H. Neyrey, *2 Peter, Jude*, AB 37c (New York: Doubleday, 1993), 120–22; Schreiner, *1, 2 Peter, Jude*, 418–19; Duane Frederick Watson, *Invention, Arrangement, and Style: Rhetorical Criticism of Jude and 2 Peter*, SBLDS 104 (Atlanta, GA: Scholars Press, 1988), 160–64; Webb, "Jude," 614.

Procedure

The analysis of Jude and 2 Peter follows the same procedure that is outlined in the previous chapter for the negative test case involving Philippians and James. In particular, perceived parallels must meet the same qualifying criteria as those established in the procedure section of chapter 3 in order to be included in the probability analysis. The present test case involving Jude and 2 Peter also adopts the same straightforward approach to textual criticism, uses the same electronically-searchable Greek documents and databases for rarity evaluations, and follows the same procedural points that are described and followed in chapter 3 for the analysis of parallels between James and Philippians (see pp. 121–123).

Unlike the analysis of James and Philippians, however, the analysis of Jude and 2 Peter involves clusters and therefore exercises the procedures described for scoring of clusters. Specifically, these include: (1) the extent of a cluster is equal to the number of lower-order parallels that form the cluster; (2) the rarity score of a cluster is equal to the score of its rarest member; and (3) since a higher-order parallel, by definition, presumes the presence of common lower-order parallels that are assessed individually for correspondence, higher-order clusters are assessed only for correspondence of meaning, correspondence of function, correspondence of structural arrangement (e.g., the sequential order of all the member parallels), and membership in other higher-order clusters.

Here again, the best-case and the worst-case scenarios for rarity of occurrence in the Greco-Roman body of literature are used in order to establish the upper and lower limits for the rarity of occurrence scores. If the entire range of values for the resulting CP_{dir} is either very high or very low, the result is conclusive and there is no need to measure the actual number of occurrences in Greco-Roman literature. However, if the range of values for the final CP_{dir} spans the mid-point of the probability scale, then a precise count of occurrences in Greco-Roman literature will be required in order to reach a conclusive outcome.

As with the negative test case involving James and Philippians, the positive test case involving Jude and 2 Peter begins with selection of an appropriate set of parallels to include in the probability analysis. The same qualifying criteria are used for both James || Philippians and Jude || 2 Peter.

Selection of Parallels

The pool of potential parallels to include in the analysis of Jude and 2 Peter has been gleaned from published studies as well as a fresh examination of the texts.[9] Application of the qualifying criteria as defined in the previous chapter results in a collection of twenty-five first-order parallels to include in the study. For convenience, each selected parallel is assigned a descriptive reference label. Nonetheless, the parallels are selected based on the rarity of occurrence and correspondence scores derived from particular features of the parallel texts, not the label descriptions. The complete list can be found in appendix J. Arrangement of the parallels is illustrated in figure 4.1, in the order in which they occur in each document. Again, the boxes representing the parallels include the reference where the parallel Greek text is found, the descriptive label that represents the parallel texts, and the assigned parallel number.

As shown in figure 4.1, the parallels between Jude and 2 Peter exhibit a much higher degree of correspondence in their arrangement than do those between James and Philippians (compare figure 3.1). In the case of Jude and 2 Peter, only seven of the twenty-five first-order parallels do not appear in the same order in both documents. Furthermore, most of the first-order word-group parallels also combine to form five higher-order parallel clusters, which are identified on the right side of figure 4.1 (WC1, WC2, WC3, WC4, and WC5).

9.   Lists of parallels between Jude and 2 Peter may be found in many works focused on these two letters, including: Bauckham, *Jude, 2 Peter*, 141–43; Davids, *Letters of 2 Peter and Jude*, 136–43; Gilmour, *Significance of Parallels*, 5, 83–91; Gene Green, *Jude and 2 Peter*, 159; Jobes, *Letters to the Church*, 380–81, 384; Johannes Kahmann, "The Second Letter of Peter and the Letter of Jude: Their Mutual Relationship," in *The New Testament in Early Christianity: La réception des écrits néotestamentaires dans le christianisme primitif*, ed. Jean-Marie Sevrin, BETL 86 (Leuven: Peeters and Leuven University Press, 1989), 105–6; Schreiner, *1, 2 Peter, Jude*, 416–17; Watson, *Invention*, 160–87.

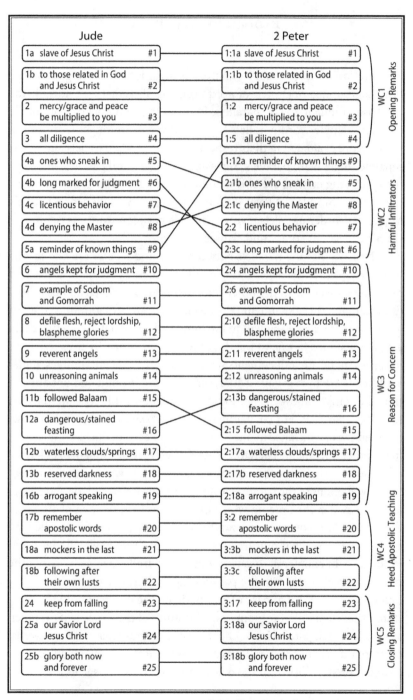

FIGURE 4.1. Arrangement of parallels (Jude ‖ 2 Peter)

Probability Analysis

Presentation of the probability analysis is organized according to the five distinct groupings or clusters of word-group parallels that are evident in the database of Jude || 2 Peter parallels. In order to avoid the error of double-counting, single-word parallels that are also part of longer word-group parallels are evaluated in their respective word-group parallels and not as separate single-word parallels. Since all the single-word parallels that meet the qualifying criteria are also members of longer word-group parallels, the analysis of Jude || 2 Peter does not include any single-word parallels. All the first-order parallels involve parallels between word-pairs, phrases, simple clauses, or compound clauses.

Nearly all of the parallels between Jude and 2 Peter are one-to-one word-group parallels, where a single instance in one document is matched by a single instance in the other document, with perhaps an occasional duplicate in either document. However, a special configuration of word-group parallels also is evident in the Jude || 2 Peter database. In two cases, a single instance in one of the documents is matched by three or more instances in the other document. Since this type of configuration resembles a folding fan, which is bound at one end to a single point and unbound at the other end to allow the fan to open, parallels of this type are referred to as "fan" parallels. For fan parallels, a distinct parallel relationship exists between the *one* instance in one document and each of the *many* instances in the other document. Therefore, fan parallels may be thought of as having multiple branches, where each branch is a separate word-group parallel.

Evaluations of the parallel clusters observed between Jude and 2 Peter are presented in the order in which they appear in both documents. Since the letter of Jude consistently holds the *one* instance of the fan parallels, all parallels within each group are presented in the order in which they occur in Jude. As in chapter 3, discussion of each parallel begins by citing the relevant Greek texts, with the parallel expressions enclosed within curly brackets ("{ . . . }"). For ease of comparison, the corresponding English translations maintain the grammatical features of the Greek texts as much as possible. Each parallel is accompanied by a diagram that illustrates verbal correspondence of the parallel expressions, with the constituent parts of each expression shown in the order in which they appear in the text of each document.[10] The block structure shows the grammatical constructs that are used to determine correspondence scores. Equivalent constructs are connected with a dashed line; identical constructs are connected with a solid line. Here too, the constructs of Jude and 2 Peter are referred to as Jn or Pn, respectively, where the variable "n" is the construct number. An explanation of the abbreviations that appear in the diagrams is found in appendix I.

At the end of each cluster or grouping of parallels, the contribution of the group to the overall probability of literary dependence is shown in a table that includes the Directness Index (DI), the Probability of Directness (IP_{dir}), and the Probability of Non-Directness (IP_{ndir}) for each individual parallel, as well as the collective probability calculations based on all the parallels presented up to that point in the analysis (CP_{ndir}, CP_{dir}). Since the overall probability of literary dependence is represented by CP_{dir}, the effect of each additional parallel on the assessment can be seen in the changes that occur in the rightmost column of each table. The tables presented in this chapter reflect the *worst*-case scores for rarity of occurrence in Greco-Roman literature because the worst-case value for the final CP_{dir} is most critical for a positive test case. Calculations for rarity of occurrence scores and verbal correspondence scores are provided in appendices K and L, respectively. All the indicator scores and probability calculations for all of the parallels are provided in appendices M (worst case) and N (best case).

First Word-Group Cluster

The first cluster of parallels, WC1, "Opening Remarks" (Jude 1–3 || 2 Pet 1:1–5), is formed by four word-group parallels that involve introductory comments in both documents. As shown in figure 4.1, the parallels that form this cluster appear in the same order in both Jude and 2 Peter. Therefore, all of the member parallels earn the highest score for membership in a higher-order cluster. Other considerations for scoring of each of the parallels are explained below, beginning with the first-order word-group parallels and ending with the second-order cluster parallel that they constitute together.

10. The only exceptions are postpositive conjunctions (e.g., δέ, γάρ, οὖν), which may be shown first in the verbal correspondence diagrams, and embedded constructs, the positions of which are indicated with ellipses.

Parallel #1:   Slave of Jesus Christ
                                                (Jude 1a || 2 Pet 1:1a)

Jude 1	2 Pet 1:1
Ἰούδας {Ἰησοῦ Χριστοῦ δοῦλος}, ἀδελφὸς δὲ Ἰακώβου, τοῖς ἐν θεῷ πατρὶ ἠγαπημένοις καὶ Ἰησοῦ Χριστῷ τετηρημένοις κλητοῖς·	Συμεὼν Πέτρος {δοῦλος καὶ ἀπόστολος Ἰησοῦ Χριστοῦ} τοῖς ἰσότιμον ἡμῖν λαχοῦσιν πίστιν ἐν δικαιοσύνῃ τοῦ θεοῦ ἡμῶν καὶ σωτῆρος Ἰησοῦ Χριστοῦ,
Jude, a {slave of Jesus Christ}, and brother of James, to those who are called, who are beloved in God the Father, and who are kept in Jesus Christ,	Simon Peter, a {slave and apostle of Jesus Christ}, to those who have received a faith of the same kind as ours in the righteousness of our God and Savior Jesus Christ,

Parallel #1, "slave of Jesus Christ" (Jude 1a || 2 Pet 1:1a), involves the authors' self-identification as a slave of Jesus Christ. Similar author identifications using a form of δοῦλος ("slave") with the genitive Ἰησοῦ Χριστου ("of Jesus Christ") are found in four other NT writings (Rom 1:1; Titus 1:1; Phil 1:1; Jas 1:1) but not in any other examined bodies of literature.

Verbal correspondence of the parallel expressions is evident in figure 4.2. All three pairs of parallel words share the same lexical roots. Therefore, they are counted as identical basic units (Ἰησοῦ, Χριστου, δοῦλος). Viewing the texts of Jude 1a and 2 Pet 1:1a as two and four grammatical constructs, respectively, reveals two pairs of constructs that are grammatically identical (J1 || P4, J2 || P1).

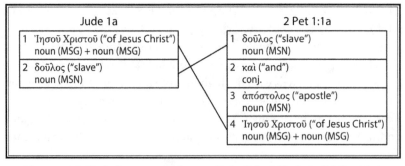

FIGURE 4.2. Verbal correspondence of parallel #1 (Jude 1a || 2 Pet 1:1a)

Figure 4.2 further shows that the parallel constructs appear in reversed order. In addition, each expression conveys the same basic idea and is used similarly in the salutation of each document to describe the author as one who belongs to, and whose authority derives from, Jesus Christ.[11] Thus the parallel is considered semantically comparable and functionally equivalent.

Parallel #2:   To Those Related in God and Jesus Christ
                            (Jude 1b || 2 Pet 1:1b)

Jude 1	2 Pet 1:1
Ἰούδας Ἰησοῦ Χριστοῦ δοῦλος, ἀδελφὸς δὲ Ἰακώβου, {τοῖς ἐν θεῷ πατρὶ ἠγαπημένοις καὶ Ἰησοῦ Χριστῷ τετηρημένοις κλητοῖς}·	Συμεὼν Πέτρος δοῦλος καὶ ἀπόστολος Ἰησοῦ Χριστοῦ {τοῖς ἰσότιμον ἡμῖν λαχοῦσιν πίστιν ἐν δικαιοσύνῃ τοῦ θεοῦ ἡμῶν καὶ σωτῆρος Ἰησοῦ Χριστοῦ},
Jude, a slave of Jesus Christ, and brother of James, {to those who are called, who are beloved in God the Father, and who are kept in Jesus Christ},	Simon Peter, a slave and apostle of Jesus Christ, {to those who have received a faith of the same kind as ours in the righteousness of our God and Savior Jesus Christ},

Parallel #2, "to those related in God and Jesus Christ" (Jude 1b || 2 Pet 1:1b), involves expressions by which the authors describe the audiences to whom their letters are addressed. Beyond this parallel, similar addresses to those who are somehow related in or through God (τοῖς ἐν θεῷ/θεοῦ) and Jesus Christ (Ἰησοῦ Χριστῷ/Χριστοῦ) are found only in Rom 1:7; 1 Cor 1:2; 2 Cor 1:1; Eph 1:1; and *1 Clem.* 1:1. The texts share six basic units with identical roots (τοῖς, ἐν, θεῷ || θεοῦ, καί, Ἰησοῦ, Χριστῷ || Χριστοῦ).[12]

11. See, e.g., Davids, *Letters of 2 Peter and Jude*, 34, 161; Gene Green, *Jude and 2 Peter*, 45, 173; Horrell, *Epistles of Peter and Jude*, 115, 147; Schreiner, *1, 2 Peter, Jude*, 284, 428.

12. Parallel #2 involves two variant readings in Jude 1. First, while the NA[27] text has the participle ἠγαπημένοις, which is well attested in early and important manuscripts, the Textus Receptus and most minuscules read ἡγιασμένοις. According to Metzger, "the latter reading, which is modeled upon 1 Cor 1.2, was introduced by copyists in order to avoid the difficult and unusual combination ἐν θεῷ πατρὶ ἠγαπημένοις" (p. 656). Second, the words καὶ Ἰησοῦ Χριστῷ τετηρημένοις are omitted in a few witnesses. The omission, however, is easily explained by copyist

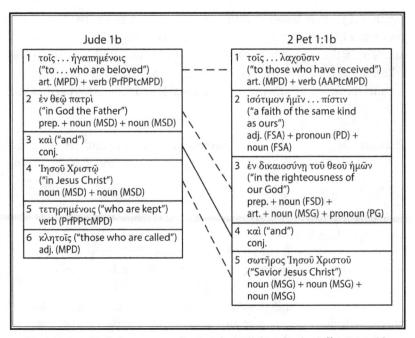

FIGURE 4.3. Verbal correspondence of parallel #2 (Jude 1b ‖ 2 Pet 1:1b)

When the parallel expressions are viewed as six and five grammatical constructs, as illustrated in figure 4.3, the syntactical structures look remarkably similar in the initial dative substantival participial clauses (J1 ‖ P1) and the subsequent compound prepositional phrases (J2 ‖ P3, J3 ‖ P4, J4 ‖ P5). The parallel terms and constructs also appear in the same order. Although the details of the two expressions differ, each is used similarly to describe the addressees and conveys the same basic idea that they have been divinely drawn into a relationship with God and Jesus Christ. Therefore, the parallel is considered functionally equivalent and semantically comparable.

error. Since neither variant reading is well attested, and both can be explained by copyist error or editing, the NA[27] text is retained for the probability analysis. See Bruce M. Metzger, *A Textual Commentary on the Greek New Testament*, 2nd ed. (Stuttgart: Deutsche Bibelgesellschaft, 1994), 656.

Parallel #3:   Mercy/Grace and Peace Be Multiplied to You
(Jude 2 || 2 Pet 1:2a)

Jude 2	2 Pet 1:2
{ἔλεος ὑμῖν καὶ εἰρήνη καὶ ἀγάπη πληθυνθείη}.	{χάρις ὑμῖν καὶ εἰρήνη πληθυνθείη} ἐν ἐπιγνώσει τοῦ θεοῦ καὶ Ἰησοῦ τοῦ κυρίου ἡμῶν.
{Mercy and peace and love be multiplied to you}.	{Grace and peace be multiplied to you} in the knowledge of God and of Jesus our Lord.

In parallel #3, "mercy/grace and peace be multiplied to you" (Jude 2 || 2 Pet 1:2a), the authors convey similar wishes ὑμῖν ("to you") using the rare optative verb πληθυνθείη ("be multiplied") together with the subjects εἰρήνη ("peace") and either ἔλεος ("mercy") or χάρις ("grace"). Similar expressions employing these same terms are found only once in the NT (1 Pet 1:2) and three times in the Apostolic Fathers (*1 Clem.* 1:1; Pol. *Phil.* 1:2; *Mart. Pol.* 1:1). This parallel exhibits four identical pairs of words (ὑμῖν, καί, εἰρήνη, πληθυνθείη).

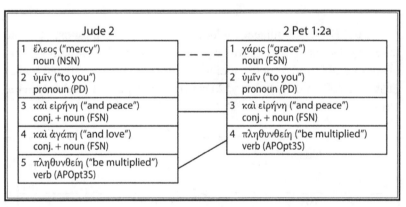

FIGURE 4.4. Verbal correspondence of parallel #3 (Jude 2 || 2 Pet 1:2a)

As shown in figure 4.4, the parallel expressions also exhibit strong grammatical correspondence. Three pairs of constructs are identical (J2 || P2, J3 || P3, J5 || P4). One additional pair is grammatically equivalent in that the two terms serve the same syntactical function in the sentence, yet they reflect a neuter-feminine gender transformation (J1 || P1). Figure 4.4 further shows that all of the parallel terms and constructs appear in the same order.

The parallel expressions convey the same basic thoughts of good will and serve equivalent functions in the introductory remarks of the two letters.

Parallel #4:   All Diligence
                                              (Jude 3 || 2 Pet 1:5)

Jude 3	2 Pet 1:5
Ἀγαπητοί, {πᾶσαν σπουδὴν} ποιούμενος γράφειν ὑμῖν περὶ τῆς κοινῆς ἡμῶν σωτηρίας ἀνάγκην ἔσχον γράψαι ὑμῖν παρακαλῶν ἐπαγωνίζεσθαι τῇ ἅπαξ παραδοθείσῃ τοῖς ἁγίοις πίστει.	Καὶ αὐτὸ τοῦτο δὲ {σπουδὴν πᾶσαν} παρεισενέγκαντες ἐπιχορηγήσατε ἐν τῇ πίστει ὑμῶν τὴν ἀρετήν, ἐν δὲ τῇ ἀρετῇ τὴν γνῶσιν,
Beloved, while making {all diligence} to write to you concerning our common salvation, I felt the necessity to write to you exhorting [you] to contend for the faith once handed down to the saints.	But also for this very reason, applying {all diligence}, supplement your faith with virtue, and virtue with knowledge,

Parallel #4, "all diligence" (Jude 3 || 2 Pet 1:5), is the shortest of the Jude || 2 Peter parallels as it involves only a pair of words. The combination of πᾶσαν ("all") and σπουδὴν ("diligence") is rare in the examined bodies of literature. Outside of Jude and 2 Peter, the word-pair is found only in the writings of Josephus (*Ant.* 6:263; 11:324; 15:114; 20:204).

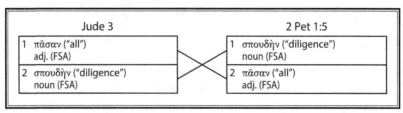

FIGURE 4.5. Verbal correspondence of parallel #4 (Jude 3 || 2 Pet 1:5)

Verbal correspondence between the parallel elements is very strong since each expression employs identical basic units and grammatical constructs. Moreover, the order of the words exhibits a reversal pattern. Semantically, the two expressions are comparable as each conveys the idea of making every effort or doing something in all earnestness or with utmost diligence. However, the word-pairs are used differently in their host documents. In Jude the word-pair is used to characterize the author's initial intention to write to the readers about their common salvation — an intention that now necessitates an exhortation for them to "contend for the faith once handed down to the saints" (Jude 3b). In 2 Peter the word-pair appears in an exhortation and describes how the readers should grow in faith. For the author of 2 Peter, this means growing in virtue.[13] Thus the parallel word-pairs are functionally dissimilar.

Parallel WC1:   Opening Remarks
                                        (Jude 1–3 || 2 Pet 1:1–5)

The final parallel associated with this first group is the second-order cluster which is formed by parallels #1, #2, #3, and #4. As shown in figure 4.1, the member parallels of this first cluster, WC1, "Opening Remarks" (Jude 1–3 || 2 Pet 1:1–5), appear in the same order in both documents. The comparable thoughts conveyed by the members also apply to the cluster as a whole, and although the two expressions of parallel #4 are functionally dissimilar, the parallel clusters serve equivalent introductory functions in their host documents. Thus cluster WC1 is classified as semantically comparable and functionally equivalent.

The worst-case probability of literary dependence based only on the first cluster and its member parallels is provided in table 4.1. At this early point in the analysis, the collective probability of directness, CP_{dir}, rises from zero to 0.135. This is already higher than the final worst-case value for James || Philippians (see chapter 3, appendices G and H).

---

13. See Bauckham, *Jude, 2 Peter*, 29–30, 184–92; Davids, *Letters of 2 Peter and Jude*, 41–43, 177–80; Gene Green, *Jude and 2 Peter*, 52–57, 188–93; Schreiner, *1, 2 Peter, Jude*, 284, 296–301, 433–34.

TABLE 4.1. Probability of directness (Jude || 2 Pet, 1st cluster, worst case)

No.	Description	Reference		Individual			Collective	
		Jude	2 Pet	DI	IP_{dir}	IP_{ndir}	CP_{ndir}	CP_{dir}
							1	0
1	slave of Jesus Christ	1a	1:1a	0.422	0.018	0.982	0.982	0.018
2	to those related in God and Jesus Christ	1b	1:1b	1.568	0.065	0.935	0.918	0.082
3	mercy/grace and peace be multiplied to you	2	1:2a	0.749	0.031	0.969	0.890	0.110
4	all diligence	3	1:5	0.283	0.012	0.988	0.879	0.121
WC1	Opening Remarks	1–3	1:1–5	0.388	0.016	0.984	0.865	0.135

Second Word-Group Cluster

The second cluster of parallels, WC2, "Harmful Infiltrators" (Jude 4 || 2 Pet 2:1–3), is formed by four word-group parallels that describe a source of trouble among the intended readers of both documents. In each case, the parallel material is found in a single sentence of the Greek texts. While the sentence of Jude constitutes only one verse, the parallel sentence in 2 Peter spans three verses. In regard to membership in a higher-order cluster, all of the parallels in this cluster receive the second highest score because, as shown in figure 4.1, they do not occur in the same order in both Jude and 2 Peter.

Parallel #5:   Ones Who Sneak In
                                                      (Jude 4a || 2 Pet 2:1b)

Jude 4	2 Pet 2:1
{παρεισέδυσαν γάρ τινες ἄνθρωποι}, οἱ πάλαι προγεγραμμένοι εἰς τοῦτο τὸ κρίμα, ἀσεβεῖς, τὴν τοῦ θεοῦ ἡμῶν χάριτα μετατιθέντες εἰς ἀσέλγειαν καὶ τὸν μόνον δεσπότην καὶ κύριον ἡμῶν Ἰησοῦν Χριστὸν ἀρνούμενοι.	Ἐγένοντο δὲ καὶ ψευδοπροφῆται ἐν τῷ λαῷ, ὡς καὶ ἐν ὑμῖν ἔσονται ψευδοδιδάσκαλοι, {οἵτινες παρεισάξουσιν αἱρέσεις ἀπωλείας} καὶ τὸν ἀγοράσαντα αὐτοὺς δεσπότην ἀρνούμενοι. ἐπάγοντες ἑαυτοῖς ταχινὴν ἀπώλειαν,
{For certain men have sneaked in}, who long ago were designated beforehand for this judgment, ungodly men, who pervert the grace of our God into licentiousness, even denying the only Master and our Lord, Jesus Christ.	But false prophets also arose among the people, just as there also will be false teachers among you, {who will sneak in heresies of destruction}, even denying the Master who bought them, bringing upon themselves swift destruction,

Parallel #5, "ones who sneak in" (Jude 4a || 2 Pet 2:1b), involves two expressions that describe the harmful factors as persons who παρεισέδυσαν ("have sneaked in") or as persons who παρεισάξουσιν ("will sneak in"). Similar expressions employing a form of the verbs found in this parallel, παρεισδύω or παρεισάγω, the similar verb παρεισέρχομαι ("sneak in"), or the cognate noun παρείσδυσις ("sneaking in") are found in the NT (Gal 2:4), the works of Philo (*Sacr.* 1:94; *Spec.* 3:88; *Opif.* 1:150; *Ebr.* 1:157; *Abr.* 1:96; *QG* 1:55; 3:21), Josephus (*J. W.* 4:571), the Pseudepigrapha (*Let. Aris.* 1:20; Dem. 4:1; *T. Jud.* 16:2; *T. Sol.* 1:11:2), and the Apostolic Fathers (*Barn.* 2:10; 4:9).

As illustrated in figure 4.6, verbal correspondence of this parallel is fairly low, with only two pairs of related words (τὶς || ὅστις, παρεισδύω || παρεισάγω) and two equivalent pairs of grammatical constructs. The verbs of J2 || P2 reflect an aorist-future morphological transformation, and the terms of J3 || P1 reflect an adjective-pronoun morphological transformation. In both cases, the parallel constructs serve similar functions in their respective sentences by referring to the source of trouble and its manner of entry into the community of faith. Since the parallel terms and constructs appear in reversed order, the parallel exhibits a recognizable structural pattern between the two expressions.

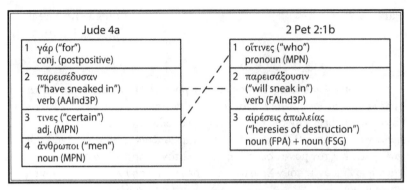

FIGURE 4.6. Verbal correspondence of parallel #5 (Jude 4a || 2 Pet 2:1b)

The thoughts conveyed by the texts of Jude 4a and 2 Pet 2:1b both involve the idea of certain persons or teachings secretly entering into the addressed early Christian faith communities. However, since the expression in Jude seems to suggest completion of what appears to be foretold in 2 Peter, the semantic relationship of the parallel texts is best understood as sequential rather than comparable. Examination of the literary contexts further shows that each clause serves a similar purpose in its host document. As indicated by the initial explanatory γάρ ("for"), the statement in Jude 4 is used to explain the impetus for the letter, namely, the dangerous situation in which the faithful assembly finds itself. In this way, the motivation for writing is based on the audience's current situation, as perceived by the author. The parallel in 2 Peter also explains the impetus for the letter, but it does so in a different way. Rather than pointing directly to the audience's current situation, the author of 2 Peter appeals to prophetic Scripture, and perhaps early Christian prophecies, as motivation for the letter (2 Pet 2:1a), with the understanding that Scripture is inherently trustworthy (2 Pet 1:19–21).[14] Since the two authors employ different methods to accomplish similar purposes, correspondence of function is classified as modified.

14. See Bauckham, *Jude, 2 Peter,* 40–41, 238–43; Davids, *Letters of 2 Peter and Jude,* 218; Gene Green, *Jude and 2 Peter,* 57, 236–38; Schreiner, *1, 2 Peter, Jude,* 284, 325–26, 436.

Parallel #6:   Long Marked for Judgment
                                                (Jude 4b || 2 Pet 2:3c)

Jude 4	2 Pet 2:3
παρεισέδυσαν γάρ τινες ἄνθρωποι, {οἱ πάλαι προγεγραμμένοι εἰς τοῦτο τὸ κρίμα}, ἀσεβεῖς, τὴν τοῦ θεοῦ ἡμῶν χάριτα μετατιθέντες εἰς ἀσέλγειαν καὶ τὸν μόνον δεσπότην καὶ κύριον ἡμῶν Ἰησοῦν Χριστὸν ἀρνούμενοι.	καὶ ἐν πλεονεξίᾳ πλαστοῖς λόγοις ὑμᾶς ἐμπορεύσονται {οἷς τὸ κρίμα ἔκπαλαι οὐκ ἀργεῖ} καὶ ἡ ἀπώλεια αὐτῶν οὐ νυστάζει.
For certain men have sneaked in, {who long ago were designated beforehand for this judgment}, ungodly men, who pervert the grace of our God into licentiousness, even denying the only Master and our Lord, Jesus Christ.	and in [their] greed they will exploit you with false words, {for whom judgment from long ago is not idle}, and their destruction is not asleep.

In parallel #6, "long marked for judgment" (Jude 4b || 2 Pet 2:3c), both authors describe the infiltrators as people for whom judgment was decreed long ago. Similar expressions using the terms τὸ κρίμα ("judgment") and either πάλαι ("long ago") or ἔκπαλαι ("from long ago") are not found elsewhere in the examined bodies of literature. The parallel expressions contain two pairs of identical words (τὸ κρίμα) and two pairs of related words (οἱ || οἷς, πάλαι || ἔκπαλαι).

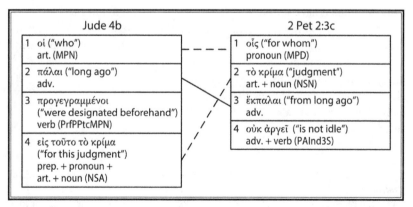

FIGURE 4.7. Verbal correspondence of parallel #6 (Jude 4b || 2 Pet 2:3c)

Grammatical correspondence is illustrated in figure 4.7. The subjects of constructs J1 and P1 reflect both nominal-pronominal and nominative-dative morphological transformations. The parallel terms in J4 || P2 reflect an accusative-nominative transformation, and the adverbs of J2 || P3 are grammatically identical. Although neither author reveals any details about the source and form of the referenced judgments, the thoughts conveyed in Jude 4b and 2 Pet 2:3c both involve the same basic idea that judgment for these infiltrators was determined long ago.[15] For this reason, the semantic relationship is considered comparable. Since the four parallels that form this cluster are all part of the same sentences in their host documents and serve the same respective functions, the functional relationship of this particular parallel is counted as modified for the same reason as that given for parallel #5 above.

Parallel #7:   Licentious Behavior
                                            (Jude 4c || 2 Pet 2:2)

Jude 4	2 Pet 2:2
παρεισέδυσαν γάρ τινες ἄνθρωποι, οἱ πάλαι προγεγραμμένοι εἰς τοῦτο τὸ κρίμα, ἀσεβεῖς, {τὴν τοῦ θεοῦ ἡμῶν χάριτα μετατιθέντες εἰς ἀσέλγειαν} καὶ τὸν μόνον δεσπότην καὶ κύριον ἡμῶν Ἰησοῦν Χριστὸν ἀρνούμενοι.	{καὶ πολλοὶ ἐξακολουθήσουσιν αὐτῶν ταῖς ἀσελγείαις} δι᾿ οὓς ἡ ὁδὸς τῆς ἀληθείας βλασφημηθήσεται,
For certain men have sneaked in, who long ago were designated beforehand for this judgment, ungodly men, {who pervert the grace of our God into licentiousness}, even denying the only Master and our Lord, Jesus Christ.	{and many will follow their licentiousness}, because of whom the way of truth will be blasphemed;

15. So, e.g., Bauckham, *Jude, 2 Peter*, 35–37, 247–48; Davids, *Letters of 2 Peter and Jude*, 43–44, 224; Gene Green, *Jude and 2 Peter*, 57–58; Kelly, *Peter and Jude*, 248–51, 329; Schreiner, *1, 2 Peter, Jude*, 436–39, 333; however, Gene Green understands the expression in 2 Pet 2:3c to mean that "judgment is not delayed for a long time" (*Jude and 2 Peter*, 246).

Parallel #7, "licentious behavior" (Jude 4c || 2 Pet 2:2), involves two expressions that associate the infiltrators with ἀσέλγεια ("licentiousness"). This parallel has a relatively low score for rarity of occurrence as various forms of the noun are found in all other examined bodies of literature.

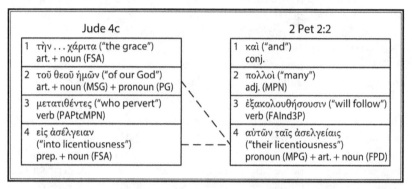

Jude 4c	2 Pet 2:2
1 τὴν ... χάριτα ("the grace") art. + noun (FSA)	1 καὶ ("and") conj.
2 τοῦ θεοῦ ἡμῶν ("of our God") art. + noun (MSG) + pronoun (PG)	2 πολλοὶ ("many") adj. (MPN)
3 μετατιθέντες ("who pervert") verb (PAPtcMPN)	3 ἐξακολουθήσουσιν ("will follow") verb (FAInd3P)
4 εἰς ἀσέλγειαν ("into licentiousness") prep. + noun (FSA)	4 αὐτῶν ταῖς ἀσελγείαις ("their licentiousness") pronoun (MPG) + art. + noun (FPD)

FIGURE 4.8. Verbal correspondence of parallel #7 (Jude 4c || 2 Pet 2:2)

Lexical-grammatical correspondence also is relatively low. As shown in figure 4.8, there are only two pairs of words with identical roots (ἀσέλγεια, ὁ). The parallel terms of J4 and P4 reflect an interesting accusative-dative morphological transformation. In addition, the grammatical structure of P4 is very similar to that of J2, with gender, number, and case transformations in the nominal terms. Although P4 shows grammatical equivalency with two of Jude's constructs, only one equivalent pair is counted in the analysis.

The thoughts of Jude 4c and 2 Pet 2:2 both involve the same basic idea that these infiltrators promote licentious behavior among the community of faith, but as part of the same sentences that began with the expressions of parallel #5, Jude seems to suggest completion of what appears to be foretold in 2 Peter. Therefore, the semantic relationship is considered sequential. So too, since the parallels that form this cluster all are part of the same sentences that exhibit a modified functional relationship in their host documents, the functional relationship of this parallel is counted as modified.

Parallel #8:   Denying the Master
                                                      (Jude 4d || 2 Pet 2:1c)

Jude 4	2 Pet 2:1
παρεισέδυσαν γάρ τινες ἄνθρωποι, οἱ πάλαι προγεγραμμένοι εἰς τοῦτο τὸ κρίμα, ἀσεβεῖς, τὴν τοῦ θεοῦ ἡμῶν χάριτα μετατιθέντες εἰς ἀσέλγειαν {καὶ τὸν μόνον δεσπότην καὶ κύριον ἡμῶν Ἰησοῦν Χριστὸν ἀρνούμενοι}.	Ἐγένοντο δὲ καὶ ψευδοπροφῆται ἐν τῷ λαῷ, ὡς καὶ ἐν ὑμῖν ἔσονται ψευδοδιδάσκαλοι, οἵτινες παρεισάξουσιν αἱρέσεις ἀπωλείας {καὶ τὸν ἀγοράσαντα αὐτοὺς δεσπότην ἀρνούμενοι}. ἐπάγοντες ἑαυτοῖς ταχινὴν ἀπώλειαν,
For certain men have sneaked in, who long ago were designated beforehand for this judgment, ungodly men, who pervert the grace of our God into licentiousness, {even denying the only Master and our Lord, Jesus Christ}.	But false prophets also arose among the people, just as there also will be false teachers among you, who will sneak in heresies of destruction, {even denying the Master who bought them}, bringing upon themselves swift destruction,

Parallel #8, "denying the Master" (Jude 4d || 2 Pet 2:1c), involves a rare use of the verb ἀρνέομαι ("deny") with the noun δεσπότην ("master") as its object. The combination is found only here in all of the examined bodies of literature. The parallel expressions share four pairs of identical words (καί, τὸν, δεσπότην, ἀρνούμενοι),[16] which also constitute three pairs of identical grammatical constructs, as illustrated in figure 4.9. All of the parallel terms and constructs appear in the same order in both documents.

In a manner similar to that of the other parallels of this cluster, the thoughts conveyed in Jude 4d and 2 Pet 2:1c involve the same basic idea that the infiltrators deny the Lord Jesus Christ. As part of the same sentences that began with parallel #5, here too, Jude seems to suggest completion of what appears to be foretold in 2 Peter. Therefore, the semantic relationship of this parallel also is considered sequential. Moreover, since the parallels

16. Parallel #8 involves two variant readings in Jude 4, according to Metzger. First, the Textus Receptus, following K L P Ψ and many minuscules, added θεόν after δεσπότην. This, however, is easily explained by a desire to "more clearly distinguish δεσπότην from the following κύριον ἡμῶν Ἰησοῦν Χριστὸν" (p. 656). Second, although the phrase ἡμῶν Ἰησοῦν Χριστὸν finds "many occasional variant readings," the wording of the NA[27] text is "strongly supported" (p. 657). Thus the NA[27] text is retained for the probability analysis. See Metzger, *Textual Commentary*, 656–57.

that form this cluster are all part of the same sentences in their host documents, the functional relationship of this parallel is counted as modified.

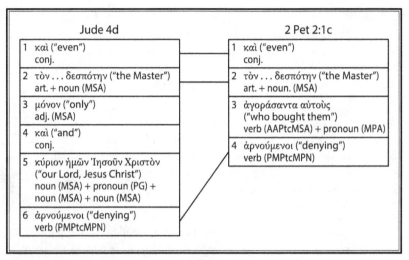

FIGURE 4.9. Verbal correspondence of parallel #8 (Jude 4d ‖ 2 Pet 2:1c)

Parallel WC2:   Harmful Infiltrators
                                               (Jude 4 ‖ 2 Pet 2:1–3)

The final parallel associated with this second group is the second-order cluster WC2, "Harmful Infiltrators" (Jude 4 ‖ 2 Pet 2:1–3), which is formed by parallels #5, #6, #7, and #8. As noted above, the member parallels appear in a different order in each document. The sequential semantic relationships exhibited by parallels #5, #7, and #8 apply to the cluster as a whole, as Jude 4 seems to suggest completion of what appears to be foretold in 2 Pet 2:1–3. The functional relationships exhibited by the parallels also apply at the cluster level. While both authors present the material as justification for their concern, they do so in different ways. Whereas Jude points directly to the audience's current situation, 2 Peter appeals to the trustworthiness of prophetic Scripture. Thus cluster WC2 is classified as semantically sequential and functionally modified.

Parallel #9:   Reminder of Known Things
                               (Jude 5a || 2 Pet 1:12a)

Jude 5	2 Pet 1:12
{Ὑπομνῆσαι δὲ ὑμᾶς βούλομαι, εἰδότας} [ὑμᾶς] πάντα ὅτι [ὁ] κύριος ἅπαξ λαὸν ἐκ γῆς Αἰγύπτου σώσας τὸ δεύτερον τοὺς μὴ πιστεύσαντας ἀπώλεσεν,	{Διὸ μελλήσω ἀεὶ ὑμᾶς ὑπομιμνήσκειν περὶ τούτων καίπερ εἰδότας} καὶ ἐστηριγμένους ἐν τῇ παρούσῃ ἀληθείᾳ.
{But I want to remind you, although you know} all things, that the Lord, having once saved the people out of the land of Egypt, later destroyed those who did not demonstrate faith,	{Therefore, I will be ready always to remind you about these things, although you know} and are established in the present truth.

Although technically not a member of a parallel cluster, parallel #9, "reminder of known things" (Jude 5a || 2 Pet 1:12a), is closely related to WC2 and therefore is discussed here with the second cluster. In this case, both authors express their desire to remind readers of things they already know. This particular parallel qualifies as a fan parallel because there is a distinct parallel relationship between the *one* instance in Jude 5a and the *many* instances in 2 Pet 1:12a, 13, 15; 3:1, as illustrated in figure 4.10.

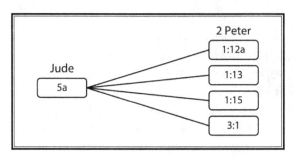

FIGURE 4.10. Configuration of fan parallel #9

For the purpose of assessing correspondence, the present study adopts a conservative approach and includes only one branch of a fan parallel in the probability analysis. In this case, the branch with 2 Pet 1:12a is selected for inclusion in the analysis. Here both authors employ an infinitive form of ὑπομιμνήσκω ("to remind") together with the participle εἰδότας ("although you know") to state explicitly their desire to remind readers of things they already know. Similar expressions employing the same terms are not found in any other examined bodies of literature. Correspondence of basic units is fairly low, with only three pairs of identical roots (ὑπομιμνήσκω, σύ, οἶδα).[17] Grammatical correspondence, however, is higher than expected.

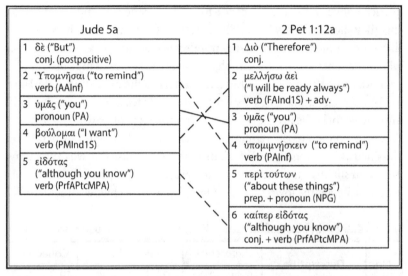

Jude 5a	2 Pet 1:12a
1 δὲ ("But") conj. (postpositive)	1 Διὸ ("Therefore") conj.
2 Ὑπομνῆσαι ("to remind") verb (AAInf)	2 μελλήσω ἀεὶ ("I will be ready always") verb (FAInd1S) + adv.
3 ὑμᾶς ("you") pronoun (PA)	3 ὑμᾶς ("you") pronoun (PA)
4 βούλομαι ("I want") verb (PMInd1S)	4 ὑπομιμνήσκειν ("to remind") verb (PAInf)
5 εἰδότας ("although you know") verb (PrfAPtcMPA)	5 περὶ τούτων ("about these things") prep. + pronoun (NPG)
	6 καίπερ εἰδότας ("although you know") conj. + verb (PrfAPtcMPA)

FIGURE 4.11. Verbal correspondence of parallel #9 (Jude 5a ‖ 2 Pet 1:12a)

As illustrated in figure 4.11, the initial coordinating conjunctions (J1 ‖ P1) and the pronouns (J3 ‖ P3) are grammatically identical. Two other pairs of constructs exhibit grammatical equivalency via tense transformations.

17. There are many variant readings for the phrase πάντα ὅτι [ὁ] κύριος ἅπαξ, which immediately follows the text of parallel #9 (Jude 5a). Some readings have ἅπαξ in the forward position, before πάντα (see Metzger, *Textual Commentary*, 657–58). Although it seems reasonable to include πάντα in the text of this parallel, given the high degree of uncertainty that surrounds the text of Jude 5, the present analysis takes a conservative approach and uses only Ὑπομνῆσαι δὲ ὑμᾶς βούλομαι, εἰδότας for the probability analysis. For detailed treatments of textual issues in Jude, see Philipp F. Bartholomä, "Did Jesus Save the People out of Egypt? A Re-examination of a Textual Problem in Jude 5," *NovT* 50, no. 2 (2008): 143–58; Jarl Fossum, "Kyrios Jesus as the Angel of the Lord in Jude 5–7," *NTS* 33, no. 2 (April 1987): 226–43; C. Landon, *A Text-Critical Study of the Epistle of Jude*, JSNTSup 135 (Sheffield: Sheffield Academic Press, 1996), 77; Bruce M. Metzger and Bart D. Ehrman, *The Text of the New Testament: Its Transmission, Corruption, and Restoration*, 4th ed. (New York: Oxford University Press, 2005), 657–58; Carroll D. Osburn, "The Text of Jude 5," *Bib* 62 (1981): 107–15.

Specifically, the infinitives reflect an aorist-present tense transformation (J2 || P4), and the indicatives reflect a present-future tense transformation (J4 || P2). Constructs J5 and P6 also exhibit equivalency as the conjunction of P6, καίπερ ("although"), makes explicit what is implicit with the stand-alone participle of J5. Semantically, the parallel expressions are comparable as each conveys the author's desire to remind readers of important things that they should already know. The contents of the reminders, however, are different. In Jude the reminder is in reference to the subsequent material which recounts historical examples of divine judgment (Jude 5b–7). The reminder in 2 Peter, on the other hand, refers to the preceding material in vv. 3–11, which outlines the trustworthy source of teaching concerning God and the gospel of Jesus Christ, and the importance of growing in virtue.[18] Since the content of the reminder in each case is different, this parallel is classified as functionally modified. In addition, because the two expressions appear in slightly different contexts and are not part of parallel clusters, this parallel receives the lowest score for membership in a higher-order parallel.

TABLE 4.2. Probability of directness (Jude || 2 Pet, 2nd cluster, worst case)

No.	Description	Reference		Individual			Collective	
		Jude	2 Pet	DI	IP_{dir}	IP_{ndir}	CP_{ndir}	CP_{dir}
5	ones who sneak in	4a	2:1b	0.349	0.015	0.985	0.852	0.148
6	long marked for judgment	4b	2:3c	0.683	0.028	0.972	0.828	0.172
7	licentious behavior	4c	2:2	0.410	0.017	0.983	0.814	0.186
8	denying the Master	4d	2:1c	0.734	0.031	0.969	0.789	0.211
WC2	Harmful Infiltrators	4	2:1–3	0.246	0.010	0.990	0.781	0.219
9	reminder of known things	5a	1:12a	0.435	0.018	0.982	0.767	0.233

18. See Bauckham, *Jude, 2 Peter*, 195–98; Davids, *Letters of 2 Peter and Jude*, 46–48, 192–93; Gene Green, *Jude and 2 Peter*, 62–66, 207–10; Horrell, *Epistles of Peter and Jude*, 120, 153–54; Schreiner, *1, 2 Peter, Jude*, 284, 307–9, 443–47.

The analysis at this point includes the first two clusters of parallels plus parallel #9. The effect of parallels #5–9 on the worst-case probability of literary dependence is shown in table 4.2. With the addition of the second group of parallels, the collective probability of directness, CP_{dir}, increases to 0.233. This value is now higher than the final best-case value for James || Philippians (see chapter 3, appendix F).

Third Word-Group Cluster

The third cluster of parallels, WC3, "Reason for Concern" (Jude 6–16b || 2 Pet 2:4–18a), is formed by ten word-group parallels that provide details which justify the authors' concerns about the infiltrators. With the exception of parallels #15 and #16, which are transposed in Jude and 2 Peter, all of the parallels in this cluster appear in the same order. Hence the cluster is best understood as a same-order cluster, and the member parallels all receive the highest score for membership in a higher-order cluster.

Parallel #10:   Angels Kept for Judgment
(Jude 6 || 2 Pet 2:4)

Jude 6	2 Pet 2:4
{ἀγγέλους τε τοὺς μὴ τηρήσαντας τὴν ἑαυτῶν ἀρχὴν ἀλλὰ ἀπολιπόντας τὸ ἴδιον οἰκητήριον εἰς κρίσιν μεγάλης ἡμέρας δεσμοῖς ἀϊδίοις ὑπὸ ζόφον τετήρηκεν},	{Εἰ γὰρ ὁ θεὸς ἀγγέλων ἁμαρτησάντων οὐκ ἐφείσατο ἀλλὰ σιροῖς ζόφου ταρταρώσας παρέδωκεν εἰς κρίσιν τηρουμένους},
{And angels who did not keep their original domain but left their own habitation, he has kept in eternal chains under gloom for judgment of the great day},	{For if God did not spare angels when they sinned, but cast them into hell and handed them over into pits of gloom, to be kept for judgment},

Parallel #10, "angels kept for judgment" (Jude 6 || 2 Pet 2:4), involves expressions that employ forms of the nouns ἄγγελος ("angel") and κρίσις ("judgment") together with the verb τηρέω ("keep") to convey the idea that

God has detained disobedient angels for future judgment. Such expressions are found only here in the examined bodies of literature.

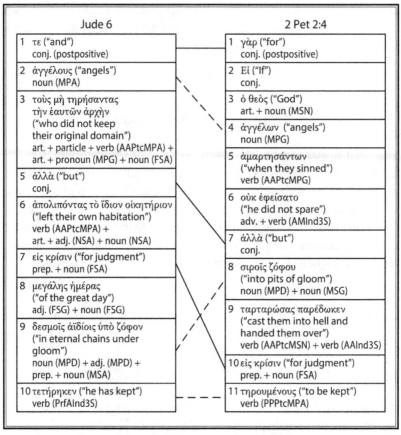

FIGURE 4.12. Verbal correspondence of parallel #10 (Jude 6 || 2 Pet 2:4)

Lexical correspondence of the parallel includes seven pairs of words with identical roots (ἄγγελος, ἀλλά, εἰς, ζόφος, κρίσις, ὁ, τηρέω) and one pair of related words (μή || οὐ).[19] When the expressions are viewed as ten and

___

19. In 2 Pet 2:4 the word σειραῖς ("chains") is replaced by σιροῖς ("pits") in many early and important manuscripts. According to Metzger, the textual evidence for both readings is "singularly evenly balanced" (*Textual Commentary*, 632). Since δεσμοῖς || σειραῖς would qualify as related basic units but δεσμοῖς || σιροῖς would not, the reading σιροῖς results in a lower correspondence score. Therefore, the variant reading σιροῖς is adopted for the correspondence evaluation.

eleven constructs, as illustrated in figure 4.12, grammatical correspondence includes three pairs of identical constructs (J1 || P1, J5 || P7, J7 || P10) and three pairs of equivalent constructs (J2 || P4, J9 || P8, J10 || P11). With the exception of J7 || P10 and J9 || P8, which are transposed, all of the parallel constructs and terms appear in the same order in both documents. Semantically, the two clauses are comparable in that both express the surety of judgment for disobedient angels, whom God has detained in chains/pits under gloom of darkness. These two clauses also serve similar purposes in their host letters. In both cases, the authors present the case of these angels as an example that demonstrates God's power and intention to keep the unrighteous under confinement, pending future judgment.[20] Thus the parallel is counted as functionally equivalent.

Parallel #11:   Example of Sodom and Gomorrah
(Jude 7 || 2 Pet 2:6)

Jude 7	2 Pet 2:6
{ὡς Σόδομα καὶ Γόμορρα καὶ αἱ περὶ αὐτὰς πόλεις τὸν ὅμοιον τρόπον τούτοις ἐκπορνεύσασαι καὶ ἀπελθοῦσαι ὀπίσω σαρκὸς ἑτέρας, πρόκεινται δεῖγμα πυρὸς αἰωνίου δίκην ὑπέχουσαι}.	{καὶ πόλεις Σοδόμων καὶ Γομόρρας τεφρώσας [καταστροφῇ] κατέκρινεν ὑπόδειγμα μελλόντων ἀσεβέ[σ]ιν τεθεικὼς}
{just as Sodom and Gomorrah and the cities around them, in the same way as these, having indulged in immorality and having gone after strange flesh, are set forth as an example by undergoing a punishment of eternal fire}.	{and [if] he condemned the cities of Sodom and Gomorrah [to destruction] by reducing [them] to ashes, making [them] an example of what is going to happen to the ungodly},

In parallel #11, "example of Sodom and Gomorrah" (Jude 7 || 2 Pet 2:6), the authors cite the example of Sodom and Gomorrah as further evidence of certain judgment for disobedience. Although not found elsewhere in

---

20. See, e.g., Bauckham, *Jude, 2 Peter*, 50–53, 248–49; Davids, *Letters of 2 Peter and Jude*, 48–51, 224–26; Gene Green, *Jude and 2 Peter*, 66–70, 249–51; Schreiner, *1, 2 Peter, Jude*, 284, 333–37, 447–51.

the NT, similar expressions that refer to Σόδομα ("Sodom") and Γόμορρα ("Gomorrah") as either a ὑπόδειγμα ("example") or a δεῖγμα ("example") appear in the LXX (3 Macc 2:5), the works of Philo (*Somn.* 1:85), and the Pseudepigrapha (*3 Macc.* 2:5).

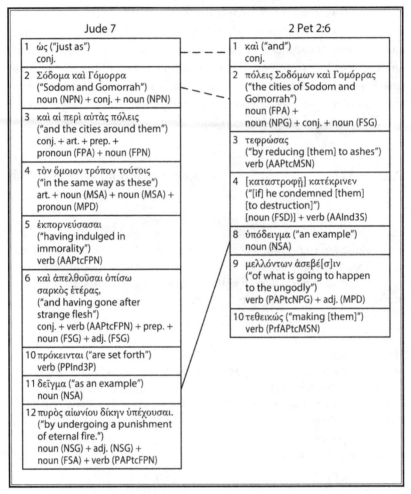

FIGURE 4.13. Verbal correspondence of parallel #11 (Jude 7 || 2 Pet 2:6)

Grammatical correspondence is quite low, as illustrated in figure 4.13. There is only one pair of grammatically identical constructs (J11 || P8). The conjunctions of J1 and P1 are considered grammatically equivalent because, while J1 serves a subordinating function, P1 serves a coordinating function. In addition, parallel constructs J2 and P2 reflect a nominative-genitive case transformation. Lexical correspondence also is relatively low, with only five pairs of words with identical roots (καί [2×], Σόδομα, Γομόρρα, πόλις) and one pair of related words (ὑπόδειγμα ‖ δεῖγμα).[21]

Despite the relatively low verbal correspondence, the two expressions convey the same basic idea that the wickedness and consequent judgment of Sodom and Gomorrah serves as an example of the certain judgment that lies ahead for those who practice and promote immorality. Continuing the line of argument set forth in the previous parallel, here too the parallel expressions serve similar purposes in their host letters. In both cases, the authors present the example of Sodom and Gomorrah as another case that demonstrates God's power and intention to punish disobedience. Hence, like parallel #10, parallel #11 is counted as semantically comparable and functionality equivalent.

Parallel #12:   Defile Flesh, Reject Lordship, Blaspheme Glories
(Jude 8 ‖ 2 Pet 2:10)

Jude 8	2 Pet 2:10
{Ὁμοίως μέντοι καὶ οὗτοι ἐνυπνιαζόμενοι σάρκα μὲν μιαίνουσιν κυριότητα δὲ ἀθετοῦσιν δόξας δὲ βλασφημοῦσιν}.	{μάλιστα δὲ τοὺς ὀπίσω σαρκὸς ἐν ἐπιθυμίᾳ μιασμοῦ πορευομένους καὶ κυριότητος καταφρονοῦντας. τολμηταὶ αὐθάδεις, δόξας οὐ τρέμουσιν βλασφημοῦντες},
{Yet in the same way even these dreamers defile the flesh and reject lordship and blaspheme glories}.	{and especially those who follow after the flesh in [its] lust of defilement and who despise lordship. Daring and self-willed, they do not tremble when they blaspheme glories},

21. Parallel #11 involves two variant readings in 2 Pet 2:6, which are indicated with square brackets in the NA[27] text. Both are well attested by early and important witnesses. See Metzger, *Textual Commentary*, 632–33. Whether ἀσεβέ[σ]ιν reads as an adjective or infinitive, the correspondence score is unaffected. Inclusion of [καταστροφῇ] also has no effect on the correspondence score. Thus [καταστροφῇ] is not included in the analysis.

Parallel #12, "defile flesh, reject lordship, blaspheme glories" (Jude 8 || 2 Pet 2:10), involves two expressions where the authors use the terms σάρξ ("flesh"), μιαίνω/μιασμός ("defile"/"defilement"), κυριότης ("lordship"), δόξα ("glory"), and βλασφημέω ("blaspheme") to describe the behavior of those who present a danger to the addressed audiences. Similar expressions are not found anywhere else in the examined bodies of literature.

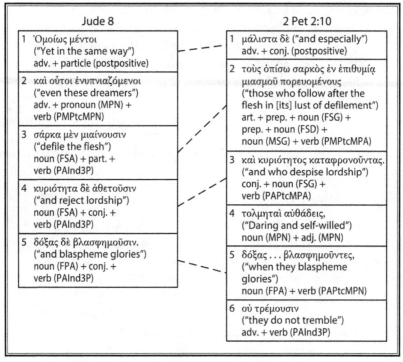

Jude 8	2 Pet 2:10
1 Ὁμοίως μέντοι ("Yet in the same way") adv. + particle (postpositive)	1 μάλιστα δὲ ("and especially") adv. + conj. (postpositive)
2 καὶ οὗτοι ἐνυπνιαζόμενοι ("even these dreamers") adv. + pronoun (MPN) + verb (PMPtcMPN)	2 τοὺς ὀπίσω σαρκὸς ἐν ἐπιθυμίᾳ μιασμοῦ πορευομένους ("those who follow after the flesh in [its] lust of defilement") art. + prep. + noun (FSG) + prep. + noun (FSD) + noun (MSG) + verb (PMPtcMPA)
3 σάρκα μὲν μιαίνουσιν ("defile the flesh") noun (FSA) + part. + verb (PAInd3P)	3 καὶ κυριότητος καταφρονοῦντας. ("and who despise lordship") conj. + noun (FSG) + verb (PAPtcMPA)
4 κυριότητα δὲ ἀθετοῦσιν ("and reject lordship") noun (FSA) + conj. + verb (PAInd3P)	4 τολμηταὶ αὐθάδεις, ("Daring and self-willed") noun (MPN) + adj. (MPN)
5 δόξας δὲ βλασφημοῦσιν. ("and blaspheme glories") noun (FPA) + conj. + verb (PAInd3P)	5 δόξας ... βλασφημοῦντες, ("when they blaspheme glories") noun (FPA) + verb (PAPtcMPN)
	6 οὐ τρέμουσιν ("they do not tremble") adv. + verb (PAInd3P)

FIGURE 4.14. Verbal correspondence of parallel #12 (Jude 8 || 2 Pet 2:10)

Verbal correspondence of the parallel texts is evident in six pairs of words with identical roots (καί, δέ, σάρξ, κυριότης, δόξα, βλασφημέω,) and one additional pair of related words (μιαίνω || μιασμός).[22] Figure 4.14 further reveals four pairs of grammatically equivalent constructs. Constructs J1 and P1 exhibit similar combinations of an adverb followed by a postpositive

22. In Jude 8, according to Metzger, "[i]nstead of the more abstract κυριότητα, a few witnesses read the plural κυριότητας" (*Textual Commentary*, 658). Since this variant reading is not well supported and makes no difference for scoring of correspondence, the NA[27] text is retained for the probability analysis.

particle or conjunction. Constructs J3 and P2 reflect an accusative-genitive case transformation (σάρκα ‖ σαρκὸς, "flesh") as well as a verbal-nominal transformation (μιαίνουσιν ‖ μιασμοῦ, "defile" ‖ "defilement"). Constructs J4 and P3 both utilize similar combinations of conjunction-noun-verb with morphological transformations in the nouns and the verbs. Finally, J5 and P5 reflect morphological transformations in the verbal components. With the exception of the conjunctions (καί, δέ), all of the parallel terms and constructs appear in the same order in both documents.

Although the descriptions given in Jude 8 and 2 Pet 2:10 differ in a few details, both texts describe the troublesome persons as engaging in defiant and immoral behavior, even speaking irreverently or inappropriately of "glories," which likely refers to supernatural angelic beings.[23] For this reason, the semantic relationship is best understood as comparable. Both authors present the material as justification for their concern; however, they do so in different ways. Whereas the author of 2 Peter uses the expression to explain further his point about God's power and intention to punish disobedient behavior, the author of Jude uses it to describe the behavior of those who are currently among the addressed audience and present a potential danger. Since the two authors employ different methods to accomplish similar purposes, correspondence of function is classified as modified.

---

23. In Jude δόξας ("glories") is widely understood to refer to good angels (e.g., Bauckham, *Jude, 2 Peter*, 57; Gene Green, *Jude and 2 Peter*, 76–77; Horrell, *Epistles of Peter and Jude*, 122). However, the term in 2 Peter has been interpreted as both good angels (e.g., Gene Green, *Jude and 2 Peter*, 269–71) and bad "fallen" angels (e.g., Bauckham, *Jude, 2 Peter*, 261; Horrell, *Epistles of Peter and Jude*, 167). Either way, the reference to angelic beings is commonly accepted.

Parallel #13: Reverent Angels
(Jude 9 || 2 Pet 2:11)

Jude 9	2 Pet 2:11
{Ὁ δὲ Μιχαὴλ ὁ ἀρχάγγελος, ὅτε τῷ διαβόλῳ διακρινόμενος διελέγετο περὶ τοῦ Μωϋσέως σώματος, οὐκ ἐτόλμησεν κρίσιν ἐπενεγκεῖν βλασφημίας ἀλλὰ εἶπεν· ἐπιτιμήσαι σοι κύριος}.	{ὅπου ἄγγελοι ἰσχύϊ καὶ δυνάμει μείζονες ὄντες οὐ φέρουσιν κατ᾽ αὐτῶν παρὰ κυρίου βλάσφημον κρίσιν}.
{But Michael the archangel, when arguing with the devil and disputing about the body of Moses, did not dare to bring against [him] a judgment of blasphemy, but said, "May the Lord rebuke you!"}	{whereas angels who are greater in strength and power do not bring against them a blasphemous judgment from the Lord}.

Parallel #13, "reverent angels" (Jude 9 || 2 Pet 2:11), which follows immediately after parallel #12 in both Jude and 2 Peter, involves parallel statements which convey the notion that even greater angels do not speak irreverently against such "glories." Similar expressions employing forms of the nouns ἀρχάγγελος ("archangel") or ἄγγελος ("angel"), the noun βλασφημία ("blasphemy") or adjective βλάσφημος ("blasphemous"), and the nouns κρίσις ("judgment") and κύριος ("Lord") occur only here in the examined bodies of literature.

The parallel statements share four pairs of words with identical roots (βλασφημ-, κρίσις, κύριος, οὐ) and two pairs of related words (ἀρχάγγελος || ἄγγελος, ἐπιφέρω || φέρω).[24] With the exception of κρίσις ("judgment") and κύριος ("Lord"), whose order is transposed, all of the parallel terms and constructs appear in the same order.

24. In 2 Pet 2:11 the prepositional phrase παρὰ κυρίου ("from the Lord") reads παρὰ κυρίῳ ("before the Lord") in many early and important witnesses. Given the absence of the phrase from a wide variety of Greek, versional, and patristic witnesses, Metzger suggests that if the phrase is to be included at all, "the least unsatisfactory decision is to adopt the reading of the great uncials," παρὰ κυρίῳ (*Textual Commentary*, 633). A clear decision, however, is difficult. Since both readings result in the same correspondence score, the NA[27] text is retained for the analysis.

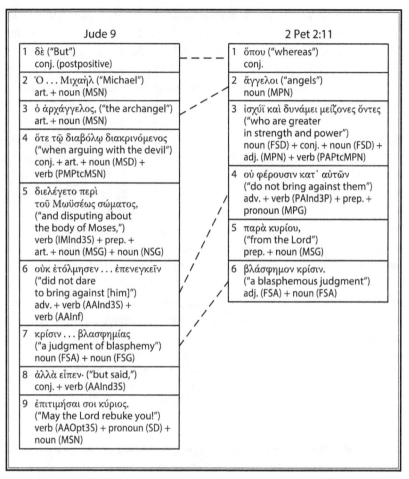

Jude 9	2 Pet 2:11
1 δὲ ("But") conj. (postpositive)	1 ὅπου ("whereas") conj.
2 Ὁ ... Μιχαὴλ ("Michael") art. + noun (MSN)	2 ἄγγελοι ("angels") noun (MPN)
3 ὁ ἀρχάγγελος, ("the archangel") art. + noun (MSN)	3 ἰσχύϊ καὶ δυνάμει μείζονες ὄντες ("who are greater in strength and power") noun (FSD) + conj. + noun (FSD) + adj. (MPN) + verb (PAPtcMPN)
4 ὅτε τῷ διαβόλῳ διακρινόμενος ("when arguing with the devil") conj. + art. + noun (MSD) + verb (PMPtcMSN)	
5 διελέγετο περὶ τοῦ Μωϋσέως σώματος, ("and disputing about the body of Moses,") verb (IMInd3S) + prep. + art. + noun (MSG) + noun (NSG)	4 οὐ φέρουσιν κατ᾽ αὐτῶν ("do not bring against them") adv. + verb (PAInd3P) + prep. + pronoun (MPG)
	5 παρὰ κυρίου, ("from the Lord") prep. + noun (MSG)
6 οὐκ ἐτόλμησεν ... ἐπενεγκεῖν ("did not dare to bring against [him]") adv. + verb (AAInd3S) + verb (AAInf)	6 βλάσφημον κρίσιν. ("a blasphemous judgment") adj. (FSA) + noun (FSA)
7 κρίσιν ... βλασφημίας ("a judgment of blasphemy") noun (FSA) + noun (FSG)	
8 ἀλλὰ εἶπεν· ("but said,") conj. + verb (AAInd3S)	
9 ἐπιτιμήσαι σοι κύριος. ("May the Lord rebuke you!") verb (AAOpt3S) + pronoun (SD) + noun (MSN)	

FIGURE 4.15. Verbal correspondence of parallel #13 (Jude 9 || 2 Pet 2:11)

The diagram in figure 4.15 further illustrates that the parallel statements exhibit four pairs of grammatically equivalent constructs, including the coordinating and subordinating conjunctions of J1 || P1 and the arthrous and anarthrous nouns of J3 || P2. The verbal components of J6 || P4 reflect transformations of tense as well as number, and constructs J7 || P6 exhibit a noun-adjective transformation between βλασφημία ("blasphemy") and βλάσφημος ("blasphemous").

Although Jude provides more detail, the two expressions convey the same basic idea that even the greater angels do not pass judgment on angelic beings, whether good or bad, because that is the Lord's prerogative.[25] In both Jude and 2 Peter, the statements are presented as a comparison or point of reference to highlight the foolish audacity of those who speak words of contempt or condemnation toward angelic beings.[26] Therefore, this parallel is classified as semantically comparable and functionally equivalent.

Parallel #14:   Unreasoning Animals
                                              (Jude 10 || 2 Pet 2:12)

Jude 10	2 Pet 2:12
{Οὗτοι δὲ ὅσα μὲν οὐκ οἴδασιν βλασφημοῦσιν, ὅσα δὲ φυσικῶς ὡς τὰ ἄλογα ζῷα ἐπίστανται, ἐν τούτοις φθείρονται}.	{Οὗτοι δὲ ὡς ἄλογα ζῷα γεγεννημένα φυσικὰ εἰς ἅλωσιν καὶ φθορὰν ἐν οἷς ἀγνοοῦσιν βλασφημοῦντες, ἐν τῇ φθορᾷ αὐτῶν καὶ φθαρήσονται}
{But these, whatever they do not know, they blaspheme, and whatever they understand instinctively like the unreasoning animals, in these things they are destroyed}.	{But these, like unreasoning animals, born as instinctive creatures for capture and destruction, blaspheming about things of which they are ignorant, in their destruction they also will be destroyed}

Parallel #14, "unreasoning animals" (Jude 10 || 2 Pet 2:12), is perhaps the most interesting of the entire collection of parallels in the Jude || 2 Peter database. The expressions that form this parallel are intriguingly different, yet remarkably similar as both authors describe the troublesome persons as being ὡς ἄλογα ζῷα ("like unreasoning animals"). Similar expressions are not found in any other examined bodies of literature.

Despite the obvious differences, verbal correspondence is relatively strong. The two expressions utilize ten pairs of words with identical roots

25. See Bauckham, *Jude, 2 Peter*, 61, 261–63; Gene Green, *Jude and 2 Peter*, 83. Even if the variant reading παρὰ κυρίῳ ("before the Lord") is adopted, the text of 2 Pet 2:11 suggests deference of judgment to the Lord, the judge of all; so Gene Green, *Jude and 2 Peter*, 273–74.

26. See, e.g., Bauckham, *Jude, 2 Peter*, 61, 261–63; Gene Green, *Jude and 2 Peter*, 83, 271–74.

(οὗτος, δέ, βλασφημ-, φυσικ-, ὡς, ἄλογος, ζῷον, ἐν, ὁ, φθείρω) and one pair of related words (οἶδα || ἀγνοέω).

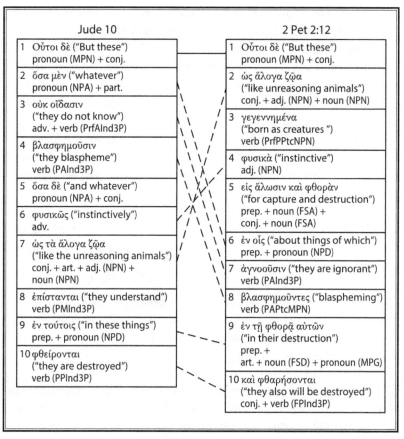

Jude 10 | 2 Pet 2:12

1 Οὗτοι δὲ ("But these") pronoun (MPN) + conj.

2 ὅσα μὲν ("whatever") pronoun (NPA) + part.

3 οὐκ οἴδασιν ("they do not know") adv. + verb (PrfAInd3P)

4 βλασφημοῦσιν ("they blaspheme") verb (PAInd3P)

5 ὅσα δὲ ("and whatever") pronoun (NPA) + conj.

6 φυσικῶς ("instinctively") adv.

7 ὡς τὰ ἄλογα ζῷα ("like the unreasoning animals") conj. + art. + adj. (NPN) + noun (NPN)

8 ἐπίστανται ("they understand") verb (PMInd3P)

9 ἐν τούτοις ("in these things") prep. + pronoun (NPD)

10 φθείρονται ("they are destroyed") verb (PPInd3P)

1 Οὗτοι δὲ ("But these") pronoun (MPN) + conj.

2 ὡς ἄλογα ζῷα ("like unreasoning animals") conj. + adj. (NPN) + noun (NPN)

3 γεγεννημένα ("born as creatures ") verb (PrfPPtcNPN)

4 φυσικὰ ("instinctive") adj. (NPN)

5 εἰς ἅλωσιν καὶ φθορὰν ("for capture and destruction") prep. + noun (FSA) + conj. + noun (FSA)

6 ἐν οἷς ("about things of which") prep. + pronoun (NPD)

7 ἀγνοοῦσιν ("they are ignorant") verb (PAInd3P)

8 βλασφημοῦντες ("blaspheming") verb (PAPtcMPN)

9 ἐν τῇ φθορᾷ αὐτῶν ("in their destruction") prep. + art. + noun (FSD) + pronoun (MPG)

10 καὶ φθαρήσονται ("they also will be destroyed") conj. + verb (FPInd3P)

FIGURE 4.16. Verbal correspondence of parallel #14 (Jude 10 || 2 Pet 2:12)

Grammatical correspondence is more difficult to delineate since there are multiple ways in which to identify parallel constructs. A good possibility is shown in figure 4.16. Based on the constructs delineated in figure 4.16, grammatical correspondence includes one pair of identical constructs (J1 || P1) and seven pairs of equivalent constructs. Constructs J2–4 and P6–8 are grammatically equivalent in that each pair serves the same function in its respective clause while reflecting slight lexical-morphological differences. Constructs J6 || P4 reflect an adverb-adjective transformation. Constructs J7 || P2 reflect an arthrous-anarthrous relationship. Constructs J9 || P9 exhibit equivalency as the prepositional phrases serve the same function in each

case, but the objects reveal differences in gender and number. Finally, the
verbs of constructs J10 and P10 reflect a morphological present-future tense
transformation. Although it might be possible to discern a pattern of some
kind in the order of the parallel terms and constructs, the correspondence
of structural arrangement is best understood as dissimilar.

Here again, although some of the details differ, the thoughts expressed
in Jude 10 and 2 Pet 2:12 are semantically comparable. Both characterize
the persons in view as blaspheming what they do not naturally understand
and as being destroyed by following what they do naturally understand.[27]
As a continuation of the arguments presented in the previous parallels, the
two expressions also serve similar purposes. In both cases, the statements
are used to describe and denounce the harmful infiltrators mentioned in
cluster WC2. Thus the parallel expressions are functionally equivalent.

Parallel #15:   Followed Balaam
(Jude 11b || 2 Pet 2:15)

Jude 11	2 Pet 2:15
οὐαὶ αὐτοῖς, ὅτι {τῇ ὁδῷ τοῦ Κάϊν ἐπορεύθησαν καὶ τῇ πλάνῃ τοῦ Βαλαὰμ μισθοῦ ἐξεχύθησαν} καὶ τῇ ἀντιλογίᾳ τοῦ Κόρε ἀπώλοντο.	{καταλείποντες εὐθεῖαν ὁδὸν ἐπλανήθησαν, ἐξακολουθήσαντες τῇ ὁδῷ τοῦ Βαλαὰμ τοῦ Βοσόρ, ὃς μισθὸν ἀδικίας ἠγάπησεν}
Woe to them! Because {in the way of Cain they went, and in the error of Balaam's wage they abandoned themselves}, and in the rebellion of Korah they perished.	{abandoning the right way, they were led astray, following in the way of Balaam, [son] of Bosor, who loved the wages of unrighteousness},

In parallel #15, "followed Balaam" (Jude 11b || 2 Pet 2:15), both authors
use similar language to inform readers that the problematic persons have
followed the misguided way of Balaam for profit. Similar expressions using
the terms ὁδός ("way"), Βαλαάμ ("Balaam"), μισθός ("wages"), and either
the noun πλάνη ("error") or the cognate verb πλανάω ("lead astray") are
not found elsewhere in the examined bodies of literature.

27. See Bauckham, *Jude, 2 Peter*, 62–63, 263–64; Gene Green, *Jude and 2 Peter*,
84–86, 274–77; Horrell, *Epistles of Peter and Jude*, 122–23, 168.

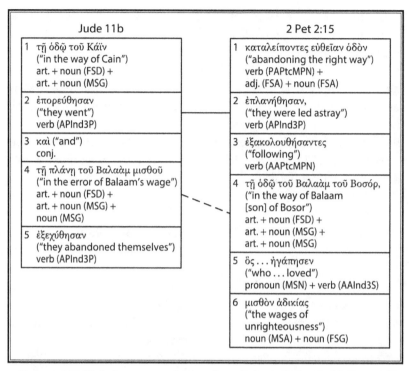

Jude 11b	2 Pet 2:15
1 τῇ ὁδῷ τοῦ Κάϊν ("in the way of Cain") art. + noun (FSD) + art. + noun (MSG)	1 καταλείποντες εὐθεῖαν ὁδὸν ("abandoning the right way") verb (PAPtcMPN) + adj. (FSA) + noun (FSA)
2 ἐπορεύθησαν ("they went") verb (APlnd3P)	2 ἐπλανήθησαν, ("they were led astray") verb (APlnd3P)
3 καὶ ("and") conj.	3 ἐξακολουθήσαντες ("following") verb (AAPtcMPN)
4 τῇ πλάνῃ τοῦ Βαλαὰμ μισθοῦ ("in the error of Balaam's wage") art. + noun (FSD) + art. + noun (MSG) + noun (MSG)	4 τῇ ὁδῷ τοῦ Βαλαὰμ τοῦ Βοσόρ, ("in the way of Balaam [son] of Bosor") art. + noun (FSD) + art. + noun (MSG) + art. + noun (MSG)
5 ἐξεχύθησαν ("they abandoned themselves") verb (APlnd3P)	5 ὃς ... ἠγάπησεν ("who ... loved") pronoun (MSN) + verb (AAlnd3S)
	6 μισθὸν ἀδικίας ("the wages of unrighteousness") noun (MSA) + noun (FSG)

FIGURE 4.17. Verbal correspondence of parallel #15 (Jude 11b || 2 Pet 2:15)

These parallel texts earn a moderately high score for lexical correspondence. Correspondence of basic units includes seven pairs of words with identical roots (ὁδός, Βαλαάμ, μισθός, πλάν-, ὁ [3×]) and two pairs of related words (πορεύομαι || ἐξακολουθέω, ἐκχέω || καταλείπω).[28] However, as shown in figure 4.17, grammatical correspondence is limited to one pair of identical constructs (J2 || P2) and one pair of equivalent constructs (J4 || P4).

Although the details differ, the parallel statements express the same basic idea that the persons of concern have followed the misguided path of Balaam for personal profit. In light of Num 31:16, and perhaps Num 31:8, which portray Balaam as having advised Moab to entice Israel to engage in sexual immorality with Moabite women and idolatry with the Moabite

28. Metzger notes that in 2 Pet 2:15 the proper name Βοσόρ ("Bosor"), which is "strongly supported by almost all Greek manuscripts, and by most early versions," is replaced by the name Βεώρ ("Beor") in some manuscripts (*Textual Commentary*, 635). Since the alternative reading is not well attested and makes no difference for the correspondence score, the NA[27] text is retained for the analysis.

gods (Num 25:1–3), the error of Balaam's way is generally understood as involving moral entrapment for profit. Other references to the infiltrators' practices of adultery and enticement to sin in 2 Pet 2:14, sexual immorality in Jude 7, and licentiousness in Jude 4 and 2 Pet 2:2, 18, further support the notion that enticement to sexual immorality leading to idolatry is in view for both authors.[29] As a continuation of the arguments presented in the previous parallels, the two expressions here also serve similar purposes as they are used to describe the behavior of the harmful infiltrators mentioned in cluster WC2. Thus the parallel is classified as semantically comparable and functionally equivalent.

Parallel #16:	Dangerous/Stained Feasting
	(Jude 12a || 2 Pet 2:13b)

Jude 12	2 Pet 2:13
{Οὗτοί εἰσιν οἱ ἐν ταῖς ἀγάπαις ὑμῶν σπιλάδες συνευωχούμενοι ἀφόβως}, ἑαυτοὺς ποιμαίνοντες, νεφέλαι ἄνυδροι ὑπὸ ἀνέμων παραφερόμεναι, δένδρα φθινοπωρινὰ ἄκαρπα δὶς ἀποθανόντα ἐκριζωθέντα,	ἀδικούμενοι μισθὸν ἀδικίας, ἡδονὴν ἡγούμενοι τὴν ἐν ἡμέρᾳ τρυφήν, {σπίλοι καὶ μῶμοι ἐντρυφῶντες ἐν ταῖς ἀπάταις αὐτῶν συνευωχούμενοι ὑμῖν},
{These are the men who are dangerous reefs in your love-feasts, feasting together [with you] without fear}, caring for themselves; clouds without water, carried along by winds; autumn trees without fruit, doubly dead, uprooted;	[they are] {stains and blemishes, reveling in their deceptions, feasting together with you},

Parallel #16, "dangerous/stained feasting" (Jude 12a \|\| 2 Pet 2:13b), involves expressions that use the terms σπιλάς ("dangerous reef") or σπίλος ("stain"), together with a participle form of συνευωχέομαι ("feast together"), in reference to the harmful persons. Not surprisingly, such expressions employing the same terms are found only here in the examined literature.

29. So, e.g., Bauckham, *Jude, 2 Peter*, 81–83, 267–68; Davids, *Letters of 2 Peter and Jude*, 66–67, 241–42; Gene Green, *Jude and 2 Peter*, 90–91, 283–84; Kelly, *Peter and Jude*, 267–68, 342–43; Schreiner, *1, 2 Peter, Jude*, 463–64, 353–54.

In addition to the use of exactly the same number of Greek words, these two parallel expressions exhibit fairly strong verbal correspondence. Correspondence of basic units shows four pairs of words with identical roots (σπιλ-, ἐν, ταῖς, συνευωχέομαι), plus two pairs of related words (ὑμῶν || αὐτῶν, ἀγάπαις || ἀπάταις).[30] Based on the constructs as shown in figure 4.18, grammatical correspondence includes two pairs of identical constructs (J4 || P5, J6 || P6). Moreover, the nouns of J5 and P1 reflect a gender transformation and therefore are considered grammatically equivalent.

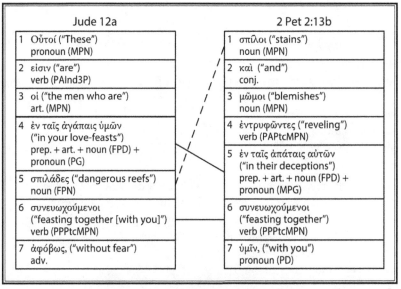

FIGURE 4.18. Verbal correspondence of parallel #16 (Jude 12a || 2 Pet 2:13b)

Although it is not clear what "feast" is in view, possibly the Eucharist or the Lord's Supper, both statements convey the idea that the persons of concern,

---

30. Parallel #16 involves related variant readings in Jude 12 and 2 Pet 2:13. In Jude 12, instead of ἀγάπαις ("love-feasts"), Metzger observes that "several witnesses, influenced by the prevailing text of 2 Pe 2.13, read ἀπάταις (82 378 460) and two read εὐωχίαις (6 224ᶜ)" (*Textual Commentary*, 658). Since neither of the variant readings in Jude 12 is well supported, the NA[27] text is retained for the analysis. In 2 Pet 2:13, instead of ἀπάταις ("deceptions"), which is strongly supported, some manuscripts read ἀγάπαις ("love-feasts"). Metzger concludes that the reading ἀγάπαις is "a scribal assimilation to the prevailing text of Jude" (*Textual Commentary*, 634). Since the variant reading in 2 Pet 2:13 is not strongly supported and can be explained by scribal assimilation, the NA[27] text is retained for the analysis.

who apparently participate together with the addressed audiences in their feasts, are dangerous and threaten the well-being of the faith community.[31] Furthermore, both expressions continue the same line of reasoning in their respective letters and are used similarly to characterize the behavior of the harmful infiltrators. Hence this parallel also is classified as semantically comparable and functionally equivalent.

Parallel #17:   Waterless Clouds/Springs
                                          (Jude 12b || 2 Pet 2:17a)

Jude 12	2 Pet 2:17
Οὗτοί εἰσιν οἱ ἐν ταῖς ἀγάπαις ὑμῶν σπιλάδες συνευωχούμενοι ἀφόβως, ἑαυτοὺς ποιμαίνοντες, {νεφέλαι ἄνυδροι ὑπὸ ἀνέμων παραφερόμεναι}, δένδρα φθινοπωρινὰ ἄκαρπα δὶς ἀποθανόντα ἐκριζωθέντα,	{οὗτοί εἰσιν πηγαὶ ἄνυδροι καὶ ὁμίχλαι ὑπὸ λαίλαπος ἐλαυνόμεναι}, οἷς ὁ ζόφος τοῦ σκότους τετήρηται.
These are the men who are dangerous reefs in your love-feasts, feasting together [with you] without fear, caring for themselves; {clouds without water, carried along by winds}; autumn trees without fruit, doubly dead, uprooted;	{These are springs without water and mists driven by a storm}, for whom the gloom of darkness has been reserved.

In parallel #17, "waterless clouds/springs" (Jude 12b || 2 Pet 2:17a), both authors characterize the persons of concern as νεφέλαι ("clouds") or πηγαὶ ("springs") ἄνυδροι ("without water"). Similar expressions using a form of νεφέλη ("cloud") or πηγή ("spring") together with a form of ἄνυδρος ("without water") are not found in any other examined bodies of literature.

---

31. So, e.g., Bauckham, *Jude, 2 Peter*, 84–87, 265–66; Davids, *Letters of 2 Peter and Jude*, 68–70, 239–40; Gene Green, *Jude and 2 Peter*, 93–97, 279–81; Horrell, *Epistles of Peter and Jude*, 124, 168–69.

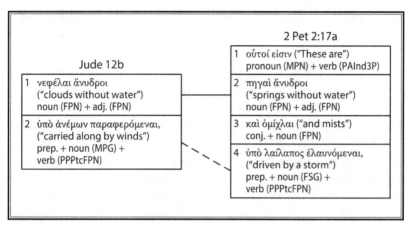

FIGURE 4.19. Verbal correspondence of parallel #17 (Jude 12b || 2 Pet 2:17a)

The parallel texts of Jude 12b and 2 Pet 2:17a contain two pairs of words with identical roots (ἄνυδρος, ὑπό) and three pairs of related words (νεφέλαι || πηγαὶ, ἀνέμων || λαίλαπος, παραφερόμεναι || ἐλαυνόμεναι). The two expressions may be delineated with two and four grammatical constructs, respectively. As shown in figure 4.19, J1 and P2 are grammatically identical. Additionally, J2 and P4 reflect gender and number transformations in the nouns and therefore are equivalent. All of the parallel terms and constructs appear in the same order in both documents.

While it is difficult to know exactly what is meant by these parallel expressions, it seems safe to say that both convey the same basic idea of being a façade without substance and which fails to provide an expected benefit.[32] Since each expression is used similarly to characterize the dangerous persons, the parallel is classified as semantically comparable and functionally equivalent.

32. So, e.g., Bauckham, *Jude, 2 Peter*, 87, 274; Davids, *Letters of 2 Peter and Jude*, 70–72, 243–44; Gene Green, *Jude and 2 Peter*, 96, 291–92; Kelly, *Peter and Jude*, 272, 344–45.

Parallel #18:   Reserved Darkness
                                                    (Jude 13b || 2 Pet 2:17b)

Jude 13	2 Pet 2:17
κύματα ἄγρια θαλάσσης ἐπαφρίζοντα τὰς ἑαυτῶν αἰσχύνας, ἀστέρες πλανῆται {οἷς ὁ ζόφος τοῦ σκότους εἰς αἰῶνα τετήρηται}.	οὗτοί εἰσιν πηγαὶ ἄνυδροι καὶ ὁμίχλαι ὑπὸ λαίλαπος ἐλαυνόμεναι, {οἷς ὁ ζόφος τοῦ σκότους τετήρηται}.
waves of the sea without control, foaming up their shame; wandering stars, {for whom the gloom of darkness has been reserved unto eternity}.	These are springs without water and mists driven by a storm, {for whom the gloom of darkness has been reserved}.

Parallel #18, "reserved darkness" (Jude 13b || 2 Pet 2:17b), involves two nearly identical clauses, both of which indicate a dark destiny for the troublesome persons. Among all the bodies of literature examined for this project, occurrences of the clause οἷς ὁ ζόφος τοῦ σκότους τετήρηται ("for whom the gloom of darkness has been reserved") are unique to the letters of Jude and 2 Peter.

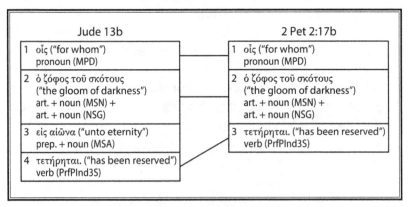

FIGURE 4.20. Verbal correspondence of parallel #18 (Jude 13b || 2 Pet 2:17b)

As shown in figure 4.20, only one of the four constructs of Jude does not find an identical construct in 2 Peter. Moreover, all six words of 2 Pet 2:17b are found in Jude 13b, and all the parallel terms and constructs appear in the same order in both documents. Here again, the parallel expressions are used in reference to the harmful infiltrators and convey the notion that a very unpleasant destiny, like that of the disobedient angels (Jude 6; 2 Pet 2:4, 9), has been divinely appointed for them.[33] Thus the parallel is counted as semantically comparable and functionally equivalent.

Parallel #19:   Arrogant Speaking
                                              (Jude 16b || 2 Pet 2:18a)

Jude 16	2 Pet 2:18
Οὗτοί εἰσιν γογγυσταὶ μεμψίμοιροι κατὰ τὰς ἐπιθυμίας ἑαυτῶν πορευόμενοι, {καὶ τὸ στόμα αὐτῶν λαλεῖ ὑπέρογκα}, θαυμάζοντες πρόσωπα ὠφελείας χάριν.	{ὑπέρογκα γὰρ ματαιότητος φθεγγόμενοι} δελεάζουσιν ἐν ἐπιθυμίαις σαρκὸς ἀσελγείαις τοὺς ὀλίγως ἀποφεύγοντας τοὺς ἐν πλάνῃ ἀναστρεφομένους,
These are grumblers, fault-finders, proceeding according to their own desires,{and their mouth speaks arrogant things}, enchanting people to gain advantage.	{For by speaking out arrogant things of vanity}, they entice by desires of the flesh, by licentiousness, those who barely escape from those who live in error.

The indictment continues with parallel #19, "arrogant speaking" (Jude 16b || 2 Pet 2:18a). Here both authors accuse the perpetrators of speaking arrogant words. Expressions employing either the verb λαλέω ("speak") or the verb φθέγγομαι ("speak out"), together with the adjective ὑπέρογκος ("arrogant") as its object, are found only here in Jude 16b || 2 Pet 2:18a and in the LXX (Dan [Th] 11:36).

Verbal correspondence of this pair of parallel expressions is fairly low. Correspondence of basic units is limited to identical instances of ὑπέρογκα ("arrogant things") and one pair of related terms (λαλέω || φθέγγομαι). Based on the grammatical constructs as illustrated in figure 4.21, the coordinating conjunctions (J1 || P1) and the substantival adjectives (J4 || P2) are grammatically identical. The verbs of J3 and P4 reflect morphological transformations and therefore are grammatically equivalent.

33. See Bauckham, *Jude, 2 Peter*, 90, 274; Davids, *Letters of 2 Peter and Jude*, 74–75, 244; Gene Green, *Jude and 2 Peter*, 99, 293.

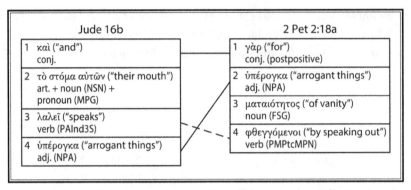

FIGURE 4.21. Verbal correspondence of parallel #19 (Jude 16b || 2 Pet 2:18a)

Despite the relatively low verbal correspondence, however, these parallel expressions appear to convey kindred thoughts and serve similar purposes. Since both expressions are used similarly to characterize the troublesome persons as voicing arrogant disregard for, or contempt of, divine moral authority,[34] the parallel is best classified as semantically comparable and functionally equivalent.

Parallel WC3:   Reason for Concern
                                (Jude 6–16b || 2 Pet 2:4–18a)

The final parallel associated with this third group is the second-order cluster WC3, "Reason for Concern" (Jude 6–16b || 2 Pet 2:4–18a), which is formed by parallels #10–19. As noted earlier, WC3 is considered a same-order cluster because nearly all of the member parallels appear in the same order. Only parallels #15 and #16 are transposed. The comparable semantic relationships exhibited by all the member parallels also apply to the cluster as a whole, as the ten parallels paint similar portraits in Jude and 2 Peter. The functional relationships exhibited by the individual parallels also apply at the cluster level. Since in both cases the portraits are used to characterize and denounce the harmful infiltrators mentioned in WC2, this ten-parallel cluster is classified as functionally equivalent.

34. See Bauckham, *Jude, 2 Peter*, 99–100, 274; Davids, *Letters of 2 Peter and Jude*, 83, 244–45; Gene Green, *Jude and 2 Peter*, 109–10, 293–94; Schreiner, *1, 2 Peter, Jude*, 474, 358.

TABLE 4.3. Probability of directness (Jude || 2 Pet, 3rd cluster, worst case)

No.	Description	Reference		Individual			Collective	
		Jude	2 Pet	DI	IP_{dir}	IP_{ndir}	CP_{ndir}	CP_{dir}
10	angels kept for judgment	6	2:4	2.343	0.098	0.902	0.692	0.308
11	example of Sodom and Gomorrah	7	2:6	1.229	0.051	0.949	0.656	0.344
12	defile flesh, reject lordship, blaspheme glories	8	2:10	1.911	0.080	0.920	0.604	0.396
13	reverent angels	9	2:11	2.111	0.088	0.912	0.551	0.449
14	unreasoning animals	10	2:12	2.379	0.099	0.901	0.496	0.504
15	followed Balaam	11b	2:15	1.550	0.065	0.935	0.464	0.536
16	dangerous/ stained feasting	12a	2:13b	1.305	0.054	0.946	0.439	0.561
17	waterless clouds/ springs	12b	2:17a	0.733	0.031	0.969	0.426	0.574
18	reserved darkness	13b	2:17b	0.959	0.040	0.960	0.409	0.591
19	arrogant speaking	16b	2:18a	0.509	0.021	0.979	0.400	0.600
WC3	Reason for Concern	6–16b	2:4–18a	0.973	0.041	0.959	0.384	0.616

The effect of adding these parallels to the probability analysis is shown in table 4.3. With the addition of this third cluster and its member parallels, more than two-thirds of all the parallels are now included in the analysis. As shown in table 4.3, the collective probability of directness, CP_{dir}, has risen above the mid-point of the probability scale (0.5) and now stands at 0.616.

Fourth Word-Group Cluster

The fourth cluster of parallels, WC4, "Heed Apostolic Teaching" (Jude 17–18 || 2 Pet 3:2–3c), is formed by three word-group parallels that involve apostolic teachings about mockers. Since the three parallels appear in the same order in both documents (see figure 4.1), the cluster is classified as a same-order cluster and each of the member parallels receives the highest score for membership in a higher-order cluster.

Parallel #20:   Remember Apostolic Words
                                                   (Jude 17b || 2 Pet 3:2)

Jude 17	2 Pet 3:2
ὑμεῖς δέ, ἀγαπητοί, {μνήσθητε τῶν ῥημάτων τῶν προειρημένων ὑπὸ τῶν ἀποστόλων τοῦ κυρίου ἡμῶν Ἰησοῦ Χριστοῦ}	{μνησθῆναι τῶν προειρημένων ῥημάτων ὑπὸ τῶν ἁγίων προφητῶν καὶ τῆς τῶν ἀποστόλων ὑμῶν ἐντολῆς τοῦ κυρίου καὶ σωτῆρος},
But you, beloved, {remember the words spoken beforehand by the apostles of our Lord Jesus Christ}	{to remember the words spoken beforehand by the holy prophets and the commandment of your apostles, of the Lord and Savior}

In parallel #20, "remember apostolic words" (Jude 17b || 2 Pet 3:2), the authors issue instructions to remember words spoken by the apostles. Similar instructions that include use of the verb μιμνήσκομαι ("remember"), the noun ῥῆμα ("word"), and the noun ἀπόστολος ("apostle") are not found elsewhere in the examined bodies of literature.

Verbal correspondence exhibited in this parallel is relatively strong. Indeed, the two statements share ten words of identical roots (μιμνήσκομαι, ὁ [4×], ῥημάτων, προειρημένων, ὑπὸ, ἀποστόλων, κυρίου). The configuration in figure 4.22 further shows that the parallel expressions exhibit two pairs of identical constructs. These are the attributive participles of J3 || P2 and the prepositions of J4 || P4. In addition, there are four pairs of grammatically equivalent constructs: (1) the verbs of J1 || P1 reflect an imperative-infinitive morphological transformation; (2) the arthrous noun of J2 is equivalent to the anarthrous noun in P3; (3) J5 || P8 differ only in the pronoun of P8; and (4) J6 || P9 differ only in the pronoun of J6. With the exception of constructs J2 || P3 and J3 ||P2, which are transposed, and one pair of articles, all of the parallel terms and constructs appear in the same order in Jude and 2 Peter.

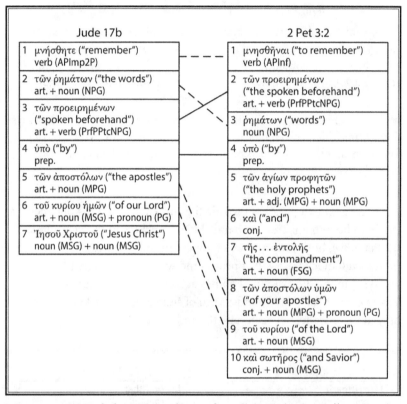

FIGURE 4.22. Verbal correspondence of parallel #20 (Jude 17b ‖ 2 Pet 3:2)

Semantically, the parallel expressions are comparable as they convey the same general idea that the readers should remember what they have already learned from the apostles (and prophets in the case of 2 Peter). While the purpose of each expression seems to be to motivate the respective audiences to heed the authors' messages and respond appropriately, they do so in slightly different ways. The author of Jude takes a direct approach and exhorts the audience to remember the apostolic words. The author of 2 Peter, on the other hand, takes an indirect approach whereby the call to remember comes through a reference to the purpose of the letter. Since the two authors employ different methods to accomplish similar purposes, correspondence of function is classified as modified.

Parallel #21:   Mockers in the Last
                                          (Jude 18a || 2 Pet 3:3b)

Jude 18	2 Pet 3:3
{ὅτι ἔλεγον ὑμῖν· [ὅτι] ἐπ᾽ ἐσχάτου [τοῦ] χρόνου ἔσονται ἐμπαῖκται} κατὰ τὰς ἑαυτῶν ἐπιθυμίας πορευόμενοι τῶν ἀσεβειῶν.	τοῦτο πρῶτον γινώσκοντες {ὅτι ἐλεύσονται ἐπ᾽ ἐσχάτων τῶν ἡμερῶν [ἐν] ἐμπαιγμονῇ ἐμπαῖκται} κατὰ τὰς ἰδίας ἐπιθυμίας αὐτῶν πορευόμενοι
{that they were saying to you, "In the last time there will be mockers}, following after their own lusts of ungodliness.	Know this first, {that in the last days mockers will come with mocking}, following after their own lusts

The next two parallels provide the content of the apostolic message that is to be remembered. In parallel #21, "mockers in the last" (Jude 18a || 2 Pet 3:3b), both Jude and 2 Peter recount the apostles' foretelling that ἐμπαῖκται ("mockers") will appear in the ἐσχάτου/ἐσχάτων ("last") time or days. Among the examined bodies of literature, such expressions using a form of ἔσχατος ("last") and a form of ἐμπαίκτης ("mocker") are found only in this parallel between Jude 18a and 2 Pet 3:3b.

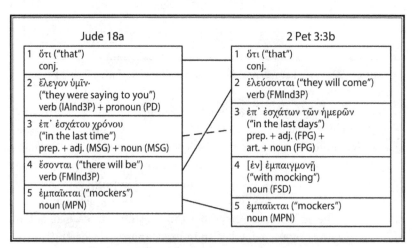

FIGURE 4.23. Verbal correspondence of parallel #21 (Jude 18a || 2 Pet 3:3b)

The expressions that form parallel #21 exhibit strong verbal correspondence. This includes four pairs of words with identical roots (ὅτι, ἐπί, ἔσχατος, ἐμπαίκτης) and one pair of related words (χρόνος || ἡμέρα). Figure 4.23 also reveals three pairs of grammatically identical constructs (J1 || P1, J4 || P2, J5 || P5). Grammatical equivalence is indicated in J3 || P3, where the nouns reflect an anarthrous-arthrous transformation, as well as gender and number transformations. The order of all the parallel terms and constructs is nearly identical in both documents. The only exception is J4 || P2.

Both statements of this parallel convey the same basic idea that the apostles said that mockers will appear in the final age. The time period in view likely refers to an apocalyptic or eschatological future that the NT writers may have understood as already underway during their lifetime.[35] Despite the comparable thoughts, however, as with the previous parallel, the authors employ different methods to accomplish similar purposes. In both cases, the statements serve as reminders of what the apostles said. In Jude this is done through the mode of direct discourse. In 2 Peter, the same thing is accomplished through the mode of indirect discourse. For this reason, parallel #21 is counted as functionally modified.

Parallel #22:	Following after Their Own Lusts
	(Jude 18b || 2 Pet 3:3c)

Jude 18	2 Pet 3:3
ὅτι ἔλεγον ὑμῖν· [ὅτι] ἐπ᾿ ἐσχάτου [τοῦ] χρόνου ἔσονται ἐμπαῖκται {κατὰ τὰς ἑαυτῶν ἐπιθυμίας πορευόμενοι} τῶν ἀσεβειῶν.	τοῦτο πρῶτον γινώσκοντες ὅτι ἐλεύσονται ἐπ᾿ ἐσχάτων τῶν ἡμερῶν [ἐν] ἐμπαιγμονῇ ἐμπαῖκται {κατὰ τὰς ἰδίας ἐπιθυμίας αὐτῶν πορευόμενοι}
that they were saying to you, "In the last time there will be mockers, {following after their own lusts} of ungodliness.	Know this first, that in the last days mockers will come with mocking, {following after their own lusts}

Parallel #22, "following after their own lusts" (Jude 18b || 2 Pet 3:3c), involves two nearly identical texts that describe the persons as πορευόμενοι ("following") κατὰ ("after") τὰς ἑαυτῶν ἐπιθυμίας or τὰς ἰδίας ἐπιθυμίας

35. So, e.g., Bauckham, *Jude, 2 Peter*, 104, 288–89; Davids, *Letters of 2 Peter and Jude*, 86–87, 263; Gene Green, *Jude and 2 Peter*, 115, 315; Kelly, *Peter and Jude*, 282–83, 355.

αὐτῶν ("their own lusts"). Similar expressions employing the same terms are not found elsewhere in the examined bodies of literature.

Here too, verbal correspondence is quite strong. The parallel texts share four identical words (κατὰ, τὰς, ἐπιθυμίας, πορευόμενοι), in addition to one pair of related words (ἑαυτῶν ‖ αὐτῶν). The strong grammatical correspondence is illustrated in figure 4.24.

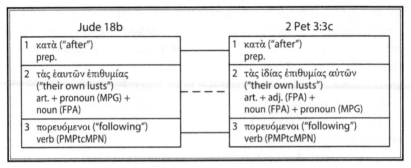

FIGURE 4.24. Verbal correspondence of parallel #22 (Jude 18b ‖ 2 Pet 3:3c)

Constructs J1 ‖ P1 and J3 ‖ P3 are identical. Constructs J2 ‖ P2 are grammatically equivalent, differing only in the presence of an additional adjective in P2. With the possible exception of the pronoun ‖ adjective-pronoun in J2 ‖ P2, all of the parallel terms and parallel constructs appear in the same order in both documents. The thoughts conveyed by these parallel texts are semantically comparable as each expresses the idea of indulging in or living according to one's own evil desires.[36] Since both are used to characterize the mockers mentioned in the previous parallel, the parallel expressions are considered functionally equivalent.

Parallel WC4:   Heed Apostolic Teaching
                                        (Jude 17b–18 ‖ 2 Pet 3:2–3c)

Parallels #20–22 combine together to form cluster parallel WC4, "Heed Apostolic Teaching" (Jude 17b–18 ‖ 2 Pet 3:2–3c). As discussed above, all the member parallels appear in the same order and convey the same basic idea that the intended audiences should be mindful of apostolic teaching that

36. See, e.g., Bauckham, *Jude, 2 Peter*, 105, 289; Davids, *Letters of 2 Peter and Jude*, 88, 263; Gene Green, *Jude and 2 Peter*, 116, 315; Kelly, *Peter and Jude*, 283, 356.

mockers would appear in the future, practicing and promoting immoral behavior that is harmful for the community of faith. Thus the cluster is semantically comparable.

Although parallel #22 is counted as functionally equivalent, the functional relationship of the cluster as a whole is governed by that of parallels #20 and #21. While it seems clear that both authors use the parallel material to motivate their respective audiences to heed their words and respond appropriately, each takes a different approach. The author of Jude takes a direct approach. He directly exhorts his readers to remember the apostolic words, which he directly quotes. The author of 2 Peter takes an indirect approach. First, he issues a call to remember the apostolic words indirectly through a reference to the purpose of the letter, and then he recounts the apostolic words through indirect discourse. Since the two authors employ different methods to accomplish similar purposes, correspondence of function at the cluster level is classified as modified.

The result of the probability analysis up to this point is provided in table 4.4. After adding the fourth cluster and its member parallels to the analysis, the collective probability of directness, CP_{dir}, increases to 0.678. This value will rise still more as the final cluster of parallels is included in the calculation.

TABLE 4.4. Probability of directness (Jude || 2 Pet, 4th cluster, worst case)

No.	Description	Reference		Individual			Collective	
		Jude	2 Pet	DI	IP_{dir}	IP_{ndir}	CP_{ndir}	CP_{dir}
20	remember apostolic words	17b	3:2	1.835	0.076	0.924	0.354	0.646
21	mockers in the last	18a	3:3b	1.173	0.049	0.951	0.337	0.663
22	following after their own lusts	18b	3:3c	0.807	0.034	0.966	0.326	0.674
WC4	Heed Apostolic Teaching	17–18	3:2–3	0.265	0.011	0.989	0.322	0.678

Fifth Word-Group Cluster

The fifth and final cluster of parallels, WC5, "Closing Remarks" (Jude 24–25 || 2 Pet 3:17–18), is formed by three word-group parallels that involve similar closing remarks from each of the two authors. As shown in figure 4.1, these final three parallels appear in the same order in both documents. Therefore, the cluster is classified as a same-order cluster, and each of the member parallels receives the highest score for membership in a higher-order cluster.

Parallel #23:   Keep from Falling
                                                         (Jude 24 || 2 Pet 3:17)

Jude 24	2 Pet 3:17
{Τῷ δὲ δυναμένῳ φυλάξαι ὑμᾶς ἀπταίστους καὶ στῆσαι κατενώπιον τῆς δόξης αὐτοῦ ἀμώμους ἐν ἀγαλλιάσει},	{ὑμεῖς οὖν, ἀγαπητοί, προγινώσκοντες φυλάσσεσθε, ἵνα μὴ τῇ τῶν ἀθέσμων πλάνῃ συναπαχθέντες ἐκπέσητε τοῦ ἰδίου στηριγμοῦ},
{Now to him who is able to keep you free from falling and make you stand firm in the presence of his glory, without blemish, with great joy},	{Therefore, you beloved, knowing this beforehand, be on your guard, so that you are not led astray by the error of lawless men and fall away from your own steadfastness},

The two statements that form parallel #23, "keep from falling" (Jude 24 || 2 Pet 3:17), involve the notion of guarding against falling and instead standing firm. Similar expressions that use the verb φυλάσσω ("keep" or "guard"), either the adjective ἄπταιστος ("free from falling") or the verb ἐκπίπτω ("fall away"), and either the verb ἵστημι ("stand") or the noun στηριγμός ("steadfastness") are not found in any other examined bodies of literature. They occur only in this parallel between Jude 24 and 2 Pet 3:17.

Verbal correspondence of the two texts includes four words of identical roots (ὁ [2×], σύ, φυλάσσω) and two pairs of related words (ἄπταιστος || ἐκπίπτω, ἵστημι || στηριγμός). Figure 4.25 further illustrates that only the coordinating conjunctions of J1 and P1 are grammatically identical. The coordinating and subordinating conjunctions of constructs J6 and P6 are considered grammatically equivalent. Two other pairs of constructs provide evidence of equivalency through a case transformation (J4 || P2) and a verbal transformation involving tense, voice, and mood (J3 ‖ P5). Two pairs of constructs reflect nominal-verbal syntactical transformations (J5 ‖ P7, J7 ‖ P9). Finally, constructs J8 and P8 are syntactically equivalent because the preposition + genitive object of J8 and the dative nominal + genitive modifier of P8 serve similar syntactical functions.

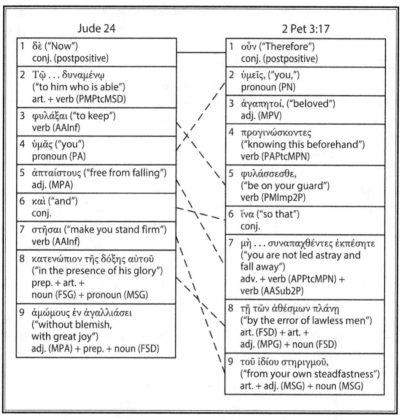

Jude 24	2 Pet 3:17
1 δὲ ("Now") conj. (postpositive)	1 οὖν ("Therefore") conj. (postpositive)
2 Τῷ ... δυναμένῳ ("to him who is able") art. + verb (PMPtcMSD)	2 ὑμεῖς, ("you,") pronoun (PN)
3 φυλάξαι ("to keep") verb (AAInf)	3 ἀγαπητοί, ("beloved") adj. (MPV)
4 ὑμᾶς ("you") pronoun (PA)	4 προγινώσκοντες ("knowing this beforehand") verb (PAPtcMPN)
5 ἀπταίστους ("free from falling") adj. (MPA)	5 φυλάσσεσθε, ("be on your guard") verb (PMImp2P)
6 καὶ ("and") conj.	6 ἵνα ("so that") conj.
7 στῆσαι ("make you stand firm") verb (AAInf)	7 μὴ ... συναπαχθέντες ἐκπέσητε ("you are not led astray and fall away") adv. + verb (APPtcMPN) + verb (AASub2P)
8 κατενώπιον τῆς δόξης αὐτοῦ ("in the presence of his glory") prep. + art. + noun (FSG) + pronoun (MSG)	8 τῇ τῶν ἀθέσμων πλάνῃ ("by the error of lawless men") art. (FSD) + art. + adj. (MPG) + noun (FSD)
9 ἀμώμους ἐν ἀγαλλιάσει ("without blemish, with great joy") adj. (MPA) + prep. + noun (FSD)	9 τοῦ ἰδίου στηριγμοῦ, ("from your own steadfastness") art. + adj. (MSG) + noun (MSG)

FIGURE 4.25. Verbal correspondence of parallel #23 (Jude 24 ‖ 2 Pet 3:17)

Despite the verbal similarity, the parallel texts convey significantly different thoughts. The expression in Jude conveys attributes of God, the one to whom a doxology is addressed. Specifically, Jude acknowledges that God is able to protect the readers from stumbling in their faith and establish them in his presence, free from blame and full of joy. On the other hand, the parallel expression in 2 Peter conveys what it is that the readers should do. Specifically, they should be on guard against false teachers and opinion leaders among them so that they are not misled and lose the stability which is founded on sound apostolic teachings.[37] Thus the semantic relationship of this parallel is best understood as dissimilar. The functional relationship also is dissimilar since Jude 24 serves to identify the addressee of a doxology and 2 Pet 3:17 functions as an exhortation.

Parallel #24: Our Savior Lord Jesus Christ
(Jude 25a || 2 Pet 3:18a)

Jude 25	2 Pet 3:18
{μόνῳ θεῷ σωτῆρι ἡμῶν διὰ Ἰησοῦ Χριστοῦ τοῦ κυρίου ἡμῶν} δόξα μεγαλωσύνη κράτος καὶ ἐξουσία πρὸ παντὸς τοῦ αἰῶνος καὶ νῦν καὶ εἰς πάντας τοὺς αἰῶνας, ἀμήν.	{αὐξάνετε δὲ ἐν χάριτι καὶ γνώσει τοῦ κυρίου ἡμῶν καὶ σωτῆρος Ἰησοῦ Χριστοῦ}. αὐτῷ ἡ δόξα καὶ νῦν καὶ εἰς ἡμέραν αἰῶνος. [ἀμήν.]
{to the only God, our Savior, through Jesus Christ our Lord}, glory, majesty, power, and authority, before all time, both now and unto all eternity, amen.	{but grow in grace and knowledge of our Lord and Savior Jesus Christ}. To him be the glory, both now and unto the day of eternity. [Amen.]

Parallel #24, "our Savior Lord Jesus Christ" (Jude 25a || 2 Pet 3:18a), involves specific references to ἡμῶν σωτῆρι/σωτῆρος ("our Savior"), Ἰησοῦ Χριστοῦ ("Jesus Christ"), and τοῦ κυρίου ἡμῶν ("our Lord"). Outside of Jude and 2 Peter, this particular combination of terms is found only twice in the Apostolic Fathers (Ign. *Phld.* 9:2; Pol. *Phil.* 1:1).

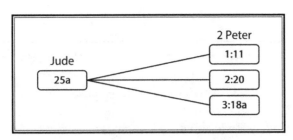

FIGURE 4.26. Configuration of fan parallel #24

---

37. See Bauckham, *Jude, 2 Peter*, 122, 337; Davids, *Letters of 2 Peter and Jude*, 109–11, 309–12; Gene Green, *Jude and 2 Peter*, 131–34, 341–43; Kelly, *Peter and Jude*, 290–91, 374; Schreiner, *1, 2 Peter, Jude*, 399–400, 490–91.

Since the parallel between Jude 25a and 2 Pet 3:18a is just one of many branches, parallel #24 qualifies as a fan parallel. The single instance in Jude 25a finds multiple parallels in 2 Pet 1:11; 2:20; and 3:18a, as illustrated in figure 4.26. As in the case of parallel #9, for the purpose of assessing correspondence, a conservative approach is adopted and only one branch of the fan parallel is included in the probability analysis. In this case, the branch with 2 Pet 3:18a is selected for inclusion in the analysis.

The texts of this particular branch contain six pairs of words with identical roots (ἡμῶν, σωτῆρ-, τοῦ, κυρίου, Ἰησοῦ, Χριστοῦ).[38] The grammatical configuration, as illustrated in figure 4.27, shows two pairs of grammatically identical constructs (J4 ‖ P8, J5 ‖ P5). In addition, constructs J2 and P7 reflect a nominal case transformation and therefore are counted as being grammatically equivalent. Equivalence is also evident in the prepositions of J3 and P3 since διὰ has a genitive object and ἐν has a dative object.

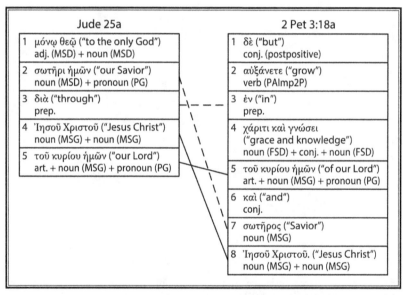

FIGURE 4.27. Verbal correspondence of parallel #24 (Jude 25a ‖ 2 Pet 3:18a)

38. Parallel #24 involves a variant reading for the text in Jude 25a. According to Metzger, "after μόνῳ, K L P and many minuscules, followed by the Textus Receptus, add σοφῷ, thus assimilating the doxology to Ro 16.27" (*Textual Commentary*, 661). Since the variant reading is not well supported by early and important manuscripts and is easily explained by scribal assimilation, the NA[27] text is retained for the probability analysis.

Despite the lexical and grammatical correspondence, the ideas conveyed by these two parallel expressions are dissimilar. A noticeable difference concerns the association of σωτήρ ("Savior"). In 2 Pet 3:18a the term is clearly associated with Jesus Christ. However, the parallel term in Jude 25a is associated with θεός ("God"). Since Jude does not directly equate Jesus Christ with "God" or "Savior" anywhere in the letter, it cannot be assumed from Jude alone that the terms also apply to "Jesus Christ our Lord."[39] Furthermore, the expression in Jude 25a as a whole indicates that what follows in Jude 25b is directed toward God. The parallel expression in 2 Pet 3:18a, on the other hand, indicates that the readers should grow in the grace and knowledge of Jesus Christ. In light of these differences, the parallel is considered semantically dissimilar. The functional relationship also is dissimilar for the same reason as that given for parallel #23. That is, Jude 25a serves to identify the addressee of a doxology, and 2 Pet 3:18a functions as an exhortation.

39. For an explanation, see the discussion of Jude's theology in Davids, *Letters of 2 Peter and Jude*, 28–32. According to Davids, "Jude does not allow for the possibility that the title 'God' is being applied to Jesus" (p. 30). Rather, God is presented as the family head and sender, while "Jesus is presented as his agent, as the leader of the people of God, as the sovereign of God's kingdom" (p. 30). Davids suggests, however, that the juxtaposition of "Lord" in v. 4 and "Lord"/"Jesus" in v. 5 might indicate that the same person is in view (p. 31). See also J. Ramsey Michaels, "Catholic Christologies in the Catholic Epistles," in *Contours of Christology in the New Testament*, ed. Richard N. Longenecker (Grand Rapids, MI: Eerdmans, 2005), 282–85; I. Howard Marshall, *New Testament Theology: Many Witnesses, One Gospel* (Downers Grove, IL: IVP Academic, 2004), 665.

Parallel #25:

Glory both Now and Forever
(Jude 25b || 2 Pet 3:18b)

Jude 25	2 Pet 3:18
μόνῳ θεῷ σωτῆρι ἡμῶν διὰ Ἰησοῦ Χριστοῦ τοῦ κυρίου ἡμῶν {δόξα μεγαλωσύνη κράτος καὶ ἐξουσία πρὸ παντὸς τοῦ αἰῶνος καὶ νῦν καὶ εἰς πάντας τοὺς αἰῶνας}, ἀμήν.	αὐξάνετε δὲ ἐν χάριτι καὶ γνώσει τοῦ κυρίου ἡμῶν καὶ σωτῆρος Ἰησοῦ Χριστοῦ. αὐτῷ {ἡ δόξα καὶ νῦν καὶ εἰς ἡμέραν αἰῶνος}. [ἀμήν.]
to the only God, our Savior, through Jesus Christ our Lord, {glory, majesty, power, and authority, before all time, both now and unto all eternity}, amen.	but grow in grace and knowledge of our Lord and Savior Jesus Christ. To him be {the glory, both now and unto the day of eternity}. [Amen.]

Parallel #25, "glory both now and forever" (Jude 25b || 2 Pet 3:18b), involves the final words of the letters. In both cases, the authors close with an expression that glorifies God and/or Jesus Christ. Similar statements employing various forms of δόξα ("glory"), αἰών ("time" or "eternity"), and the distinctive phrase καὶ νῦν καὶ εἰς ("both now and unto") occur elsewhere only in the writings of the Apostolic Fathers (*1 Clem.* 61:3; 64:1; *Mart. Pol.* 14:3). Other similar statements with slight variations of the καὶ νῦν καὶ εἰς phrase are found in the Pseudepigrapha (*Gk. Apoc. Ezra* 7:16; *T. Ab.* 2:14:9; *Apoc. Mos.* 43:4).

Verbal correspondence of the parallel statements includes seven pairs of words with identical roots (δόξα, καί [2×], νῦν, εἰς, αἰών, ὁ).[40] Moreover, when the parallel expressions are viewed as four and three grammatical constructs, as illustrated in figure 4.28, one pair of identical constructs is revealed in the common καὶ νῦν καὶ phrases (J3 || P2). Constructs J1 || P1 and J4 || P3 serve the same syntactical functions in their respective sentences, albeit with some structural variances, and therefore are considered equivalent. With the exception of the definite articles, all of the parallel terms and constructs appear in the same order in both documents.

---

40. The prepositional phrase πρὸ παντὸς τοῦ αἰῶνος ("before all time") in Jude 25b is omitted in several of the later uncials and most minuscules. However, since the phrase is strongly supported by many early and important witnesses, the NA[27] text is retained for the analysis. See Metzger, *Textual Commentary*, 661.

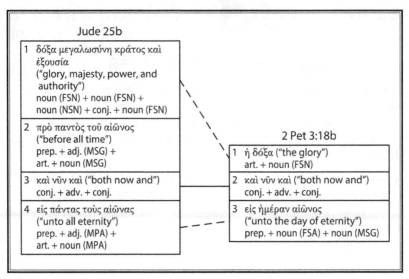

Fɪɢᴜʀᴇ 4.28. Verbal correspondence of parallel #25 (Jude 25b || 2 Pet 3:18b)

Although Jude 25b includes additional details, both texts convey the same basic idea that glory belongs to God and/or Jesus Christ forever. Furthermore, since both expressions are used in a closing doxology, they serve similar purposes in the two letters. Therefore, the parallel expressions are considered functionally equivalent.

Parallel WC5:   Closing Remarks
                                        (Jude 24–25 || 2 Pet 3:17–18)

The cluster that is formed by parallels #23–25, WC5, "Closing Remarks" (Jude 24–25 || 2 Pet 3:17–18), is the last parallel to be included in the analysis. Since the three member parallels appear in the same order in both documents, correspondence of structural arrangement at the cluster level is identical. Semantic and functional correspondence, however, is another matter. Although the similar doxological expressions of parallel #25 are semantically comparable and functionally equivalent, parallel #23 and parallel #24 are more representative of the cluster as a whole. As explained in the discussion of these parallels above, the expression in Jude 24–25a identifies and characterizes the one who is to be glorified. Therefore, it functions as an exposition which clarifies the address of a doxology. The parallel expression in 2 Pet 3:17–18a is quite different. It instructs the readers to be on guard and grow in the grace and knowledge of Jesus Christ, and thereby functions as a direct exhortation. Given the dissimilarities evident in parallel #23 and parallel #24, the cluster as a whole is most appropriately classified as semantically and functionally dissimilar.

The effect of including this fifth cluster of parallels in the probability analysis is shown in table 4.5. With the addition of WC5 and its member parallels, the worst case collective probability of directness, CP_{dir}, between Jude and 2 Peter reaches its final value of 0.724.

TABLE 4.5. Probability of directness (Jude || 2 Pet, 5th cluster, worst case)

No.	Description	Reference		Individual			Collective	
		Jude	2 Pet	DI	IP_{dir}	IP_{ndir}	CP_{ndir}	CP_{dir}
23	keep from falling	24	3:17	1.395	0.058	0.942	0.303	0.697
24	our Savior Lord Jesus Christ	25a	3:18a	0.908	0.038	0.962	0.292	0.708
25	glory both now and forever	25b	3:18b	1.103	0.046	0.954	0.279	0.721
WC5	Closing Remarks	24–25	3:17–18	0.185	0.008	0.992	0.276	0.724

The Likelihood of Literary Dependence

Before reaching a conclusion about the likelihood of literary dependence between Jude and 2 Peter, it is important to note that the result shown in table 4.5 is based on rarity of occurrence scores that include the worst-case values for Greco-Roman literature. When the best-case scores for rarity of occurrence are used for this same set of parallels, the final value for CP_{dir} rises to 0.831 (see appendix N). Thus the range of values for the final CP_{dir} is 0.724–0.831. In effect, this result is equivalent to that of a pair of documents which contain a single parallel that is formed by 81–93 consecutive verbatim words, earns the highest possible scores for correspondence of parallel elements, and is found in no other examined bodies of literature. Since the entire range of final values for CP_{dir} is significantly above the mid-point of the probability scale, there is no need to measure the actual number of occurrences in Greco-Roman literature. The probability analysis is conclusive using the best-case scores and the worst-case scores for rarity of occurrence in the Greco-Roman body of literature.

Thus the probability analysis of Jude and 2 Peter has produced the expected positive result that a direct literary connection is highly likely. Although the non-deterministic nature of probability disallows specific claims about direct literary connections for individual parallels, this part of the study concludes that, at the whole document level, Jude and 2 Peter are very likely to be related through direct literary dependence. This does not preclude the possibility that some of the parallels might derive from independent use of common traditions or from coincidence. The study concludes only that it is highly unlikely that *all* of the parallels are due to non-direct or non-existent influences. There is a high probability that *at least one* of the parallels is due to a direct literary connection.

The case of Jude and 2 Peter therefore demonstrates credibility of the assessment methodology at the high end of the probability scale. Application of the methodology to two documents that are strikingly similar does indeed yield an expected positive result. Together, the negative and positive test cases also show that the results are independent of the length of the documents, since James and Philippians, at 1,742 and 1,629 Greek words, respectively, are considerably longer than the 461 and 1,099 Greek words of Jude and 2 Peter. The strong positive result for Jude and 2 Peter, then, is significant and warrants proceeding to the next stage of the methodology demonstration. Since literary dependence is highly likely, the question of who borrowed from whom is valid. Hence, we now turn our attention to assessing the most likely direction of borrowing between Jude and 2 Peter.

CHAPTER 5

Positive Test Case:
Direction of Borrowing
between Jude and 2 Peter

A high probability of literary dependence between documents raises many questions. How did one of the authors become acquainted with the other document? Why did the author borrow material from the other document? How does the author interpret the borrowed material? Why did the author deviate from the borrowed material? These and other important questions, however, can only be addressed if the direction of borrowing is known.

The second stage of the assessment methodology, which is presented in chapter 2, provides a disciplined analytical approach to assessing the most likely direction of borrowing between two documents that have a high probability of being related through literary dependence. The methodology, however, is only useful if it produces consistent and credible results. Again, the best way to demonstrate reliability of the direction-assessing methodology is to apply it to two literarily-dependent documents where scholarly opinion already favors a particular borrowing scenario. Jude and 2 Peter present such a test case. As demonstrated in the previous chapter, these two documents are highly likely to be related through literary dependence of one upon the other. Moreover, scholarly opinion does in fact favor one of the two authors as more likely to be the borrower.

Expected Outcome

A survey of published commentaries and focused studies on the relationship between Jude and 2 Peter reveals disparate levels of support for each
borrowing scenario. For the scenario in which the author of Jude borrowed
from 2 Peter, support primarily is found in older works that emphasize
Peter's prominence in the early Christian community.[1] As an apostle of Jesus
Christ, according to this view, the Petrine author would not have borrowed
material from a lesser figure such as Jude. Proponents of this view find
further support for Jude's position as borrower in Jude 4 and 17–18, where
the language seems to suggest fulfillment of what is stated in 2 Pet 2:1–3
and 3:2–3. The vast majority of contemporary scholarly works, however,
favor the scenario in which the author of 2 Peter borrowed from Jude.[2]

---

1. So, e.g., Charles Bigg, *The Epistles of St. Peter and St. Jude*, ICC (Edin-
burgh: T&T Clark, 1901), 216–24; Martin Luther, "Sermons on the Second Epistle
of St. Peter," and "Sermons on the Epistle of St. Jude," trans. M. H. Bertram, in *The
Catholic Epistles*, ed. J. Pelikan and W. A. Hansen, Luther's Works 30 (St. Louis,
MO: Concordia Publishing House, 1967); J. B. Mayor, *The Epistle of St. Jude and
the Second Epistle of St. Peter* (London: Macmillan, 1907; reprint, Grand Rapids:
Baker, 1965), i–xxv; Douglas J. Moo, *2 Peter and Jude*, NIV Application Commentary
(Grand Rapids, MI: Zondervan, 1996), 16–21.

2. So, e.g., Gary M. Burge, Lynn H. Cohick, and Gene L. Green, *The New
Testament in Antiquity: A Survey of the New Testament within Its Cultural Contexts*
(Grand Rapids, MI: Zondervan, 2009), 405; Peter H. Davids, *The Letters of 2 Peter
and Jude*, The Pillar New Testament Commentary (Grand Rapids, MI: Eerdmans,
2006), 141–43; Michael J. Gilmour, *The Significance of Parallels between 2 Peter and
Other Early Christian Literature*, AcBib 10 (Leiden, The Netherlands: Brill Academic,
2002), 83–91; Gene L. Green, *Jude and 2 Peter*, BECNT (Grand Rapids, MI: Baker
Academic, 2008), 159–62; David G. Horrell, *The Epistles of Peter and Jude* (London:
Epworth, 1998), 142; Johannes Kahmann, "The Second Letter of Peter and the Letter
of Jude: Their Mutual Relationship," in *The New Testament in Early Christianity: La
réception des écrits néotestamentaires dans le christianisme primitif*, ed. Jean-Marie
Sevrin, BETL 86 (Leuven: Peeters and Leuven University Press, 1989), 106–7; J. N. D.
Kelly, *A Commentary on the Epistles of Peter and of Jude*, BNTC (London: Adam &
Charles Black, 1969), 225–27; James Moffatt, *An Introduction to the Literature of the
New Testament*, The International Theological Library (New York: Charles Scribner's
Sons, 1911, reprinted 1929), 351; Jerome H. Neyrey, *2 Peter, Jude*, AB 37c (New York:
Doubleday, 1993), 120–22; Thomas R. Schreiner, *1, 2 Peter, Jude*, NAC 37 (Nashville:
Broadman & Holman, 2003), 418–19; Lauri Thurén, "The Relationship between
2 Peter and Jude—A Classical Problem Resolved?" in *The Catholic Epistles and the
Tradition*, ed. Jacques Schlosser, BETL 176 (Leuven: Peeters, 2004), 451–60; J. W. C.

Arguments for this scenario frequently maintain that since nearly all of Jude is paralleled in 2 Peter, Jude must be prior because there would have been no need to write the letter if 2 Peter were already available.[3] Furthermore, if Jude borrowed from 2 Peter, then why did the author exclude important material from chapters 1 and 3 of 2 Peter? It also has been claimed that since Jude alone draws material from the apocryphal books of *1 Enoch* and the *Testament (Assumption) of Moses*, it is more likely that the author of 2 Peter held a stricter view of Scripture and therefore was reluctant to include Jude's apocryphal material than that the author of Jude augmented the work borrowed from 2 Peter with apocryphal material.[4] The scenario in which the author of 2 Peter borrowed from the letter of Jude has been further supported by rhetorical criticism, as Duane Frederick Watson maintains that an observed shift in the rhetorical pattern between Jude and 2 Peter fits rhetorical conventions if 2 Peter borrowed from Jude, but not if Jude borrowed from 2 Peter.[5]

Although the weight of scholarly opinion favors the author of 2 Peter as borrower, plausible arguments to the contrary do cast a shadow of doubt over such a conclusion. Thus the question of who used whom remains a matter of scholarly interest, especially since the direction of borrowing has potential implications for relative dating, authorship, and exegetical study of the letters. Moreover, none of the earlier studies consulted for this project employ an objective mathematical approach to assessing the relationship between Jude and 2 Peter. All of them reflect subjective appraisals of the relationship, based primarily on the indirect-chronological and indirect-logical types of indicators discussed in chapter 2.[6] Nevertheless, the strength

---

Wand, ed., *The General Epistles of St. Peter and St. Jude*, WC (London: Methuen & Co. Ltd., 1934), 135–37; Duane Frederick Watson, *Invention, Arrangement, and Style: Rhetorical Criticism of Jude and 2 Peter*, SBLDS 104 (Atlanta, GA: Scholars Press, 1988), 160–87; Richard J. Bauckham, *Jude, 2 Peter*, WBC 50 (Nashville, TN: Thomas Nelson, 1983), 141–43.

3. So, e.g., Davids, *Letters of 2 Peter and Jude*, 141–42; Gilmour, *Significance of Parallels*, 83–86; Kelly, *Peter and Jude*, 226; Moffatt, *Introduction*, 351; John A. T. Robinson, *Redating the New Testament* (London: SCM Press Ltd., 1976), 192; Schreiner, *1, 2 Peter, Jude*, 419.

4. So Werner Georg Kümmel, *Introduction to the New Testament*, rev. ed., trans. Howard Clark Kee (Nashville, TN: Abingdon, 1975), 431; Kelly, *Peter and Jude*, 227.

5. Watson, *Invention*, 170.

6. Examples involving Jude || 2 Peter are cited on pp. 72, 73, 76–79.

of the majority opinion makes Jude || 2 Peter an excellent test case for the direction-assessing methodology. When the two documents are analyzed for the likelihood of borrowing in each directional scenario, we should expect a result which points to the author of 2 Peter as most likely to have borrowed from Jude.

Procedure

Having established in the previous chapter a high probability that at least one of the parallels between Jude and 2 Peter is very likely due to literary dependence, the next step of the assessment process is to try to discern who is most likely to have borrowed from whom. Investigation of the question proceeds by re-evaluating the parallels according to the methodology prescribed in chapter 2, which focuses on directionality as indicated by evidence of borrowing. Of particular interest is evidence of disturbance in the host document, consistency of borrowing practices, logical progression between parallel elements, and identification of a likely external source for one of the parallel elements. Since both authors are potential borrowers, it is necessary to evaluate two directional scenarios: (1) the probability that the author of Jude borrowed from 2 Peter; and (2) the probability that the author of 2 Peter borrowed from Jude. The final assessment of directionality is based on the combination of the two results.

Three observations about the study are in order before proceeding. First, since a legitimate assessment of the direction of borrowing assumes that a high probability of literary dependence has already been established, this next step of the analysis is based on the same set of parallels that were used to determine the probability of literary dependence.[7] Second, the evaluation of parallels for evidence of a likely external source takes into consideration the LXX, the Hebrew Bible, and the OT Pseudepigrapha as possible sources that surely would have been in circulation when the NT documents were written. Finally, since each directional scenario must be

---

7.   Because probability is non-deterministic, the identity of the direct-connect parallel(s) is unknown. For this reason, assessment of directionality must be based on cumulative evidence over the same set of parallels that was used in the probability analysis presented in chapter 4.

evaluated separately, the presentation of results is organized accordingly, beginning with the probability that the author of Jude borrowed at least one of the parallel elements from 2 Peter.

Probability that Jude Borrowed

According to the methodology presented in chapter 2, the probability that an author borrowed material is based on specific indicators of borrowing. Even though the present analysis of Jude || 2 Peter includes all the parallels that were used to establish the probability of literary dependence, not all of these parallels exhibit such evidence. Therefore, only the parallels that show evidence of having been borrowed are included in the discussion below. As it turns out, this particular borrowing scenario is supported only by evidence of logical progression from 2 Peter to Jude.

Logical Progression between Parallel Elements

Evaluation of the parallels between Jude and 2 Peter from the perspective that the author of Jude might be the borrower reveals only four parallels that exhibit evidence of having been borrowed. All four of these parallels involve progression of language. As explained in chapter 2, progression of language is evidenced primarily by a difference in verbal tense between the parallel elements where the tenses may be understood to indicate the relative time frame and not just the aspect of the action that is in view (p. 100). Such evidence is found in four parallels associated with cluster WC2, "Harmful Infiltrators" (Jude 4 || 2 Pet 2:1–3). As explained in the previous chapter, Jude 4 seems to suggest completion of what appears to be foretold in 2 Peter 2:1–3. Specifically, readers of 2 Peter are warned that troublesome people who have been long marked for judgment will sneak in among them and cause harm to the faith community through their licentious behavior and denial of the Master. According to Jude 4, such harmful infiltration has in fact occurred in the addressed community. Although the parallel statements which identify the infiltrators as having been long marked for judgment do not provide evidence of different time frames for the respective infiltrations (parallel #6), the other member parallels (#5, #7, #8) and the cluster as a whole (WC2) do provide evidence of language progression from 2 Peter to Jude (see the discussion of these parallels in chapter 4).

Summary of Results

Examination of the Jude || 2 Peter parallels for other signs of having been borrowed yields no additional evidence that meets the criteria defined in chapter 2. Therefore, the evidence is limited to progression of language indicators exhibited by four of the parallels associated with WC2.

The probability of borrowing based on these observed indicators is shown in table 5.1, which shows the Borrowing Index (BI), the Probability of Borrowing (IP_{bor}), and the Probability of Not-Borrowed (IP_{nbor}) for each of these parallels, as well as the collective probability calculations for each successive parallel (CP_{nbor}, CP_{bor}). It is not necessary to include all 30 parallels in the borrowing probability calculation tables shown in this chapter. See the illustrative example in chapter 2 for an explanation (p. 91). Indicator scores and probability calculations for all the parallels are provided in appendix O.

TABLE 5.1. Probability of borrowing (Jude)

No.	Description	Reference		Individual			Collective	
		Jude	2 Pet	BI	IP_{bor}	IP_{nbor}	CP_{nbor}	CP_{bor}
							1	0
5	ones who sneak in	4a	2:1b	1	0.08	0.92	0.92	0.08
7	licentious behavior	4c	2:2	1	0.08	0.92	0.85	0.15
8	denying the Master	4d	2:1c	1	0.08	0.92	0.79	0.21
WC2	Harmful Infiltrators	4	2:1–3	1	0.08	0.92	0.73	0.27

As shown in table 5.1, the collective probability that Jude borrowed, CP_{bor}, is only 0.27. This relatively low value indicates that the author of Jude is unlikely to be the borrower. This, however, does not necessarily mean that the author of 2 Peter is the borrower. The direction of borrowing cannot be discerned without also assessing the probability that 2 Peter borrowed material from Jude.

Probability that 2 Peter Borrowed

The probability that the author of 2 Peter borrowed any of the parallel material is determined using the same method that is employed above for Jude. Here again, although all of the parallels are included in the analysis, not all of them exhibit evidence of having been borrowed. Hence only the parallels that show evidence of having been borrowed are discussed below. Presentation of the results is organized according to the major categories of borrowing indicators, with a summary table of probability calculations at the end of the presentation. For this directional scenario, evidence is found for three categories of indicators. These include disturbance in the host document, logical progression between parallel elements, and identification of a likely external source for one of the parallel elements.

Disturbance in the Host Document

According to the methodology presented in chapter 2, a disturbance may appear as anything that looks like an intrusion of foreign matter into the discourse of the document (p. 92). Examination of the parallel material in 2 Peter reveals five distinct cases of disturbance involving six parallels (#12–14, #17, #20, #24), all of which concern a matter of style. Disturbance of style is evident when there is a noticeable difference in the presentation of the parallel material as compared to the overall flow of the document. The phenomenon can take many different forms, including awkward editing, an unusual pattern of writing, syntactical or stylistic tension, and even editorial fatigue (see pp. 93–95).

The first case of style disturbance involves the interaction between parallel #12, "defile flesh, reject lordship, blaspheme glories" (Jude 8 ∥ 2 Pet 2:10) and parallel #13, "reverent angels" (Jude 9 ∥ 2 Pet 2:11). In the text that constitutes these two parallels, the author of 2 Peter writes:

> 10b τολμηταὶ αὐθάδεις, δόξας οὐ τρέμουσιν βλασφημοῦντες, 11 ὅπου ἄγγελοι ἰσχύϊ καὶ δυνάμει μείζονες ὄντες οὐ φέρουσιν κατ᾽ αὐτῶν παρὰ κυρίου βλάσφημον κρίσιν (2 Pet 2:10b–11).

> 10b Daring and self-willed, they do not tremble when they blaspheme *glories*, 11 whereas angels who are greater in strength and power do not bring against *them* a blasphemous judgment from the Lord (2 Pet 2:10b–11).

Here the author contrasts the behavior of the infiltrators with that of greater angels. In light of the comparison, it is reasonable to assume that the object of blasphemous judgment is the same in both cases. In other words, the antecedent of αὐτῶν ("them") is δόξας ("glories"). Since this is preceded by a passage where the author accuses the infiltrators of ungodly behavior which will not escape God's judgment (2 Pet 2:1–10a), it is most natural to interpret this instance of δόξας ("glories") as good angelic beings.[8] The second part of the sentence, however, suggests that the antecedent of αὐτῶν ("them") is deserving of blasphemous judgment and therefore should be understood as bad angels.[9] The apparent inconsistency in the text of 2 Peter presents an interpretive conundrum.[10] Indeed, it might be the result of awkward editing as the author leveraged the text of Jude 8–9. The reference to Michael's dispute with the devil in Jude 9 clearly indicates that the one who deserves blasphemous judgment is the devil, not the "glories" whom the infiltrators blaspheme. The parallel in 2 Pet 2:11, however, does not include the reference to Michael's confrontation with the devil. Without it, the intended object of blasphemous judgment, that is, the antecedent of

---

8. So, e.g., Gene Green, *Jude and 2 Peter*, 269–71; Kelly, *Peter and Jude*, 337; Schreiner, *1, 2 Peter, Jude*, 347.

9. See Bauckham, *Jude, 2 Peter*, 261; Gilmour, *Significance of Parallels*, 84; Schreiner, *1, 2 Peter, Jude*, 348.

10. The interpretive difficulty in 2 Pet 2:10b–11 is widely recognized. See, e.g., Bauckham, *Jude, 2 Peter*, 261–63; Davids, *Letters of 2 Peter and Jude*, 234–36; Gene Green, *Jude and 2 Peter*, 269–74; Kelly, *Peter and Jude*, 337–38; Schreiner, *1, 2 Peter, Jude*, 347–49.

αὐτῶν ("them"), is lost. Instead, αὐτῶν ("them") seems to refer to δόξας ("glories"), which results in the awkward contradiction.[11] Thus the apparent inconsistency involving parallel #12 and parallel #13 exhibits evidence of borrowing in the form of a disturbance of style. Although this disturbance involves two parallels, it is a single disturbance. Therefore, the borrowing indicator is counted for only one of the parallels (#13).

The text of parallel #14, "unreasoning animals" (Jude 10 || 2 Pet 2:12), also is uncharacteristically awkward in the flow of 2 Peter. The construction of 2 Pet 2:12, in fact, has been described as "cumbersome and artificial,"[12] and has given the impression that "the writer is expanding material taken almost word for word from Jude 10, and rearranging it rather clumsily."[13] As written, the verse presents significant interpretive difficulties, particularly for the final clause, ἐν τῇ φθορᾷ αὐτῶν καὶ φθαρήσονται ("in their destruction they also will be destroyed"), where both the antecedent of αὐτῶν ("their") and the subject of the verb φθαρήσονται ("they will be destroyed") are unclear.[14] It is not difficult to see how this problematic expression might have arisen from an awkward use of the parallel material in Jude 10, ἐν τούτοις φθείρονται ("in these things they are destroyed"), which clearly refers to the troublesome infiltrators as being destroyed by what they know instinctively. Use of the masculine plural demonstrative pronoun Οὗτοι ("These") at the beginning of 2 Pet 2:12 also is unusual in the letter. Of the twenty-two demonstrative pronouns that appear in 2 Peter, only three are masculine. A singular masculine form appears in the quotation, ὁ υἱός μου ὁ ἀγαπητός μου οὗτός ἐστιν εἰς ὃν ἐγὼ εὐδόκησα ("My beloved Son *this* is, with whom I am well pleased," 2 Pet 1:17). The other two masculine forms are plural and involve parallels with Jude (#14, #17). Curiously, other than the quotation found in 2 Pet 1:17, these are the only instances where the author uses a demonstrative pronoun in reference to people. All other demonstrative pronouns, which are feminine or neuter, refer to inanimate objects or concepts such as promises, purposes, character traits, an earthly dwelling, an utterance, facts, corruption, defilements of the world, the letter

---

11. So also Gilmour, who understands the confusion evident in 2 Pet 2:10b–11 as "an instance of clumsy editing" that meets the criterion for awkward editing (*Significance of Parallels*, 85).

12. Kahmann, "Second Peter and Jude," 109.

13. Kelly, *Peter and Jude*, 338.

14. See, e.g., Bauckham, *Jude, 2 Peter*, 263–64; Davids, *Letters of 2 Peter and Jude*, 236–38; Gene Green, *Jude and 2 Peter*, 274–77; Schreiner, *1, 2 Peter, Jude*, 349–50.

itself, false claims, heaven, and earth. Hence the use of a demonstrative pronoun in reference to the troublesome infiltrators is uncharacteristic and therefore constitutes a disturbance in the discourse of 2 Peter.

A second unusual occurrence of οὗτοί ("these") is found in parallel #17, "waterless clouds/springs" (Jude 12b || 2 Pet 2:17a). Here again, the pronoun refers to the troublesome infiltrators. While such a practice is characteristic of Jude, where οὗτοί is used to reference harmful persons five times, the practice in 2 Peter is uncharacteristic. Therefore, although this particular instance of οὗτοί ("these") may be understood as part of a "rhetorical marker" (οὗτοί εἰσιν, "these are") in the flow of the discourse,[15] it provides additional evidence of disturbance in the normal style of writing found in 2 Peter.

Another case of style disturbance is found in parallel #20, "remember apostolic words" (Jude 17b || 2 Pet 3:2). The text of 2 Pet 3:2 is disturbing in at least two ways. First, the expression, τῆς τῶν ἀποστόλων ὑμῶν ἐντολῆς τοῦ κυρίου καὶ σωτῆρος ("the commandment of your apostles, of the Lord and Savior"), with its double genitive, is very difficult and awkward.[16] The syntax alone constitutes evidence of awkward editing. Second, the short expression τῶν ἀποστόλων ὑμῶν ("your apostles") seems to exclude the author. Although it is possible that the author includes himself in the reference to "your apostles," such an interpretation would be inconsistent with the author's normal style of referring to himself in the first person (e.g., the first-person verbs in 2 Pet 1:12, 13, 15, 16, 18, 19; 3:1, 13; and the first person personal pronouns in 2 Pet 1:1, 2, 3, 4, 8, 11, 14, 16, 18; 2:20; 3:15, 18). This would be the only case where he refers to himself in the third person. Thus it seems likely that "your apostles" does not include the author. Such an exclusion is quite odd since the author claims to be an apostle of Jesus Christ (2 Pet 1:1) and an eyewitness who previously "made known to you the power and coming of our Lord Jesus Christ" (2 Pet 1:16). Some scholars have understood the apparent contradiction as evidence of pseudonymous authorship of the letter sometime in the post-apostolic period.[17] Others have attempted to explain the anomaly by claiming that this particular instance of "apostle" refers more broadly to an apostolic "college" or to the

15. Gene Green, *Jude and 2 Peter*, 292.

16. Awkwardness of the Greek syntax is widely recognized. See, e.g., Bauckham, *Jude, 2 Peter*, 287; Davids, *Letters of 2 Peter and Jude*, 261; Kelly, *Peter and Jude*, 354; Schreiner, *1, 2 Peter, Jude*, 370.

17. So, e.g., Kelly, *Peter and Jude*, 354.

early missionaries who preached the Christian message and founded the addressed congregation(s).[18] Such explanations, however, would require a different meaning of "apostle" than what is implied in 2 Pet 1:1, 16. In any case, the expression "your apostles" seems out of place in a letter that claims to have been written by an eyewitness apostle. Thus the awkward and unexpected nature of the expression in 2 Pet 3:2 presents evidence of a style disturbance in 2 Peter.

The final case of style disturbance found in 2 Peter involves parallel #24, "our Savior Lord Jesus Christ" (Jude 25a ‖ 2 Pet 3:18a). The author's instruction to "grow in grace and knowledge of our Lord and Savior Jesus Christ" reflects an unusual grammatical construction in the Greek text. Typical usages of the nouns χάριτι ("grace") and γνώσει ("knowledge") in the NT suggest that in this verse Christ should be understood as the *source* of grace and the *object* of knowledge (e.g., Rom 5:15; 1 Cor 1:5; 2 Cor 1:12; 11:6; Gal 1:6). This results in a highly unusual case where a genitive construct, τοῦ κυρίου ἡμῶν καὶ σωτῆρος Ἰησοῦ Χριστου ("of our Lord and Savior Jesus Christ"), simultaneously functions as both a subjective and objective genitive.[19] The ambiguous construction may be the result of awkward editing as the author of 2 Peter incorporated the genitive of Jude 25a, Ἰησοῦ Χριστοῦ τοῦ κυρίου ἡμῶν ("Jesus Christ our Lord"), into his instruction for readers, αὐξάνετε ἐν χάριτι καὶ γνώσει ("grow in grace and knowledge"). As such, the text of 2 Pet 3:18a constitutes a disturbance of style in the discourse of 2 Peter.

Logical Progression between Parallel Elements

Borrowing from Jude is further evidenced by fifteen indicators of logical progression, which are found in fourteen parallels. The evidence spans three of the four sub-categories of progression, including progression of structure, progression of thought, and progression of function.

18. So, e.g., Bauckham, *Jude, 2 Peter*, 287; Davids, *Letters of 2 Peter and Jude*, 262; Gene Green, *Jude and 2 Peter*, 313; Moo, *2 Peter and Jude*, 164–65; Horrell, *Epistles of Peter and Jude*, 175; Schreiner, *1, 2 Peter, Jude*, 371.

19. Grammatical difficulty involving the function of the genitive in 2 Pet 3:18a is widely recognized by scholars. E.g., Bauckham, *Jude, 2 Peter*, 337; Davids, *Letters of 2 Peter and Jude*, 315–17; Kelly, *Peter and Jude*, 375; Schreiner, *1, 2 Peter, Jude*, 401.

Progression of Structure

According to chapter 2, progression of formal structure may be observed in the phenomenon of *dispersion*, which in this methodology is defined as "the expansion of clustered elements, generally in the same order, to a higher level of discourse with evidence of content development" (p. 102). The phenomenon of dispersion is evident in three of the second-order cluster parallels, as well as the two first-order fan parallels.

The first cluster, WC1, "Opening Remarks" (Jude 1–3 || 2 Pet 1:1–5), provides evidence of significant development from Jude to 2 Peter in two of its member parallels. In parallel #3, "mercy/grace and peace be multiplied to you" (Jude 2 || 2 Pet 1:2a), both authors convey similar wishes of well-being for their respective audiences. While Jude simply states his desire that mercy, peace, and love be multiplied, the author of 2 Peter not only makes a similar statement, but he goes on to explain how such indicators of well-being are multiplied. Specifically, the Petrine author explains that multiplication occurs through "the knowledge of God and of Jesus our Lord" (2 Pet 1:2b–11). Parallel #4, "all diligence" (Jude 3 || 2 Pet 1:5), evidences a similar case of dispersion regarding the chief concern of "all diligence," namely, salvation and faith. In Jude 3 the author simply states his initial intention to write to the readers about their common salvation — apparently an intention that now necessitates an exhortation for them to "contend for the faith once handed down to the saints" (Jude 3b).[20] The author of 2 Peter develops the notion of "all diligence" concerning salvation and faith in two ways. First, the readers must apply "all diligence" in the way they live their lives. Specifically, the author instructs his audience on how to live out their faith in a manner that reflects the cleansing of former sins which comes through knowledge of Jesus Christ (2 Pet 1:5b–11). For the author of 2 Peter, this means growing in virtue.[21] Second, the author holds himself responsible to be a diligent teacher of these things so that his readers will be able to recall them long after he is gone (2 Pet 1:12–15). The author further explains that they need to pay attention because his teaching about Christ is the truth (2 Pet 1:16–21). In this way, the concise statement of Jude 3 is expanded in 2 Pet 1:5–21 to explain how, why, and by whom all

20. So, e.g., Gene Green, *Jude and 2 Peter*, 52–57; Davids, *Letters of 2 Peter and Jude*, 41–43; Schreiner, *1, 2 Peter, Jude*, 433–34.

21. So, e.g., Gene Green, *Jude and 2 Peter*, 188–93; Davids, *Letters of 2 Peter and Jude*, 177–80; Schreiner, *1, 2 Peter, Jude*, 296–301.

diligence must be applied in the matters of faith and salvation. Since WC1 provides evidence of content development with two of its members, and all of the member parallels appear in the same order in both documents, WC1 exhibits progression of structure in the form of dispersion.

Cluster parallel WC3, "Reason for Concern" (Jude 6–16b || 2 Pet 2:4–18a), also provides evidence of dispersion through content development associated with five of its ten member parallels. In parallel #10, "angels kept for judgment" (Jude 6 || 2 Pet 2:4), both texts convey the idea that God has detained disobedient angels for future judgment. In 2 Pet 2:5 the notion of judgment by God is further developed in two significant ways. First, using the familiar example of Noah and the flood, the author provides evidence that God has already demonstrated his power and intention to severely judge the ungodly (2 Pet 2:5a). Second, from the same example, the author also shows that God has already demonstrated his power and intention to save the righteous, in this case, Noah and his family (2 Pet 2:5b). In parallel #11, "example of Sodom and Gomorrah" (Jude 7 || 2 Pet 2:6), both authors cite the example of Sodom and Gomorrah as further evidence of certain judgment for disobedience. Here again, the author of 2 Peter develops the notion of judgment by showing that the example of Sodom and Gomorrah also involves saving the righteous, namely, Lot (2 Pet 2:7–9). Thus the basic thought is developed in 2 Peter to show that God not only punishes the unrighteous but also saves the righteous.[22]

The next two parallels of cluster WC3 that exhibit evidence of content development appear together in the two letters, albeit in reversed order. In parallel #15, "followed Balaam" (Jude 11b || 2 Pet 2:15), both authors claim that the troublesome persons have followed the misguided way of Balaam for profit. While Jude says no more about Balaam's error, the author of 2 Peter provides additional details about the event recorded in Numbers 22–24. In particular, the text of 2 Pet 2:15–16 adds that Balaam was the son of Bosor, he loved to profit from wrongdoing, and he was rebuked for his wrongdoing and restrained by a donkey. By including these details, the author leaves no doubt as to what event is in view and the seriousness of the error. Parallel #16, "dangerous/stained feasting" (Jude 12a || 2 Pet 2:13b), also finds content development in 2 Pet 2:14, where the troublesome persons

---

22. See Bauckham, *Jude, 2 Peter*, 246–57; Davids, *Letters of 2 Peter and Jude*, 226–32; Gene Green, *Jude and 2 Peter*, 251–65; Schreiner, *1, 2 Peter, Jude*, 337–45; Kelly, *Peter and Jude*, 331–36.

who feast together with the addressed audiences are more fully described as adulterous, ever-sinning, seductive, greedy, and accursed.

The final parallel of cluster WC3 that exhibits evidence of content development is parallel #19, "arrogant speaking" (Jude 16b || 2 Pet 2:18a), where both authors accuse the perpetrators of speaking arrogant words. While Jude adds only that they flatter or enchant audiences in order to gain favor, the author of 2 Peter offers a more detailed description of the dangerous nature of the perpetrators' arrogance. Following the accusation of arrogant speaking, the letter goes on to explain that by such empty words these hypocrites appeal to the lustful desires of the flesh and entice those who are vulnerable, making promises of freedom, while they themselves are slaves of corruption. The author further warns that after having been freed from worldly sins through knowledge of the Lord and Savior Jesus Christ, returning to the former corrupt way of life constitutes a rejection of the way of righteousness that comes through such knowledge (2 Pet 2:18b–22). Here the author of 2 Peter apparently develops the notion of arrogant speaking in order to highlight the grave danger posed by the harmful infiltrators. Thus cluster WC3 exhibits dispersion through significant content development associated with parallels #10, #11, #15, #16, and #19.

Dispersion at the cluster level is also evident with the fourth cluster WC4, "Heed Apostolic Teaching" (Jude 17b–18 || 2 Pet 3:2–3c). Although the individual member parallels (#20–22) do not exhibit dispersion, the idea conveyed by WC4 receives significant development in the text that immediately follows the cluster material in 2 Peter. In particular, the author elaborates that the nature of their mocking involves claims that the Day of the Lord and the associated judgment would never come. In response, he points out the foolishness of such mocking, explaining that God created and maintains the world by his word and that the seemingly long delay in the Lord's coming is not slowness, but merciful patience. Indeed, the promised Day of the Lord and future judgment will surely come (2 Pet 3:4–10). Thus the general idea of Jude 17b–18, that the intended audiences should be mindful of apostolic teaching about the appearance of future mockers, is given specificity in 2 Peter, which highlights the gross error of the mockers' claims and thereby stresses the importance of heeding such apostolic teaching.

Additional evidence of structural progression is found in the two fan parallels. Whereas a typical case of dispersion involves the expansion and development of multiple elements, fan parallels involve the multiplication and development of a single element. Thus fan parallels may be understood as exhibiting a special case of dispersion. Such is the case with fan parallels #9 and #24. In the case of fan parallel #9, "reminder of known things" (Jude 5a || 2 Pet 1:12a), content development in 2 Peter involves the reason for writing. As shown in chapter 4, parallel #9 exhibits a fan structure because there is a distinct parallel relationship between the *one* instance in Jude 5a and the *many* instances found in 2 Pet 1:12a, 13, 15; 3:1 (figure 4.10). The author of Jude simply states his desire to remind the audience of important things they already know, which in Jude's case are the historical examples of divine judgment mentioned in the subsequent material (Jude 5b–7). The author of 2 Peter also states a similar desire to remind his readers of things they already know (2 Pet 1:12a), which in this case refers to the preceding discussion outlining the trustworthy source of teaching concerning God and the gospel of Jesus Christ, and the importance of growing in virtue (2 Pet 1:3–11).[23] Through the fan structure, the Petrine author then goes on to explain that it is right for him to remind his audience because his death is imminent (2 Pet 1:13–14), that diligent reminders are necessary so that the audience will be able to recall these things long after his departure (2 Pet 1:15), and that by this letter he demonstrates his commitment to remind them (2 Pet 3:1). In this way, the idea of the reminder found in Jude 5a is further developed in 2 Peter to impress upon the readers why it is so important that the author remind them of what they already know.

In parallel #24, "our Savior Lord Jesus Christ" (Jude 25a || 2 Pet 3:18a), the author of 2 Peter uses the fan structure to develop another important component of the discourse. Here the *one* instance in Jude 25a is developed through the *many* instances found in 2 Pet 1:11; 2:20; 3:18a (figure 4.26). In this case, content development concerns the identity and importance of Jesus Christ. The expression in Jude 25a is part of the final doxology and identifies the person to whom glory is due. As noted in chapter 4, the term σωτήρ ("Savior") is associated with θεός ("God"). Since Jude does not directly equate Jesus Christ with "God" or "Savior" anywhere in the letter, it cannot be assumed from Jude alone that the terms also apply to the one identified as "Jesus Christ our Lord." The identity of Jesus is clarified and developed in 2 Peter. The first branch with 2 Pet 1:11 clearly associates σωτῆρος ("Savior") with Jesus Christ. Moreover, the author adds that he is Lord over an eternal kingdom, the entry into which involves practicing the

---

23. See Bauckham, *Jude, 2 Peter*, 48–49, 197; Davids, *Letters of 2 Peter and Jude*, 46–47, 193; Gene Green, *Jude and 2 Peter*, 63, 207–8; Horrell, *Epistles of Peter and Jude*, 120, 153–54; Schreiner, *1, 2 Peter, Jude*, 308, 443–44.

230 PROBABILITY OF INTERTEXTUAL BORROWING

virtues listed in 2 Pet 1:5–10. The second branch with 2 Pet 2:20 not only associates σωτῆρος ("Savior") with Jesus Christ, but also explains that it is "by knowledge of the Lord and Savior Jesus Christ" that the addressees have "escaped the defilements of the world." Finally, the third branch with 2 Pet 3:18a stresses the importance of growing in such knowledge. After issuing a stern warning not to be led astray (2 Pet 3:17), the author exhorts his addressees instead to "grow in grace and knowledge of our Lord and Savior Jesus Christ." Thus, through the fan structure, the identity and importance of Jesus Christ is developed to show that "the only God our Savior" of Jude 25a and "Jesus Christ our Lord" are one, that salvation involves Christ's eternal kingdom, and that knowledge of Christ is essential for entry into the kingdom and maintaining godly behavior.

A second type of structural difference between parallel elements that suggests logical progression concerns the *portability* of the parallel material. As explained in chapter 2, portable material is identified by the presence of certain features that are believed to facilitate widespread ease of use. Such features may include strophic arrangement, participial construction, relative clauses, and parallelism (e.g., repetition, chiastic arrangement, rhythm, antithesis). Progression of formal structure may be indicated when parallels exhibit a significant difference in the portability features of each element, with the direction moving from more to less portable (see pp. 102–105). This situation occurs with seven of the Jude ‖ 2 Peter parallels, as much of the Greek text between Jude 8 and Jude 19 contains portable features.

Most of the portable features in Jude 8–19 occur in the third cluster, WC3, "Reason for Concern" (Jude 6–16b ‖ 2 Pet 2:4–18a), which is formed by parallels #10–19. A curiously distinctive characteristic is repetition of the demonstrative pronoun οὗτοι ("these") in reference to the troublesome infiltrators (Jude 8, 10, 12, 16; also 19). The author's repeated use of οὗτοι ("these") serves as a formula that makes the indictment against the harmful persons particularly memorable and therefore portable.[24] Since this section of the letter also exhibits a significantly higher concentration of relative clauses, participial constructions, and various types of parallelism than does the parallel cluster in 2 Pet 2:4–18a, cluster WC3 provides evidence of structural progression from more to less portable at the cluster level.[25]

---

24. See Bauckham, *Jude, 2 Peter*, 45.

25. Even though WC3 exhibits both dispersion and more-to-less portability, it still receives only one point for progression of structure.

In addition, the more-to-less portable phenomenon is evident with six of the member parallels of cluster WC3.

The first case of more-to-less portability in the member parallels of WC3 is found in parallel #12, "defile flesh, reject lordship, blaspheme glories" (Jude 8 ‖ 2 Pet 2:10). Here Jude employs a triplet of expressions to show that the behavior of the infiltrators is similar to that of those mentioned in vv. 5–7 who were judged and destroyed by God for their sinful behavior.[26] While figure 4.14 (chapter 4) shows that constructs J3, J4, and J5 all have structures of the form: noun (FA) + particle/conjunction + verb (PAInd3P), parallelism in the verse is more easily seen in figure 5.1.

Jude 8		
1 Ὁμοίως μέντοι καὶ οὗτοι ἐνυπνιαζόμενοι Yet in the same way even these dreamers		
2 σάρκα the flesh	μὲν	μιαίνουσιν defile
3 κυριότητα lordship	δὲ and	ἀθετοῦσιν reject
4 δόξας glories	δὲ and	βλασφημοῦσιν. blaspheme.

FIGURE 5.1. Parallelism in Jude 8 (parallel #12)

Through the use of parallel structures and rhyming of the noun and verb endings (-α / -ας, -οῦσιν), the triplet in Jude 8 (lines 2, 3, 4) exhibits a style of synonymous parallelism that makes the entire trifold expression highly portable.[27] Since the parallel text in 2 Pet 2:10 lacks such portable features, the parallel provides evidence of structural progression from more to less portable.

The second case of more-to-less portability in WC3 involves parallel #14, "unreasoning animals" (Jude 10 ‖ 2 Pet 2:12). Although not obvious from figure 4.16 (chapter 4), the author uses a pair of parallel expressions to contrast the behavior of the infiltrators with that of Michael the archangel (Jude 9). Parallelism of the doublet is more clearly illustrated in figure 5.2.

---

26. Jude's fondness of triplets is widely recognized by scholars. See, e.g., Davids, *Letters of 2 Peter and Jude*, 25; Neyrey, *2 Peter, Jude*, 28; Watson, *Invention*, 42.

27. Rhyming of parallel terms in Jude 8 is also noted in Bauckham, *Jude, 2 Peter*, 44. See also, Gene Green, *Jude and 2 Peter*, 75n4; Kelly, *Peter and Jude*, 261.

Jude 10				
1 Οὗτοι δὲ But these				
2 ὅσα μὲν whatever		οὐκ οἴδασιν they do not know		βλασφημοῦσιν they blaspheme
3 ὅσα δὲ and whatever	φυσικῶς ὡς τὰ ἄλογα ζῷα instinctively like the unreasoning animals	ἐπίστανται they understand	ἐν τούτοις in these things	φθείρονται. they are destroyed.

FIGURE 5.2. Parallelism in Jude 10 (parallel #14)

Following the initial Οὗτοι δὲ ("But these"), the text of Jude 10 consists of a pair of contrastive μέν-δέ relative clauses (lines 2, 3). Each clause begins with the relative pronoun ὅσα ("whatever"), which is followed by μέν/δέ. The referents of the pronouns, which are found in the middle of each clause, are opposites. Whereas the first pronoun refers to what "they do not know," the second pronoun refers to what "they understand." Finally, the clauses end with contrasting actions associated with the referents. Whereas they blaspheme the former, they are destroyed by the latter. Thus even though the second clause supplements the basic idea with additional phrases, the relative clauses reflect antithetical parallelism in that they employ similar structures and convey contrastive ideas. Here again, the parallel text in 2 Pet 2:12 does not exhibit any evidence of similar parallelism.[28] Hence parallel #14 evidences the phenomenon of more-to-less portability.

A third case of more-to-less portable structure in WC3 is found in parallel #15, "followed Balaam" (Jude 11b || 2 Pet 2:15), where the author of Jude again uses a triplet of expressions to declare that the troublesome persons have followed the misguided way of Balaam for profit. Parallelism in the verse is apparent in figure 5.3.

28. See Bauckham, *Jude, 2 Peter*, 6, 263.

Jude 11

1 οὐαὶ αὐτοῖς,
   Woe to them,

2 ὅτι   τῇ ὁδῷ   τοῦ Κάϊν   ἐπορεύθησαν
   for   in the way   of Cain   they went

3 καὶ   τῇ πλάνῃ   τοῦ Βαλαὰμ μισθοῦ   ἐξεχύθησαν
   and   in the error   of Balaam's wage   they abandoned themselves

4 καὶ   τῇ ἀντιλογίᾳ   τοῦ Κόρε   ἀπώλοντο.
   and   in the rebellion   of Korah   they perished.

FIGURE 5.3. Parallelism in Jude 11 (parallel #15)

After issuing the warning, οὐαὶ αὐτοῖς ("Woe to them"), in line 1, the author of Jude then explains why the warning is warranted using the three parallel statements in lines 2, 3, and 4. Each of these three lines exhibits the same structure: conjunction + articular dative + articular genitive + aorist indicative verb. In addition to structural-grammatical parallelism, this triplet reflects synonymous parallelism in that each of the three lines presents an OT example which highlights the surety of unpleasant consequences for those who follow their own selfish desires. Since the parallel text in 2 Pet 2:15 exhibits a much lower degree of portability, this parallel shows evidence of structural progression from more to less portable.

Three additional parallels that provide evidence of parallelism are parallel #16, "dangerous/stained feasting" (Jude 12a || 2 Pet 2:13b), parallel #17, "waterless clouds/springs" (Jude 12b || 2 Pet 2:17a), and parallel #18, "reserved darkness" (Jude 13b || 2 Pet 2:17b). In the letter of Jude, the texts of these three parallels are part of the well-constructed sentence found in Jude 12–13, which is shown in figure 5.4.

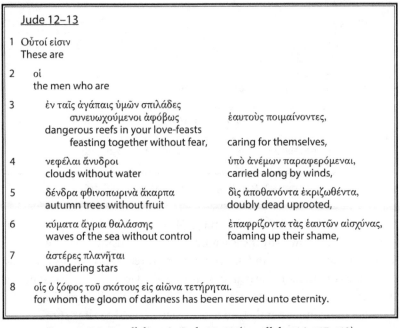

FIGURE 5.4. Parallelism in Jude 12–13 (parallels #16, #17, #18)

Here again the author begins the long sentence with a reference to "these" people (line 1). He then employs a series of poetic parallel statements to describe them (lines 2–7), followed by a relative clause which affirms their fate (line 8). Synonymous parallelism is particularly evident in lines 3, 4, 5, and 6. The first half of each of these lines compares "these" people to a particular natural phenomenon that lacks an important feature, the absence of which renders it useless or even harmful. Moreover, each of the noted deficiencies begins with the same sound as each word starts with the letter ἀ (ἀφόβως, ἄνυδροι, ἄκαρπα, ἄγρια). The defective phenomenon identified in line 7 also begins with the letter ἀ (ἀστέρες). The second half of lines 3–6 all are participial clauses that further highlight the folly of their ways (ποιμαίνοντες, παραφερόμεναι, ἀποθανόντα ἐκριζωθέντα, ἐπαφρίζοντα). The relative pronoun οἷς ("for whom") in line 8 parallels the definite article οἱ ("the men who are") in line 2, both of which follow from Οὗτοί εἰσιν ("These are") in line 1. Given the relatively high degree of portability displayed in Jude 12–13 as compared to the parallel text in 2 Peter, the three parallels that are involved in these verses all meet the defined criteria for more-to-less portable (#16, #17, #18).

Progression of Thought

As explained in chapter 2, progression of thought may be indicated when the thoughts conveyed by two parallel elements reflect a continuation or progression of events or circumstances from the perspective of the two authors (p. 105). The phenomenon is evident in parallel #4, "all diligence" (Jude 3 || 2 Pet 1:5). In Jude 3 the author states that his initial intention was to write to the audience about their common salvation, but now he must exhort them to "contend for the faith." It would appear that, due to unspecified circumstances, he did not follow through with his original intention for writing. The desire to write about salvation was an intention unfulfilled. The author of 2 Peter, however, did write about salvation in 2 Pet 1:3–11, seemingly as if to fulfill Jude's original intention. In 2 Pet 1:3–4 the author succinctly establishes the basis of their shared community of faith as having been rooted in God's redemptive plan accomplished in Christ. This is followed in verses 5–10 with a description of moral conduct that demonstrates and reinforces effective faith. Finally, in 2 Pet 1:11 the author explains that God's plan of salvation culminates with entrance into Christ's eternal kingdom.[29] Thus parallel #4 provides evidence of borrowing from Jude according to the progression of thought indicator. Jude intended to write about salvation and the author of 2 Peter fulfilled the intention by actually writing about details pertaining to salvation.[30]

Progression of Function

As explained in chapter 2, logical progression might also be evidenced by a shift in the rhetorical function of parallel elements from exposition in one document to exhortation in the other document (pp. 106–108). Such a shift occurs with word-group cluster WC5, "Closing Remarks" (Jude 24–25 || 2 Pet 3:17–18), and two of its three member parallels, parallel #23, "keep

---

29. The salvation teaching found in 2 Pet 1:3–11 is widely noted by NT scholars. E.g., Bauckham, *Jude, 2 Peter*, 172–93, esp. 192–93.

30. The intention-fulfillment relationship between Jude and 2 Peter in regard to writing about salvation is also noted in Robinson, *Redating the New Testament*, 193–95. Robinson understands the relationship as indicting common authorship of both letters by Jude, and that the previous letter mentioned in 2 Pet 3:1 is actually the letter of Jude.

from falling" (Jude 24 || 2 Pet 3:17), and parallel #24, "our Savior Lord Jesus Christ" (Jude 25a || 2 Pet 3:18a). The expression in Jude 24–25a appears in the closing doxology of the letter, where the author identifies the one to whom glory is due. In so doing, the author also includes expositional material about the one so identified. Specifically, he is "able to keep you free from falling and make you stand firm in the presence of his glory, without blemish, with great joy," and he is "the only God our Savior, through Jesus Christ our Lord." The parallel expression in 2 Pet 3:17–18a, on the other hand, appears as a direct exhortation to the addressed audience. Readers are warned to be on guard so that they are not misled by false teaching and thereby fall away from steadfast living. Rather, they should focus on sound teaching and grow in grace and knowledge of "our Lord and Savior Jesus Christ." Thus while Jude informs readers that God is able to keep them from falling, the author of 2 Peter instructs his readers not to fall; and while Jude informs readers that God saves through Jesus Christ, the author of 2 Peter instructs his readers to grow in grace and knowledge of Jesus Christ. In each case, the basis for the exhortation logically precedes the exhortation. Therefore, both parallels present evidence of having been borrowed according to the progression of function indicator. In addition, since parallels #23 and #24 best represent the cluster as a whole, the cluster parallel, WC5, also exhibits the same progression of function.

External Source

Borrowing may also be indicated if one of the parallel elements finds a likely source in another document that would have been available to the NT writers, and the other element does not (see chapter 2, pp. 108–109). Such sources might include the writings of the LXX, the Hebrew Bible, or the OT Pseudepigrapha. A likely external source may be evidenced by verbal correspondence with a clearly identified source document, along with other contextual indicators that the NT author had the particular source in view. For the directional scenario where 2 Peter borrowed from Jude, this means that an external source can be identified for the parallel text in Jude, but not for the text in 2 Peter. The possibilities, however, are limited. Although Jude frequently refers to people and events from the OT, the letter does not contain any quotations from the LXX or the Hebrew Scriptures. All the references are in the form of allusions. Hence verbal correspondence to specific sources is difficult to ascertain.[31] The few cases where it might be possible to identify an OT source for a text in Jude fail to meet the criteria for an external source, either because the source is also likely for the parallel in 2 Peter (e.g., Jude 11b || 2 Pet 2:15 || Numbers 22–24, 31:8, 16), the allusive text in Jude is not included in the parallel text of 2 Peter (e.g., "feeding themselves," Jude 12a || Ezek 34:2; cf. 2 Pet 2:13b), or the literary context of the parallel material lacks sufficient evidence to suggest that the connection was intended by the author (Jude 12b || 2 Pet 2:17a || Prov 25:14 Hebrew). Thus none of the OT allusions in Jude provide evidence of borrowing according to the external source indicator. Jude's use of pseudepigraphal material, however, does provide such evidence.

Reference to the OT Pseudepigrapha in the letter of Jude has received a great deal of attention by NT scholars. Indeed, there is little doubt that the author of Jude alluded to or quoted from *1 Enoch* and the *Testament (Assumption) of Moses*, while the author of 2 Peter made no references to such writings.[32] Although there is much speculation about why one author chose to use these writings and the other did not, for the present analysis it is sufficient simply to identify the relevant parallels.

Jude's familiarity with *1 Enoch* is evident in verses 6 and 12–16, the contents of which involve three of the Jude || 2 Peter parallels. In parallel #10, "angels kept for judgment" (Jude 6 || 2 Pet 2:4), the author of Jude refers to an angelic fall, which has roots in Gen 6:1–4 and is elaborated extensively in *1 Enoch* 6–19.[33] The Jude text of parallel #18, "reserved darkness" (Jude 13b || 2 Pet 2:17b), also bears evidence of a literary connection to *1 Enoch*. The expression found in Jude 13b is linked directly through the relative pronoun οἷς ("for whom") to the preceding ἀστέρες πλανῆται ("wandering stars"), which is commonly understood as having derived from *1 Enoch*

---

31. Karen H. Jobes notes that identification of specific OT sources for Jude is particularly difficult since many of the allusions suggest that the author drew from the Hebrew Scriptures rather than the Greek (*Letters to the Church: A Survey of Hebrews and the General Epistles* [Grand Rapids, MI: Zondervan, 2011], 249–52).

32. So, e.g., Jobes, *Letters to the Church*, 252–58; Burge, Cohick, and Green, *New Testament in Antiquity*, 407; Gilmour, *Significance of Parallels*, 83–85; Gene Green, *Jude and 2 Peter*, 26, 249; Horrell, *Epistles of Peter and Jude*, 110, 140.

33. The influence of *1 Enoch* on Jude 6 is widely recognized in NT scholarship. See, e.g., Bauckham, *Jude, 2 Peter*, 7, 50–53; Burge, Cohick, and Green, *New Testament in Antiquity*, 407; Davids, *Letters of 2 Peter and Jude*, 48–51; Gene Green, *Jude and 2 Peter*, 26, 66–70; Horrell, *Epistles of Peter and Jude*, 120–21; Schreiner, *1, 2 Peter, Jude*, 447–51.

(*1 En.* 18:13–16; 21:3–6; 80:2–8).[34] Similarity of the text in Jude 13b to the thought and language found in Jude 6 (τηρέω, "keep"/"reserve"; ζόφος, "gloom"; and ἀϊδίοις/εἰς αἰῶνα, "eternal"/"unto eternity") suggests that the thought of Jude 13b also derives from *1 Enoch* (*1 En.* 46:6; 63:6; 103:8; 108:14).[35] Although many of the ideas underlying Jude 6 and 13 may be found in other documents of the time period, a direct quotation of *1 En.* 1:9 in Jude 14–15 confirms that the author did in fact have *1 Enoch* in view as he wrote, and that a literary connection was intentional.[36] Therefore, there is good reason to believe that a connection to *1 Enoch* in verses 6 and 13 also was intended by the author. So too for parallel #19, "arrogant speaking" (Jude 16b ‖ 2 Pet 2:18a), where the author of Jude comments on τῶν σκληρῶν ("the harsh things") spoken by the ungodly persons in the quoted text of *1 En.* 1:9. To be specific, the author of Jude states that τὸ στόμα αὐτῶν λαλεῖ ὑπέρογκα ("their mouth speaks arrogant [lit. "huge"] things," Jude 16). This expression finds parallels in *1 En.* 5:4 and 101:3, where the perpetrators are accused of speaking μεγάλους/μεγάλα καὶ σκληροὺς/σκληρὰ ("great and harsh") words with their mouth. Although Jude 16 uses ὑπέρογκα (lit. "huge") in place of μεγάλους/μεγάλα ("great") in connection with σκληρός ("harsh") speaking by the mouth, in light of the preceding quotation of *1 En.* 1:9, a deliberate connection to *1 Enoch* seems very likely in Jude 16.[37]

The parallel texts in 2 Peter, however, cannot be traced to *1 Enoch* or any other specific source. Although the reference to angels in 2 Pet 2:4 (parallel #10) likely is based on an interpretation of Gen 6:1–4, the verbal echoes are insufficient to tie it to any particular source.[38] So too for the reserved darkness mentioned in 2 Pet 2:17b (parallel #18). Without the accompanying reference to "wandering stars" as it is found in Jude, the

34. So, e.g., Bauckham, *Jude, 2 Peter*, 89–91, 274; Kahmann, "Second Peter and Jude," 109–10; Kelly, *Peter and Jude*, 274, 345.

35. Bauckham, *Jude, 2 Peter*, 90.

36. See, e.g., Bauckham, *Jude, 2 Peter*, 93–101; Gilmour, *Significance of Parallels*, 85; Gene Green, *Jude and 2 Peter*, 26, 67, 101–8; Horrell, *Epistles of Peter and Jude*, 125–26; Jobes, *Letters to the Church*, 255; Schreiner, *1, 2 Peter, Jude*, 468–73.

37. Bauckham, *Jude, 2 Peter*, 98–99. See also Davids, *Letters of 2 Peter and Jude*, 83–84; Kelly, *Peter and Jude*, 279.

38. See Gene Green, *Jude and 2 Peter*, 249–51; Bauckham, *Jude, 2 Peter*, 248; Davids, *Letters of 2 Peter and Jude*, 225–26; Kelly, *Peter and Jude*, 331; Schreiner, *1, 2 Peter, Jude*, 335–36.

expression is untraceable.[39] The accusation of arrogant speaking found in 2 Pet 2:18a (parallel #19) also lacks sufficient verbal cues to identify a source for the expression.

Jude's use of the *Testament (Assumption) of Moses* is evident in parallel #13, "reverent angels" (Jude 9 || 2 Pet 2:11), where both authors highlight the seriousness of the infiltrators' blasphemous speech against angelic beings by declaring that even greater angels dare not speak blasphemous judgments against such "glories." While 2 Peter simply states that "angels who are greater in strength and power do not bring against them a blasphemous judgment from the Lord," Jude includes significant details. The angel is specifically identified as "Michael the archangel," the situation is described as a dispute between Michael and the devil about the body of Moses, and the declaration that Michael dared not pass judgment is supported with a quotation, "May the Lord rebuke you!" While the quoted words may derive from Zech 3:2, the notion of a contest between Satan and the angel of the Lord over the body of Moses is commonly understood to have come from the lost ending of the *Testament of Moses*. Although the ending is no longer extant, the substance of its content appears to be preserved in multiple ancient sources.[40] Moreover, several of the Apostolic Fathers attribute the source of Jude 9 to a work they refer to as the *Assumption of Moses*.[41] The relationship between the *Testament of Moses* and the so-called *Assumption of Moses* cannot be definitively determined. Nevertheless, there is little doubt that the author of Jude knew and used material from this pseudepigraphal work.[42]

Additional evidence of Jude's use of the *Testament of Moses* is found at the end of Jude 16, where the author accuses the arrogant speakers of θαυμάζοντες πρόσωπα ὠφελείας χάριν ("enchanting people to gain advantage"). The expression may have been influenced by a part of the *Testament*

---

39. See Bauckham, *Jude, 2 Peter*, 274; Davids, *Letters of 2 Peter and Jude*, 243–44; Gene Green, *Jude and 2 Peter*, 293; Kelly, *Peter and Jude*, 344–45; Schreiner, *1, 2 Peter, Jude*, 356–57.

40. For a good summary, see Bauckham, *Jude, 2 Peter*, 67–73.

41. These include Clement of Alexandria (Fragm. in *Ep. Jud.*), Didymus the Blind (in *ep. Jud. enarr.*), Origen (*De Princ.* 3:2:1), and Gelasius Cyzicenus (*Hist. eccl.* 2.17.17; 2.21.7). See the discussion in Bauckham, *Jude, 2 Peter*, 73–76.

42. So, e.g., Bauckham, *Jude, 2 Peter*, 47–48, 59–62, 65–76, 261; Davids, *Letters of 2 Peter and Jude*, 59–60; Gene Green, *Jude and 2 Peter*, 26, 79–84; Horrell, *Epistles of Peter and Jude*, 122; Jobes, *Letters to the Church*, 255; Kelly, *Peter and Jude*, 265; Schreiner, *1, 2 Peter, Jude*, 459–60.

of Moses that is extant (*T. Mos.* 5:5).[43] Although not included in a parallel with 2 Peter, the expression does add support for claims that the author knew and used the *Testament (Assumption) of Moses* in the crafting of the letter. Hence it is reasonable to conclude that Jude 9 finds a likely source in the *Testament (Assumption) of Moses*. The same cannot be claimed of the parallel text in 2 Pet 2:11. Without a similar reference to Michael, the expression in 2 Peter cannot be traced with confidence to any particular source. Thus parallels #10, #18, #19, and #13 exhibit evidence of borrowing according to the external source indicator.

Summary of Results

The preceding presentation identifies a total of eighteen parallels in 2 Peter that exhibit evidence of having been borrowed. Five parallels show disturbance of style (#13, #14, #17, #20, #24). Fourteen parallels exhibit fifteen indicators of logical progression from Jude. Of these fourteen parallels, five exhibit progression of structure in the form of dispersion (WC1, WC3, WC4, #9, #24), seven parallels show progression of structure according to the more-to-less portable indicator (WC3, #12, #14, #15, #16, #17, #18), one parallel exhibits progression of thought (#4), and three parallels show progression of function (#23, #24, WC5). Finally, for four of the parallels, the element in Jude has a likely external source while the parallel element in 2 Peter does not (#10, #13, #18, #19).

    The probability of borrowing based on all the observed indicators is shown in table 5.2. As noted earlier, it is not necessary to include all 30 parallels in the borrowing probability calculation tables shown in this chapter. See the illustrative example in chapter 2 for an explanation (p. 91). The indicator scores and the probability calculations for all the parallels are provided in appendix P. As shown in table 5.2, the collective probability of borrowing, CP_{bor}, is 0.86. Since this is a relatively high value, it is safe to conclude that the author of 2 Peter is likely to have borrowed material from Jude for at least one of the intertextual parallels.

---

43. NT scholars have suggested this as a likely possibility. See, e.g., Bauckham, *Jude, 2 Peter*, 100; Davids, *Letters of 2 Peter and Jude*, 83–84.

TABLE 5.2. Probability of borrowing (2 Peter)

No.	Description	Reference		Individual			Collective	
		Jude	2 Pet	BI	IP_{bor}	IP_{nbor}	CP_{nbor}	CP_{bor}
							1	0
4	all diligence	3	1:5	1	0.08	0.92	0.92	0.08
WC1	Opening Remarks	1–3	1:1–5	1	0.08	0.92	0.85	0.15
9	reminder of known things	5a	1:12a	1	0.08	0.92	0.79	0.21
10	angels kept for judgment	6	2:4	1	0.08	0.92	0.73	0.27
12	defile flesh, reject lordship, blaspheme glories	8	2:10	1	0.08	0.92	0.67	0.33
13	reverent angels	9	2:11	2	0.15	0.85	0.57	0.43
14	unreasoning animals	10	2:12	2	0.15	0.85	0.48	0.52
15	followed Balaam	11b	2:15	1	0.08	0.92	0.44	0.56
16	dangerous/ stained feasting	12a	2:13b	1	0.08	0.92	0.41	0.59
17	waterless clouds/ springs	12b	2:17a	2	0.15	0.85	0.35	0.65
18	reserved darkness	13b	2:17b	2	0.15	0.85	0.29	0.71
19	arrogant speaking	16b	2:18a	1	0.08	0.92	0.27	0.73
WC3	Reason for Concern	6–16	2:4–18a	1	0.08	0.92	0.25	0.75
20	remember apostolic words	17b	3:2	1	0.08	0.92	0.23	0.77
WC4	Heed Apostolic Teaching	17–18	3:2–3	1	0.08	0.92	0.21	0.79
23	keep from falling	24	3:17	1	0.08	0.92	0.20	0.80
24	our Savior Lord Jesus Christ	25a	3:18a	3	0.23	0.77	0.15	0.85
WC5	Closing Remarks	24–25	3:17–18	1	0.08	0.92	0.14	0.86

Evaluation of Alternative Scenarios

Having determined the collective probability of borrowing for each of the two directional scenarios, the next step is to evaluate the results to see which, if any, scenario is more likely. The final assessment depends on the combination of the two results.

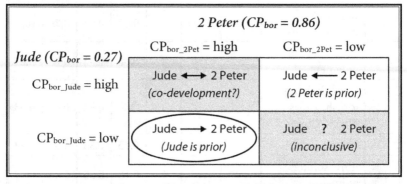

FIGURE 5.5. Significance of borrowing probabilities (Jude || 2 Peter)

According to the probability analysis of Jude's borrowing potential, the collective probability that the author of Jude borrowed parallel material is 0.27. Since this is a relatively low value, the final assessment of significance will be indicated by one of the two options on the bottom row of the chart in figure 5.5. The collective probability that the author of 2 Peter borrowed is relatively high at 0.86. Therefore, the final assessment will be indicated by one of the two options in the left column of the chart in figure 5.5. The significance of the two calculated borrowing probabilities is found at the intersection of the bottom row and the left column. Here the combination of the two results indicates that the author of 2 Peter most likely borrowed from the letter of Jude. Accordingly, the letter of Jude most likely is the prior document.

The Most Likely Direction of Borrowing

The probability analysis presented in this chapter produces a conclusive answer to the question of directionality. Specifically, the author of 2 Peter most likely borrowed material from Jude. This outcome is supported, not only by the majority scholarly opinion, but also by the sheer weight of evidence, as seen in a summary of the observed borrowing indicators.

TABLE 5.3. Summary of borrowing indicators (Jude || 2 Peter)

Scenario	Number of Parallels	Number of Indicators				
		Disturbance	Consistency	Progression	External Source	Total
1. The author of Jude borrowed from 2 Peter	4	0	0	4	0	4
2. The author of 2 Peter borrowed from Jude	18	5	0	15	4	24

As shown in table 5.3, there are six times more borrowing indicators for the second scenario in which the author of 2 Peter borrowed from Jude than there are for the first scenario in which the author of Jude borrowed from 2 Peter. Moreover, while Jude evidences only one type of borrowing indicator, 2 Peter exhibits evidence of three major categories of indicators. The strength of evidence for the second scenario is further apparent in the distribution of indicators across the parallels in each document. While the four indicators found for Jude are isolated in cluster WC2 (Jude 4), the twenty-four indicators found for 2 Peter are distributed across eighteen parallels that span much of the document. Five of these parallels show multiple indicators of having been borrowed (#13, #14, #17, #18, #24). Hence the weight of evidence favors the scenario in which the author of 2 Peter borrowed from Jude, not only because of the greater number of borrowing indicators, but also because of the broader distribution of parallels that show evidence of having been borrowed, and the higher average strength of evidence per parallel.

Although the identity of the borrowed parallel(s) remains unknown due to the non-deterministic nature of probability, application of stage 2 of the assessment methodology, as described in chapter 2, has produced the expected result that the author of 2 Peter is more likely to have borrowed material from the letter of Jude. Thus the test case involving Jude and 2 Peter demonstrates credibility of the assessment methodology at the high end of the probability scale. Application of the methodology to two documents that are strikingly similar does indeed yield an expected positive result, both for the likelihood of literary dependence and for the most likely direction of borrowing.

Conclusion

This book addresses a weakness in the growing field of New Testament Intertextuality Studies, which is founded on the belief that connections exist between NT writings and other ancient texts. As noted in the introduction, scholars historically have applied personal subjective reasoning to infer the likelihood of such connections based on perceived verbal and conceptual parallels between two texts. In the absence of commonly accepted criteria and objective analysis methods, however, claims of intertextual borrowing and the associated implications for interpretation have been inconsistent and often have lacked credibility, so much so that charges of speculation and misuse have been laid upon the field of parallels-study. NT scholarship, in particular, has been accused of "parallelomania," a practice of presuming an underlying literary connection and a given direction of borrowing based on perceived similarities between texts.[1] In the interest of establishing a more disciplined approach to the phenomena of intertextual parallels, this

---

1. The term "parallelomania" was coined by Samuel Sandmel in his 1961 Presidential Address to the Society of Biblical Literature ("Parallelomania," *JBL* 81, no. 1 [March 1962]: 1).

book has presented an innovative analytical assessment methodology for determining the significance of such literary parallels for the likelihood of intertextual borrowing.

The assessment methodology involves two separate stages, each of which follows a systematic approach that is designed to assess the likelihood of a particular event of interest, based on specific evidence of distinguishing characteristics of the particular event. The first stage addresses the question of literary dependence between two NT documents, independent of the direction of borrowing. The relevant indicators of literary dependence pertain to relational directness as evidenced by rarity of occurrence and degree of correspondence. The second stage then addresses the question of directionality, or who is most likely to have borrowed from whom. The relevant indicators of directionality involve direct-logical relationships related to the notion of borrowing, as evidenced by disturbance in the host document, consistency of borrowing practices, logical progression between parallel elements, and identification of a likely external source for one of the parallel elements.

The two-stage methodology is developed within the objective mathematical framework of probability theory. Each of the two stages focuses on cumulative evidence of directness or directionality that is observed in the intertextual parallels across entire documents. For stage 1, the final result is a collective probability of directness which represents the probability that *at least one* of the parallels derives from a direct literary connection. Similarly, stage 2 produces, for each of two interdependent documents, a collective probability of borrowing which represents the probability that *at least one* of the parallels was borrowed from the other document. The most likely direction of borrowing then is revealed by the combination of the two borrowing probabilities.

Two test cases demonstrate usage and reliability of the methodology for both negative and positive outcomes. In the negative test case involving two NT books that bear little resemblance to one another, namely James and Philippians, application of the methodology produces the expected negative result which indicates that literary dependence is highly unlikely. In the positive test case involving two NT documents that are remarkably similar, namely Jude and 2 Peter, application of the methodology produces the expected positive result which indicates that literary dependence is highly likely and that the author of 2 Peter most likely borrowed material from Jude. Together, these negative and positive test cases also demonstrate that the results are independent of the length of the documents, since James and Philippians are considerably longer than Jude and 2 Peter. Rather, the assessment methodology produces results that are based on cumulative evidence of relevant literary indicators.

Adoption of the analytical assessment methodology described in this book extends a much needed degree of objectivity to the task of evaluating NT literary parallels for the likelihood of intertextual borrowing. The test cases involving parallels between James and Philippians and between Jude and 2 Peter show that it is feasible to determine the likelihood of direct literary connections and the most likely direction of borrowing between two documents through mathematical analysis based on probability theory and relevant literary indicators. Rather than basing conclusions on what seems most reasonable in the eyes of individual interpreters, the assessment methodology allows for consistent and reliable results, regardless of who performs the assessment.

The repeatable analytical nature of the methodology gives rise to a host of potentially broad-sweeping implications. Most immediate are a variety of implications for pairs of documents for which the likelihood of literary dependence is positive and the direction of borrowing is conclusive. First, intertextual borrowing has obvious implications for relative dating of the documents. If the author of one document is highly likely to have borrowed material from another document, then it may be concluded with a high level of confidence that the borrowed document predates the borrowing document. Second, intertextual borrowing can help clarify text critical issues involving variant readings in the Greek manuscript traditions of the NT. Indeed, certain variants might be best explained by intertextual borrowing in the original composition process rather than by deviations in the later transmission process. Third, in the case of NT || NT parallels that involve LXX quotations, the borrowed NT text must be considered as a potential source for the quotations in the borrowing document. This may help identify the most likely source of such quotations, especially if verbal correspondence is much higher with the borrowed NT text than with all known LXX texts. Fourth, intertextual borrowing provides justification for interpreting parallel passages in light of one another since the borrowing document most likely reflects the author's interpretation of the borrowed text. This may help clarify the intended meanings of difficult or ambiguous texts that have long been a point of conflict among biblical scholars. Fifth, application to multiple pairs of documents can result in a literary relationship map that shows how the pieces of the early Christian literary puzzle might relate to one another. Such a map would establish a literary basis from which to evaluate NT development scenarios, including matters of origin, circulation patterns, and limits for dating of the documents. In light of these types of broad-sweeping implications, application of the methodology to selected pairs of NT documents has the potential to shed new light on some of the most intriguing mysteries of the NT, including the order of the Synoptic Gospels, the background of thought and chronology of the NT epistles, and even authorship of the writings.[2]

This assessment methodology might also have important indirect implications for popular tradition source theories and their significance for NT intertextuality studies. As noted in the preceding pages, intertextual borrowing is only one of the proposed explanations offered for the curious presence of so many literary parallels between books of the NT. The major alternative explanation is that NT || NT parallels arise from the authors having made independent use of common traditions. Independent use of shared traditions, in fact, is a very popular explanation for intertextual parallels that exhibit a low degree of verbal correspondence. Although such parallels raise questions of possible direct literary relationships between the documents, they are viewed more often as supporting evidence for theories about the existence, nature, and use of common source traditions. While such theories are certainly possible and perhaps even likely in many cases, the methodology presented in this book calls to question those explanations that point to the use of shared hypothetical traditions.

Arguments which claim that intertextual parallels derive from the authors' independent use of common traditions exhibit a weakness in the deductive reasoning process that is used to link intertextual parallels with traditions. The basic argument is exemplified in E. G. Selwyn's influential study of traditions in 1 Peter.[3] Selwyn approaches the question of documentary interdependence from a *Formgeschichte* perspective in an attempt

---

2. For example, application of the assessment methodology to 1 Peter and Hebrews reveals, not only a high probability of intertextual borrowing, but also new evidence for authorship of both NT books. See Elizabeth A. Myers, *Intertextual Borrowing between 1 Peter and Hebrews: Probability of Literary Dependence and the Most Likely Direction of Borrowing* (Cody, WY: Pistos Ktistes Publishing LLC, 2020); Elizabeth A. Myers, *Authorship of 1 Peter and Hebrews: New Evidence in Light of Probable Intertextual Borrowing* (Cody, WY: Pistos Ktistes Publishing LLC, 2020).

3. Edward Gordon Selwyn, "Essay II: Bearing of Evidence on the Supposed Dependence of 1 Peter on Other Epistles," in *The First Epistle of St. Peter: The Greek Text with Introduction, Notes and Essays* (London: Macmillan & Co. Ltd., 1955), 365–466.

to understand "the nature and history of the Forms in which the earliest Christian preaching and teaching were drawn up and transmitted."[4] He assumes that traditions of the early church developed in a wide variety of forms due to the different needs of various communities and the different styles and objectives of those called to preach and teach. Thus, according to Selwyn, the various forms serve as windows through which to discover the developmental shape of early Christian traditions. Assuming that intertextual parallels are founded on underlying forms, Selwyn hypothesizes the nature of the forms from selected sets of parallels and then shows how the forms might reflect different stages of development in early Christian tradition. According to Selwyn, the idea that common catechetical and liturgical sources underlie most of the epistles is "proven beyond a doubt; but the isolation and differentiation of the sources, and the attribution of particular pieces of teaching to this or to that source, are a more difficult and more dubious matter."[5] The problem of sources raised by Selwyn highlights a key weakness in the deductive approach. Since the forms are hypothesized, there are no tangible sources with which to demonstrate an indirect genealogical relationship between parallel texts through a common tradition form. From Selwyn's *Formgeschichte* perspective, an indirect genealogical relationship is inferred from the existence of intertextual parallels, which are used to define the shape of the forms.

Deductive reasoning is also employed from the parallels perspective, where scholars attempt to explain the existence of NT || NT parallels. The arguments generally assume the existence of underlying traditions and then show how parallels might be traced to certain traditions.[6] The necessary indirect genealogical relationship that would enable the rise of intertextual parallels is implicitly inferred from the presumed existence of common tradition forms. As mentioned above, however, Selwyn infers an indirect

---

4. Selwyn, "Essay II," 365.

5. Selwyn, "Essay II," 459.

6. For examples involving 1 Peter and Hebrews, see L. D. Hurst, *The Epistle to the Hebrews: Its Background of Thought*, SNTSMS 65 (Cambridge: Cambridge University Press, 1990), 129; Paul J. Achtemeier, *1 Peter: A Commentary on First Peter*, Hermeneia (Minneapolis, MN: Fortress Press, 1996), 12–23; Harold W. Attridge, *The Epistle to the Hebrews: A Commentary on the Epistle to the Hebrews*, Hermeneia (Philadelphia, PA: Fortress Press, 1989), 28–31; John H. Elliott, *1 Peter*, AB 37B (New Haven: Yale University Press, 2001), 20–40; J. N. D. Kelly, *A Commentary on the Epistles of Peter and of Jude*, BNTC (London: Adam & Charles Black, 1969), 12–13; Ceslas Spicq, "La Iª Petri et le témoignage évangélique de Saint Pierre," *ST* 20 (1966): 37–61.

genealogical relationship from the existence of intertextual parallels. In both cases, then, the relationship that links parallels to hypothesized traditional forms is inferred. The combination of these two perspectives of deductive reasoning adds an element of circularity to the whole argument. While the explanation for intertextual parallels is based on the presumed existence of tradition forms, the hypothesized tradition forms are based on the existence of intertextual parallels. Moreover, the entire argument rests on the existence of an indirect genealogical relationship that is inferred from both perspectives. This does not necessarily imply that tradition source theories are misguided, only that the arguments are not conclusive and therefore should be applied with caution.

The assessment methodology presented in this book differs from the *Formgeschichte* approach in that the nature of a parallel relationship is derived directly from evidence of directness and borrowing that is found in tangible intertextual parallels. Given the soundness and relevance of the selected literary indicators, direct demonstration of directness and directionality in an intertextual relationship seems more defensible than claims of an indirect relationship that is inferred from hypothesized forms, which in turn are based on an indirect relationship that is inferred from the observed intertextual parallels. Hence the direct analytical nature of this assessment methodology calls to question both the rationale behind commonly accepted tradition source theories and the widespread practice of attributing NT || NT intertextual parallels to such traditions.

It is hoped that the assessment methodology presented in this book will not only help illuminate the mystery of NT || NT parallels, but also stimulate further research and scholarly dialogue on NT intertextuality assessment methods. The potential implications are far reaching, as the present methodology demonstrates feasibility of a mathematical approach and is directly applicable to any of the NT documents. Moreover, it can easily be adapted for use with documents in other collections of ancient works, including the Septuagint, the Pseudepigrapha, and even the Hebrew Bible. Applications such as these have important implications for exegetical study of interdependent books as well as for investigation of the full extent of intertextuality involving the books of the NT and other early Christian and Jewish writings. Through the use of analytical methodologies such as this, future studies of New Testament intertextuality have the potential, not just to contribute significant historical-hermeneutical insights, but to do so in a manner that avoids charges of speculation and misuse that are often associated with "parallelomania."

APPENDIX A

Probability of Directness
(Illustrative Example)

TABLE A.1. Indicator Scores (Illustrative Example)

No.	Rarity	Basic Units	Gram.	Struc.	Mean.	Funct.	Mem.
1	10.00	0.00	2.00	0	2	0	1
2	7.00	0.00	2.00	0	2	1	2
3	4.00	0.00	1.00	0	2	2	0
4	8.00	1.00	0.50	1	2	2	2
5	7.00	0.50	0.33	2	2	2	2
6	6.00	0.60	0.20	2	2	1	2
7	5.00	1.33	2.00	1	1	1	3
8	7.00	0.80	0.75	2	1	2	3
9	3.00	1.33	1.00	1	2	1	3
10	9.00	1.75	2.00	1	2	1	4
11	8.00	0.75	0.75	1	2	1	4
12	8.00	1.50	1.50	1	2	1	4

TABLE A.1. *continued*

No.	Rarity	Basic Units	Gram.	Struc.	Mean.	Funct.	Mem.
13	7.00	0.00	0.00	0	1	1	0
14	9.00	0.00	0.00	2	2	1	0

NOTE: Data is fabricated to illustrate the assessment methodology and does not represent any actual intertextual parallels.

TABLE A.2. Probability Calculation (Illustrative Example)

No.	EM	DI	IP_{dir}	IP_{ndir}	CP_{ndir}	CP_{dir}
					1	0
1	0.009	0.134	0.006	0.994	0.994	0.006
2	0.009	0.125	0.005	0.995	0.989	0.011
3	0.009	0.080	0.003	0.997	0.986	0.014
4	0.054	0.884	0.037	0.963	0.950	0.050
5	0.027	0.424	0.018	0.982	0.933	0.067
6	0.071	0.986	0.041	0.959	0.895	0.105
7	0.134	1.920	0.080	0.920	0.823	0.177
8	0.152	2.512	0.105	0.895	0.737	0.263
9	0.214	2.643	0.110	0.890	0.656	0.344
10	0.313	6.484	0.270	0.730	0.479	0.521
11	0.366	6.406	0.267	0.733	0.351	0.649
12	0.339	6.446	0.269	0.731	0.257	0.743
13	0.027	0.241	0.010	0.990	0.254	0.746
14	0.027	0.375	0.016	0.984	0.250	0.750

Probability of Borrowing
(Illustrative Example)

TABLE B.1. Indicator Scores (document_A)

No.	DL	DS	DM	DF	CL	CS	CI	CF	PL	PS	PT	PF	ES
1	0	0	0	0	0	0	0	0	0	0	0	0	0
2	0	0	1	0	0	0	0	0	0	0	0	0	0
3	0	0	1	0	0	0	0	0	0	0	0	0	0
4	0	0	0	0	0	1	0	0	0	0	0	0	1
5	0	1	0	0	0	1	0	0	0	0	0	0	0
6	0	1	1	0	0	1	0	0	0	0	0	0	0
7	0	1	0	0	0	0	0	0	0	0	1	0	1
8	0	0	0	0	0	0	0	0	0	0	1	0	0
9	1	0	0	0	0	0	0	0	0	0	1	0	1
10	0	1	0	0	0	0	0	0	0	1	0	1	0
11	0	1	0	0	0	0	0	0	0	1	0	1	0
12	0	1	0	0	0	0	0	0	0	0	0	1	0

TABLE B.1. *continued*

No.	DL	DS	DM	DF	CL	CS	CI	CF	PL	PS	PT	PF	ES
13	0	0	0	0	0	0	0	0	0	0	0	0	0
14	0	0	0	0	0	0	0	0	0	0	0	1	0

NOTE: Data is fabricated to illustrate the assessment methodology and does not represent any actual intertextual parallels.

TABLE B.2. Probability Calculation (document_A)

No.	BI	IP_{bor}	IP_{nbor}	CP_{nbor}	CP_{bor}
				1	0
1	0	0.00	1.00	1.00	0.00
2	1	0.08	0.92	0.92	0.08
3	1	0.08	0.92	0.85	0.15
4	2	0.15	0.85	0.72	0.28
5	2	0.15	0.85	0.61	0.39
6	3	0.23	0.77	0.47	0.53
7	3	0.23	0.77	0.36	0.64
8	1	0.08	0.92	0.33	0.67
9	3	0.23	0.77	0.26	0.74
10	3	0.23	0.77	0.20	0.80
11	3	0.23	0.77	0.15	0.85
12	2	0.15	0.85	0.13	0.87
13	0	0.00	1.00	0.13	0.87
14	1	0.08	0.92	0.12	0.88

TABLE B.3. Indicator Scores (document_B)

No.	DL	DS	DM	DF	CL	CS	CI	CF	PL	PS	PT	PF	ES
1	0	0	0	0	0	0	0	0	1	0	0	0	0
2	1	0	0	0	0	0	0	0	1	0	0	0	0
3	0	0	0	0	0	0	0	0	0	0	0	0	0
4	0	0	0	0	0	0	0	0	0	0	0	0	0
5	0	0	0	0	0	0	0	0	0	0	0	0	0
6	0	0	0	0	0	0	0	0	0	0	0	0	0
7	0	0	0	0	0	0	0	0	0	0	0	0	0
8	0	0	0	0	0	0	0	0	0	0	0	0	0
9	0	0	0	0	0	0	0	0	0	0	0	0	0
10	0	0	0	0	0	0	0	0	0	0	0	0	0
11	0	0	0	0	0	0	0	0	0	0	0	0	0
12	0	1	0	0	0	0	0	0	0	0	0	0	0
13	0	0	0	0	0	0	0	0	0	0	0	0	0
14	0	0	0	0	0	0	0	0	0	0	0	0	0

NOTE: Data is fabricated to illustrate the assessment methodology and does not represent any actual intertextual parallels.

TABLE B.4. Probability Calculation (document_B)

No.	BI	IP_{bor}	IP_{nbor}	CP_{nbor}	CP_{bor}
				1	0
1	1	0.08	0.92	0.92	0.08
2	2	0.15	0.85	0.78	0.22
3	0	0.00	1.00	0.78	0.22
4	0	0.00	1.00	0.78	0.22
5	0	0.00	1.00	0.78	0.22
6	0	0.00	1.00	0.78	0.22
7	0	0.00	1.00	0.78	0.22
8	0	0.00	1.00	0.78	0.22
9	0	0.00	1.00	0.78	0.22
10	0	0.00	1.00	0.78	0.22
11	0	0.00	1.00	0.78	0.22
12	1	0.08	0.92	0.72	0.28
13	0	0.00	1.00	0.72	0.28
14	0	0.00	1.00	0.72	0.28

Appendix C

List of Parallels
(James || Philippians)

The list of parallels selected for the probability analysis is based on the qualifying criteria established for the project. These involve the rarity of occurrence and correspondence scores derived from particular features of the parallel texts, as stipulated in the procedure section of chapter 3. For convenience, each parallel that meets the qualifying condition is assigned a number and a descriptive reference label.

TABLE C.1. Parallels (James || Philippians)

No.	Descriptive Label	Reference	
		Jas	Phil
1	suppose (οἴομαι)	1:7	1:17
2	boast (καυχάομαι)	1:9	3:3
3	giving (δόσις)	1:17	4:15
4	remain (παραμένω)	1:25	1:25
5	thoughts/disputes (διαλογισμός)	2:4	2:14

Table C.1. *continued*

No.	Descriptive Label	Reference	
		Jas	Phil
6	selfish ambition (ἐριθεία)	3:14	2:3
7	earthly (ἐπίγειος)	3:15	3:19
8	pure (ἁγνός)	3:17	4:8
9	gentle (ἐπιεικής)	3:17	4:5
10	envy (φθόνος)	4:5	1:15
11	yearn (ἐπιποθέω)	4:5	1:8
12	gain (κερδαίνω)	4:13	3:8
13	coming (παρουσία)	5:7	1:26
14	confess (ἐξομολογέω)	5:16	2:11
15	slave of Jesus Christ	1:1	1:1
16	perfect work	1:4	1:6
17	if anyone thinks	1:26	3:4
18	fruit of righteousness	3:18	1:11
19	the Lord is near	5:8	4:5
20	in the name of the Lord/Jesus	5:10	2:10

Rarity of Occurrence Scores
(James || Philippians)

Rarity of occurrence scores are based on the total number of occurrences and the number of works in which they occur in the NT, the Septuagint, the works of Philo, the works of Josephus, the Greek Pseudepigrapha, and the Apostolic Fathers, plus the worst-case and best-case scenarios for Greco-Roman literature.

TABLE D.1. Number of occurrences and works (NT, LXX, Philo)

No.	NT		LXX		Philo	
	#occur	#works	#occur	#works	#occur	#works
1	1	1	22	8	228	34
2	34	5	41	13	0	0
3	0	0	23	5	4	3
4	2	2	9	5	14	11
5	12	6	25	8	0	0
6	3	3	0	0	0	0

TABLE D.1. *continued*

No.	NT		LXX		Philo	
	#occur	#works	#occur	#works	#occur	#works
7	4	3	0	0	24	13
8	6	5	13	6	7	4
9	3	3	4	3	21	11
10	7	7	4	3	45	19
11	6	5	13	6	6	4
12	15	6	0	0	5	5
13	20	7	4	3	5	5
14	8	5	136	16	7	1
15	4	4	0	0	0	0
16	0	0	14	9	8	6
17	5	2	0	0	0	0
18	1	1	4	2	0	0
19	0	0	13	8	1	1
20	3	1	0	0	0	0

TABLE D.2. Number of occurrences and works (Jos., Pseud., AF)

No.	Josephus		Pseudepigrapha		Apostolic Fathers	
	#occur	#works	#occur	#works	#occur	#works
1	189	4	11	5	10	4
2	1	1	10	8	5	3
3	21	3	7	2	1	1
4	47	3	2	2	5	5
5	1	1	8	4	1	1
6	0	0	0	0	1	1
7	2	1	9	7	12	6
8	5	2	38	5	11	4
9	23	3	8	4	4	2
10	49	4	25	11	4	1
11	0	0	0	0	0	0
12	27	2	2	2	1	1
13	32	3	12	9	4	3
14	8	2	12	6	15	8
15	0	0	0	0	0	0
16	8	2	2	2	4	4
17	0	0	0	0	0	0
18	0	0	1	1	1	1
19	0	0	1	1	2	2
20	0	0	0	0	1	1

TABLE D.3. Rarity of occurrence scores (James || Philippians, worst case)

No.	rarity_NT	rarity_LXX	rarity_Philo	rarity_Jos.	rarity_Pseud.	rarity_AF	rarity_G-R (worst)	Weighted Sum	Rarity Score
1	1.33	0.28	0.06	0.34	0.44	0.50	0.00	0.22	1.10
2	0.34	0.18	2.00	1.33	0.37	0.69	0.00	0.31	1.56
3	2.00	0.37	0.73	0.49	0.72	1.33	0.00	0.43	2.14
4	1.00	0.47	0.28	0.44	1.00	0.57	0.00	0.33	1.66
5	0.39	0.27	2.00	1.33	0.53	1.33	0.00	0.40	2.02
6	0.80	2.00	2.00	2.00	2.00	1.33	0.00	0.86	4.31
7	0.73	2.00	0.21	1.17	0.40	0.39	0.00	0.40	2.00
8	0.54	0.38	0.56	0.79	0.34	0.49	0.00	0.21	1.07
9	0.80	0.73	0.24	0.48	0.53	0.83	0.00	0.30	1.51
10	0.44	0.73	0.14	0.37	0.23	1.00	0.00	0.24	1.21
11	0.54	0.38	0.58	2.00	2.00	2.00	0.00	0.60	2.98
12	0.37	2.00	0.57	0.57	1.00	1.33	0.00	0.57	2.84
13	0.31	0.73	0.57	0.46	0.32	0.73	0.00	0.26	1.30
14	0.49	0.13	0.89	0.70	0.39	0.32	0.00	0.20	1.00
15	0.67	2.00	2.00	2.00	2.00	2.00	0.00	0.91	4.54
16	2.00	0.31	0.45	0.70	1.00	0.67	0.00	0.39	1.94
17	0.79	2.00	2.00	2.00	2.00	2.00	0.00	0.91	4.57
18	1.33	0.83	2.00	2.00	1.33	1.33	0.00	0.65	3.24
19	2.00	0.33	1.33	2.00	1.33	1.00	0.00	0.55	2.73
20	1.07	2.00	2.00	2.00	2.00	1.33	0.00	0.88	4.38

Table D.4. Rarity of occurrence scores (James || Philippians, best case)

No.	rarity_NT	rarity_LXX	rarity_Philo	rarity_Jos.	rarity_Pseud.	rarity_AF	rarity_G-R (best)	Weighted Sum	Rarity Score
1	1.33	0.28	0.06	0.34	0.44	0.50	2.00	1.24	6.20
2	0.34	0.18	2.00	1.33	0.37	0.69	2.00	1.33	6.66
3	2.00	0.37	0.73	0.49	0.72	1.33	2.00	1.45	7.24
4	1.00	0.47	0.28	0.44	1.00	0.57	2.00	1.35	6.76
5	0.39	0.27	2.00	1.33	0.53	1.33	2.00	1.42	7.12
6	0.80	2.00	2.00	2.00	2.00	1.33	2.00	1.88	9.41
7	0.73	2.00	0.21	1.17	0.40	0.39	2.00	1.42	7.10
8	0.54	0.38	0.56	0.79	0.34	0.49	2.00	1.23	6.17
9	0.80	0.73	0.24	0.48	0.53	0.83	2.00	1.32	6.61
10	0.44	0.73	0.14	0.37	0.23	1.00	2.00	1.26	6.31
11	0.54	0.38	0.58	2.00	2.00	2.00	2.00	1.62	8.08
12	0.37	2.00	0.57	0.57	1.00	1.33	2.00	1.59	7.94
13	0.31	0.73	0.57	0.46	0.32	0.73	2.00	1.28	6.40
14	0.49	0.13	0.89	0.70	0.39	0.32	2.00	1.22	6.10
15	0.67	2.00	2.00	2.00	2.00	2.00	2.00	1.93	9.64
16	2.00	0.31	0.45	0.70	1.00	0.67	2.00	1.41	7.04
17	0.79	2.00	2.00	2.00	2.00	2.00	2.00	1.93	9.67
18	1.33	0.83	2.00	2.00	1.33	1.33	2.00	1.67	8.34
19	2.00	0.33	1.33	2.00	1.33	1.00	2.00	1.57	7.83
20	1.07	2.00	2.00	2.00	2.00	1.33	2.00	1.90	9.48

Verbal Correspondence Scores
(James || Philippians)

Table E.1. Lexical, grammatical correspondence (James || Philippians)

No.	James		Philippians		Basic Units			Gram. Constructs		
	#units	#const.	#units	#const.	#ident.	#relate	score	#ident.	#equiv.	score
1	1	1	1	1	NA	NA	0.00	0	1	1.00
2	1	1	1	1	NA	NA	0.00	0	1	1.00
3	1	1	1	1	NA	NA	0.00	0	1	1.00
4	1	1	1	1	NA	NA	0.00	0	1	1.00
5	1	1	1	1	NA	NA	0.00	1	0	2.00
6	1	1	1	1	NA	NA	0.00	1	0	2.00
7	1	1	1	1	NA	NA	0.00	0	1	1.00
8	1	1	1	1	NA	NA	0.00	0	1	1.00
9	1	1	1	1	NA	NA	0.00	0	1	1.00
10	1	1	1	1	NA	NA	0.00	1	0	2.00
11	1	1	1	1	NA	NA	0.00	0	1	1.00
12	1	1	1	1	NA	NA	0.00	0	1	1.00

TABLE E.1. *continued*

No.	James		Philippians		Basic Units			Gram. Constructs		
	#units	#const.	#units	#const.	#ident.	#relate	score	#ident.	#equiv.	score
13	1	1	1	1	NA	NA	0.00	1	0	2.00
14	1	1	1	1	NA	NA	0.00	0	1	1.00
15	3	3	3	3	3	0	2.00	2	1	1.67
16	6	5	7	5	2	1	0.71	1	1	0.60
17	3	3	3	3	3	0	2.00	3	0	2.00
18	3	3	2	2	2	0	1.33	1	1	1.00
19	5	3	3	2	3	0	1.20	0	2	0.67
20	4	3	4	3	3	1	1.75	3	0	2.00

Probability of Directness
(James || Philippians, Best Case)

TABLE F.1. Indicator Scores (James || Philippians, best case)

No.	Rarity	Basic Units	Gram.	Struc.	Mean.	Funct.	Mem.
1	6.20	0.00	1.00	0	2	0	0
2	6.66	0.00	1.00	0	2	1	0
3	7.24	0.00	1.00	0	2	0	0
4	6.76	0.00	1.00	0	2	0	0
5	7.12	0.00	2.00	0	0	0	0
6	9.41	0.00	2.00	0	2	1	0
7	7.10	0.00	1.00	0	2	2	0
8	6.17	0.00	1.00	0	2	1	0
9	6.61	0.00	1.00	0	2	1	0
10	6.31	0.00	2.00	0	2	0	0
11	8.08	0.00	1.00	0	2	0	0
12	7.94	0.00	1.00	0	2	0	0

TABLE F.1. *continued*

No.	Rarity	Basic Units	Gram.	Struc.	Mean.	Funct.	Mem.
13	6.40	0.00	2.00	0	2	0	0
14	6.10	0.00	1.00	0	2	0	0
15	9.64	2.00	1.67	1	2	2	0
16	7.04	0.71	0.60	0	0	0	0
17	9.67	2.00	2.00	2	2	1	0
18	8.34	1.33	1.00	2	0	0	0
19	7.83	1.20	0.67	2	2	1	0
20	9.48	1.75	2.00	2	0	1	0

NOTE: Scores include the best-case values for rarity of occurrence.

TABLE F.2. Probability Calculation (James || Philippians, best case)

No.	EM	DI	IP_{dir}	IP_{ndir}	CP_{ndir}	CP_{dir}
					1	0
1	0.009	0.082	0.003	0.997	0.997	0.003
2	0.009	0.095	0.004	0.996	0.993	0.007
3	0.009	0.091	0.004	0.996	0.989	0.011
4	0.009	0.087	0.004	0.996	0.985	0.015
5	0.009	0.081	0.003	0.997	0.982	0.018
6	0.009	0.129	0.005	0.995	0.977	0.023
7	0.009	0.108	0.005	0.995	0.972	0.028
8	0.009	0.091	0.004	0.996	0.969	0.031
9	0.009	0.095	0.004	0.996	0.965	0.035
10	0.009	0.092	0.004	0.996	0.961	0.039
11	0.009	0.099	0.004	0.996	0.957	0.043
12	0.009	0.098	0.004	0.996	0.953	0.047
13	0.009	0.093	0.004	0.996	0.950	0.050
14	0.009	0.081	0.003	0.997	0.946	0.054
15	0.027	0.490	0.020	0.980	0.927	0.073
16	0.054	0.448	0.019	0.981	0.910	0.090
17	0.027	0.500	0.021	0.979	0.891	0.109
18	0.018	0.226	0.009	0.991	0.882	0.118
19	0.027	0.394	0.016	0.984	0.868	0.132
20	0.036	0.580	0.024	0.976	0.847	0.153

NOTE: Calculation uses the best-case values for rarity of occurrence.

Probability of Directness
(James || Philippians, Worse Case)

TABLE G.1. Indicator Scores (James || Philippians, worse case)

No.	Rarity	Basic Units	Gram.	Struc.	Mean.	Funct.	Mem.
1	1.10	0.00	1.00	0	2	0	0
2	1.56	0.00	1.00	0	2	1	0
3	2.14	0.00	1.00	0	2	0	0
4	1.66	0.00	1.00	0	2	0	0
5	2.02	0.00	2.00	0	0	0	0
6	4.31	0.00	2.00	0	2	1	0
7	2.00	0.00	1.00	0	2	2	0
8	1.07	0.00	1.00	0	2	1	0
9	1.51	0.00	1.00	0	2	1	0
10	1.21	0.00	2.00	0	2	0	0
11	2.98	0.00	1.00	0	2	0	0
12	2.84	0.00	1.00	0	2	0	0

TABLE G.1. *continued*

No.	Rarity	Basic Units	Gram.	Struc.	Mean.	Funct.	Mem.
13	1.30	0.00	2.00	0	2	0	0
14	1.00	0.00	1.00	0	2	0	0
15	4.54	2.00	1.67	1	2	2	0
16	1.94	0.71	0.60	0	0	0	0
17	4.57	2.00	2.00	2	2	1	0
18	3.24	1.33	1.00	2	0	0	0
19	2.73	1.20	0.67	2	2	1	0
20	4.38	1.75	2.00	2	0	1	0

NOTE: Scores include the worst-case values for rarity of occurrence.

Table G.2. Probability Calculation (James || Philippians, worse case)

No.	EM	DI	IP_{dir}	IP_{ndir}	CP_{ndir}	CP_{dir}
					1	0
1	0.009	0.037	0.002	0.998	0.998	0.002
2	0.009	0.050	0.002	0.998	0.996	0.004
3	0.009	0.046	0.002	0.998	0.995	0.005
4	0.009	0.042	0.002	0.998	0.993	0.007
5	0.009	0.036	0.001	0.999	0.991	0.009
6	0.009	0.083	0.003	0.997	0.988	0.012
7	0.009	0.063	0.003	0.997	0.985	0.015
8	0.009	0.045	0.002	0.998	0.983	0.017
9	0.009	0.049	0.002	0.998	0.981	0.019
10	0.009	0.046	0.002	0.998	0.980	0.020
11	0.009	0.053	0.002	0.998	0.977	0.023
12	0.009	0.052	0.002	0.998	0.975	0.025
13	0.009	0.047	0.002	0.998	0.973	0.027
14	0.009	0.036	0.001	0.999	0.972	0.028
15	0.027	0.354	0.015	0.985	0.958	0.042
16	0.054	0.174	0.007	0.993	0.951	0.049
17	0.027	0.364	0.015	0.985	0.936	0.064
18	0.018	0.135	0.006	0.994	0.931	0.069
19	0.027	0.257	0.011	0.989	0.921	0.079
20	0.036	0.398	0.017	0.983	0.906	0.094

Note: Calculation uses the worst-case values for rarity of occurrence.

Probability of Directness
(James || Philippians, Worst Case)

TABLE H.1. Indicator Scores (James || Philippians, worst case)

No.	Rarity	Basic Units	Gram.	Struc.	Mean.	Funct.	Mem.
3	2.14	0.00	1.00	0	2	0	0
5	2.02	0.00	2.00	0	0	0	0
6	4.31	0.00	2.00	0	2	1	0
7	2.00	0.00	1.00	0	2	2	0
11	2.98	0.00	1.00	0	2	0	0
12	2.84	0.00	1.00	0	2	0	0
15	4.54	2.00	1.67	1	2	2	0
17	4.57	2.00	2.00	2	2	1	0
18	3.24	1.33	1.00	2	0	0	0
19	2.73	1.20	0.67	2	2	1	0
20	4.38	1.75	2.00	2	0	1	0

NOTE: Scores include the worst-case values for rarity of occurrence.

TABLE H.2. Probability Calculation (James || Philippians, worst case)

No.	EM	DI	IP_{dir}	IP_{ndir}	CP_{ndir}	CP_{dir}
					1	0
3	0.009	0.046	0.002	0.998	0.998	0.002
5	0.009	0.036	0.001	0.999	0.997	0.003
6	0.009	0.083	0.003	0.997	0.993	0.007
7	0.009	0.063	0.003	0.997	0.991	0.009
11	0.009	0.053	0.002	0.998	0.988	0.012
12	0.009	0.052	0.002	0.998	0.986	0.014
15	0.027	0.354	0.015	0.985	0.972	0.028
17	0.027	0.364	0.015	0.985	0.957	0.043
18	0.018	0.135	0.006	0.994	0.952	0.048
19	0.027	0.257	0.011	0.989	0.941	0.059
20	0.036	0.398	0.017	0.983	0.926	0.074

NOTE: Calculation uses the worst-case values for rarity of occurrence.

Abbreviations for Grammatical Properties

The abbreviations used in this book to describe grammatical properties of parallel texts are defined in the tables below. The different parts of speech are parsed as follows:

Finite Verbs: Tense-Voice-Mood-Person-Number
Participles: Tense-Voice-Type-Gender-Number-Case
Infinitives: Tense-Voice-Type
Nouns and Nominals: Gender-Number-Case

TABLE I.1. Abbreviations (verbs and verbals)

Tense	P = present; I = imperfect; A = aorist; F = future; Prf = perfect; Plu = pluperfect
Voice	A = active; M = middle; P = passive
Mood	Ind = indicative; Sub = subjunctive; Opt = optative; Imp = imperative;
Type	Ptc = participle; Inf = infinitive
Person	1 = 1st person; 2 = 2nd person; 3 = 3rd person
Number	S = singular; P = plural

TABLE I.2. Abbreviations (nouns and nominals)

Gender	M = masculine; F = feminine
Number	S = singular; P = plural
Case	N = nominative; V = vocative; G = genitive; D = dative; A = accusative

APPENDIX J

List of Parallels
(Jude || 2 Peter)

The list of parallels selected for the probability analysis is based on the qualifying criteria established for the project. These involve the rarity of occurrence and correspondence scores derived from particular features of the parallel texts, as stipulated in the procedure section of chapter 4 (same as in chapter 3). For convenience, each parallel that meets the qualifying condition is assigned a number and a descriptive reference label.

Table J.1. Parallels (Jude || 2 Peter)

No.	Descriptive Label	Reference	
		Jude	2 Pet
1	slave of Jesus Christ	1a	1:1a
2	to those related in God and Jesus Christ	1b	1:1b
3	mercy/grace and peace be multiplied to you	2	1:2a
4	all diligence	3	1:5
WC1	Opening Remarks	1–3	1:1–5

TABLE J.1. *continued*

No.	Descriptive Label	Reference	
		Jude	2 Pet
5	ones who sneak in	4a	2:1b
6	long marked for judgment	4b	2:3c
7	licentious behavior	4c	2:2
8	denying the Master	4d	2:1c
WC2	Harmful Infiltrators	4	2:1–3
9	reminder of known things	5a	1:12a
10	angels kept for judgment	6	2:4
11	example of Sodom and Gomorrah	7	2:6
12	defile flesh, reject lordship, blaspheme glories	8	2:10
13	reverent angels	9	2:11
14	unreasoning animals	10	2:12
15	followed Balaam	11b	2:15
16	dangerous/stained feasting	12a	2:13b
17	waterless clouds/springs	12b	2:17a
18	reserved darkness	13b	2:17b
19	arrogant speaking	16b	2:18a
WC3	Reason for Concern	6–16	2:4–18a
20	remember apostolic words	17b	3:2
21	mockers in the last	18a	3:3b
22	following after their own lusts	18b	3:3c
WC4	Heed Apostolic Teaching	17–18	3:2–3
23	keep from falling	24	3:17
24	our Savior Lord Jesus Christ	25a	3:18a
25	glory both now and forever	25b	3:18b
WC5	Closing Remarks	24–25	3:17–18

Rarity of Occurrence Scores
(Jude || 2 Peter)

Rarity of occurrence scores are based on the total number of occurrences and the number of works in which they occur in the NT, the Septuagint, the works of Philo, the works of Josephus, the Greek Pseudepigrapha, and the Apostolic Fathers, plus the worst-case and best-case scenarios for Greco-Roman literature. For this project, the rarity score of a cluster is equal to the score of its rarest member.

TABLE K.1. Number of occurrences and works (NT, LXX, Philo)

No.	NT		LXX		Philo	
	#occur	#works	#occur	#works	#occur	#works
1	4	4	0	0	0	0
2	4	4	0	0	0	0
3	1	1	0	0	0	0
4	0	0	0	0	0	0
5	1	1	0	0	7	6

Table K.1. *continued*

No.	NT		LXX		Philo	
	#occur	#works	#occur	#works	#occur	#works
6	0	0	0	0	0	0
7	6	6	2	2	3	2
8	0	0	0	0	0	0
9	0	0	0	0	0	0
10	0	0	0	0	0	0
11	0	0	1	1	1	1
12	0	0	0	0	0	0
13	0	0	0	0	0	0
14	0	0	0	0	0	0
15	0	0	0	0	0	0
16	0	0	0	0	0	0
17	0	0	0	0	0	0
18	0	0	0	0	0	0
19	0	0	1	1	0	0
20	0	0	0	0	0	0
21	0	0	0	0	0	0
22	0	0	0	0	0	0
23	0	0	0	0	0	0
24	0	0	0	0	0	0
25	0	0	0	0	0	0

TABLE K.2. Number of occurrences and works (Jos., Pseud., AF)

No.	Josephus		Pseudepigrapha		Apostolic Fathers	
	#occur	#works	#occur	#works	#occur	#works
1	0	0	0	0	0	0
2	0	0	0	0	1	1
3	0	0	0	0	3	3
4	4	1	0	0	0	0
5	1	1	4	4	2	1
6	0	0	0	0	0	0
7	10	2	5	4	3	3
8	0	0	0	0	0	0
9	0	0	0	0	0	0
10	0	0	0	0	0	0
11	0	0	1	1	0	0
12	0	0	0	0	0	0
13	0	0	0	0	0	0
14	0	0	0	0	0	0
15	0	0	0	0	0	0
16	0	0	0	0	0	0
17	0	0	0	0	0	0
18	0	0	0	0	0	0
19	0	0	0	0	0	0
20	0	0	0	0	0	0
21	0	0	0	0	0	0
22	0	0	0	0	0	0
23	0	0	0	0	0	0
24	0	0	0	0	2	2
25	0	0	3	3	3	2

TABLE K.3. Rarity of occurrence scores (Jude || 2 Peter, worst case)

No.	rarity_NT	rarity_LXX	rarity_Philo	rarity_Jos.	rarity_Pseud.	rarity_AF	rarity_G-R (worst)	Weighted Sum	Rarity Score
1	0.67	2.00	2.00	2.00	2.00	2.00	0.00	0.91	4.54
2	0.67	2.00	2.00	2.00	2.00	1.33	0.00	0.85	4.27
3	1.33	2.00	2.00	2.00	2.00	0.80	0.00	0.85	4.24
4	2.00	2.00	2.00	1.00	2.00	2.00	0.00	0.97	4.86
5	1.33	2.00	0.47	1.33	0.67	1.17	0.00	0.56	2.78
6	2.00	2.00	2.00	2.00	2.00	2.00	0.00	0.98	4.90
7	0.50	1.00	0.90	0.67	0.62	0.80	0.00	0.38	1.90
8	2.00	2.00	2.00	2.00	2.00	2.00	0.00	0.98	4.90
9	2.00	2.00	2.00	2.00	2.00	2.00	0.00	0.98	4.90
10	2.00	2.00	2.00	2.00	2.00	2.00	0.00	0.98	4.90
11	2.00	1.33	1.33	2.00	1.33	2.00	0.00	0.75	3.74
12	2.00	2.00	2.00	2.00	2.00	2.00	0.00	0.98	4.90
13	2.00	2.00	2.00	2.00	2.00	2.00	0.00	0.98	4.90
14	2.00	2.00	2.00	2.00	2.00	2.00	0.00	0.98	4.90
15	2.00	2.00	2.00	2.00	2.00	2.00	0.00	0.98	4.90
16	2.00	2.00	2.00	2.00	2.00	2.00	0.00	0.98	4.90
17	2.00	2.00	2.00	2.00	2.00	2.00	0.00	0.98	4.90
18	2.00	2.00	2.00	2.00	2.00	2.00	0.00	0.98	4.90
19	2.00	1.33	2.00	2.00	2.00	2.00	0.00	0.90	4.49
20	2.00	2.00	2.00	2.00	2.00	2.00	0.00	0.98	4.90
21	2.00	2.00	2.00	2.00	2.00	2.00	0.00	0.98	4.90
22	2.00	2.00	2.00	2.00	2.00	2.00	0.00	0.98	4.90
23	2.00	2.00	2.00	2.00	2.00	2.00	0.00	0.98	4.90
24	2.00	2.00	2.00	2.00	2.00	1.00	0.00	0.90	4.50
25	2.00	2.00	2.00	2.00	0.80	0.90	0.00	0.71	3.56

TABLE K.4. Rarity of occurrence scores (Jude || 2 Peter, best case)

No.	rarity_NT	rarity_LXX	rarity_Philo	rarity_Jos.	rarity_Pseud.	rarity_AF	rarity_G-R (best)	Weighted Sum	Rarity Score
1	0.67	2.00	2.00	2.00	2.00	2.00	2.00	1.93	9.64
2	0.67	2.00	2.00	2.00	2.00	1.33	2.00	1.87	9.37
3	1.33	2.00	2.00	2.00	2.00	0.80	2.00	1.87	9.34
4	2.00	2.00	2.00	1.00	2.00	2.00	2.00	1.99	9.96
5	1.33	2.00	0.47	1.33	0.67	1.17	2.00	1.58	7.88
6	2.00	2.00	2.00	2.00	2.00	2.00	2.00	2.00	10.00
7	0.50	1.00	0.90	0.67	0.62	0.80	2.00	1.40	7.00
8	2.00	2.00	2.00	2.00	2.00	2.00	2.00	2.00	10.00
9	2.00	2.00	2.00	2.00	2.00	2.00	2.00	2.00	10.00
10	2.00	2.00	2.00	2.00	2.00	2.00	2.00	2.00	10.00
11	2.00	1.33	1.33	2.00	1.33	2.00	2.00	1.77	8.84
12	2.00	2.00	2.00	2.00	2.00	2.00	2.00	2.00	10.00
13	2.00	2.00	2.00	2.00	2.00	2.00	2.00	2.00	10.00
14	2.00	2.00	2.00	2.00	2.00	2.00	2.00	2.00	10.00
15	2.00	2.00	2.00	2.00	2.00	2.00	2.00	2.00	10.00
16	2.00	2.00	2.00	2.00	2.00	2.00	2.00	2.00	10.00
17	2.00	2.00	2.00	2.00	2.00	2.00	2.00	2.00	10.00
18	2.00	2.00	2.00	2.00	2.00	2.00	2.00	2.00	10.00
19	2.00	1.33	2.00	2.00	2.00	2.00	2.00	1.92	9.59
20	2.00	2.00	2.00	2.00	2.00	2.00	2.00	2.00	10.00
21	2.00	2.00	2.00	2.00	2.00	2.00	2.00	2.00	10.00
22	2.00	2.00	2.00	2.00	2.00	2.00	2.00	2.00	10.00
23	2.00	2.00	2.00	2.00	2.00	2.00	2.00	2.00	10.00
24	2.00	2.00	2.00	2.00	2.00	1.00	2.00	1.92	9.60
25	2.00	2.00	2.00	2.00	0.80	0.90	2.00	1.73	8.66

Verbal Correspondence Scores
(Jude || 2 Peter)

TABLE L.1. Lexical, grammatical correspondence (Jude || 2 Peter)

No.	Jude		2 Peter		Basic Units			Gram. Constructs		
	#units	#const.	#units	#const.	#ident.	#relate	score	#ident.	#equiv.	score
1	3	2	5	4	3	0	1.20	2	0	1.00
2	11	6	14	5	6	0	0.86	1	3	0.83
3	7	5	5	4	4	0	1.14	3	1	1.40
4	2	2	2	2	2	0	2.00	2	0	2.00
5	4	4	4	3	0	2	0.50	0	2	0.50
6	7	4	6	4	2	2	0.86	1	2	1.00
7	8	4	6	4	2	0	0.50	0	1	0.25
8	10	6	6	4	4	0	0.80	3	0	1.00
9	5	5	9	6	3	0	0.67	2	3	1.17
10	22	10	16	11	7	1	0.68	3	3	0.82
11	25	12	11	10	5	1	0.44	1	2	0.33
12	14	5	18	6	6	1	0.72	0	4	0.67

TABLE L.1. *continued*

No.	Jude		2 Peter		Basic Units			Gram. Constructs		
	#units	#const.	#units	#const.	#ident.	#relate	score	#ident.	#equiv.	score
13	24	9	15	6	4	2	0.42	0	4	0.44
14	18	10	21	10	10	1	1.00	1	7	0.90
15	12	5	15	6	7	2	1.07	1	1	0.50
16	10	7	10	7	4	2	1.00	2	1	0.71
17	5	2	9	4	2	3	0.78	1	1	0.75
18	8	4	6	3	6	0	1.50	3	0	1.50
19	6	4	4	4	1	1	0.50	2	1	1.25
20	13	7	18	10	10	0	1.11	2	4	0.80
21	8	5	8	5	4	1	1.13	3	1	1.40
22	5	3	6	3	4	1	1.50	2	1	1.67
23	15	9	16	9	4	2	0.63	1	6	0.89
24	10	5	13	8	6	0	0.92	2	2	0.75
25	16	4	8	3	7	0	0.88	1	2	1.00

Probability of Directness
(Jude || 2 Peter, Worst Case)

Table M.1. Indicator Scores (Jude || 2 Peter, worst case)

No.	Rarity	Basic Units	Gram.	Struc.	Mean.	Funct.	Mem.
1	4.54	1.20	1.00	1	2	2	4
2	4.27	0.86	0.83	2	2	2	4
3	4.24	1.14	1.40	2	2	2	4
4	4.86	2.00	2.00	1	2	0	4
WC1	4.86	0.00	0.00	2	2	2	0
5	2.78	0.50	0.50	1	1	1	3
6	4.90	0.86	1.00	0	2	1	3
7	1.90	0.50	0.25	0	1	1	3
8	4.90	0.80	1.00	2	1	1	3
WC2	4.90	0.00	0.00	0	1	1	0
9	4.90	0.67	1.17	0	2	1	0
10	4.90	0.68	0.82	2	2	2	4

TABLE M.1. *continued*

No.	Rarity	Basic Units	Gram.	Struc.	Mean.	Funct.	Mem.
11	3.74	0.44	0.33	0	2	2	4
12	4.90	0.72	0.67	2	2	1	4
13	4.90	0.42	0.44	2	2	2	4
14	4.90	1.00	0.90	0	2	2	4
15	4.90	1.07	0.50	0	2	2	4
16	4.90	1.00	0.71	0	2	2	4
17	4.90	0.78	0.75	2	2	2	4
18	4.90	1.50	1.50	2	2	2	4
19	4.49	0.50	1.25	0	2	2	4
WC3	4.90	0.00	0.00	2	2	2	0
20	4.90	1.11	0.80	2	2	1	4
21	4.90	1.13	1.40	2	2	1	4
22	4.90	1.50	1.67	2	2	2	4
WC4	4.90	0.00	0.00	2	2	1	0
23	4.90	0.63	0.89	0	0	0	4
24	4.50	0.92	0.75	0	0	0	4
25	3.56	0.88	1.00	2	2	2	4
WC5	4.90	0.00	0.00	2	0	0	0

NOTE: Scores include the worst-case values for rarity of occurrence.

TABLE M.2. Probability Calculation (Jude || 2 Peter, worst case)

No.	EM	DI	IP_{dir}	IP_{ndir}	CP_{ndir}	CP_{dir}
					1	0
1	0.027	0.422	0.018	0.982	0.982	0.018
2	0.098	1.568	0.065	0.935	0.918	0.082
3	0.045	0.749	0.031	0.969	0.890	0.110
4	0.018	0.283	0.012	0.988	0.879	0.121
WC1	0.036	0.388	0.016	0.984	0.865	0.135

Table M.2. *continued*

No.	EM	DI	IP_{dir}	IP_{ndir}	CP_{ndir}	CP_{dir}
5	0.036	0.349	0.015	0.985	0.852	0.148
6	0.054	0.683	0.028	0.972	0.828	0.172
7	0.054	0.410	0.017	0.983	0.814	0.186
8	0.054	0.734	0.031	0.969	0.789	0.211
WC2	0.036	0.246	0.010	0.990	0.781	0.219
9	0.045	0.435	0.018	0.982	0.767	0.233
10	0.143	2.343	0.098	0.902	0.692	0.308
11	0.098	1.229	0.051	0.949	0.656	0.344
12	0.125	1.911	0.080	0.920	0.604	0.396
13	0.134	2.111	0.088	0.912	0.551	0.449
14	0.161	2.379	0.099	0.901	0.496	0.504
15	0.107	1.550	0.065	0.935	0.464	0.536
16	0.089	1.305	0.054	0.946	0.439	0.561
17	0.045	0.733	0.031	0.969	0.426	0.574
18	0.054	0.959	0.040	0.960	0.409	0.591
19	0.036	0.509	0.021	0.979	0.400	0.600
WC3	0.089	0.973	0.041	0.959	0.384	0.616
20	0.116	1.835	0.076	0.924	0.354	0.646
21	0.071	1.173	0.049	0.951	0.337	0.663
22	0.045	0.807	0.034	0.966	0.326	0.674
WC4	0.027	0.265	0.011	0.989	0.322	0.678
23	0.134	1.395	0.058	0.942	0.303	0.697
24	0.089	0.908	0.038	0.962	0.292	0.708
25	0.071	1.103	0.046	0.954	0.279	0.721
WC5	0.027	0.185	0.008	0.992	0.276	0.724

Note: Calculation uses the worst-case values for rarity of occurrence.

Probability of Directness
(Jude || 2 Peter, Best Case)

TABLE N.1. Indicator Scores (Jude || 2 Peter, best case)

No.	Rarity	Basic Units	Gram.	Struc.	Mean.	Funct.	Mem.
1	9.64	1.20	1.00	1	2	2	4
2	9.37	0.86	0.83	2	2	2	4
3	9.34	1.14	1.40	2	2	2	4
4	9.96	2.00	2.00	1	2	0	4
WC1	9.96	0.00	0.00	2	2	2	0
5	7.88	0.50	0.50	1	1	1	3
6	10.00	0.86	1.00	0	2	1	3
7	7.00	0.50	0.25	0	1	1	3
8	10.00	0.80	1.00	2	1	1	3
WC2	10.00	0.00	0.00	0	1	1	0
9	10.00	0.67	1.17	0	2	1	0
10	10.00	0.68	0.82	2	2	2	4

TABLE N.1. *continued*

No.	Rarity	Basic Units	Gram.	Struc.	Mean.	Funct.	Mem.
11	8.84	0.44	0.33	0	2	2	4
12	10.00	0.72	0.67	2	2	1	4
13	10.00	0.42	0.44	2	2	2	4
14	10.00	1.00	0.90	0	2	2	4
15	10.00	1.07	0.50	0	2	2	4
16	10.00	1.00	0.71	0	2	2	4
17	10.00	0.78	0.75	2	2	2	4
18	10.00	1.50	1.50	2	2	2	4
19	9.59	0.50	1.25	0	2	2	4
WC3	10.00	0.00	0.00	2	2	2	0
20	10.00	1.11	0.80	2	2	1	4
21	10.00	1.13	1.40	2	2	1	4
22	10.00	1.50	1.67	2	2	2	4
WC4	10.00	0.00	0.00	2	2	1	0
23	10.00	0.63	0.89	0	0	0	4
24	9.60	0.92	0.75	0	0	0	4
25	8.66	0.88	1.00	2	2	2	4
WC5	10.00	0.00	0.00	2	0	0	0

NOTE: Scores include the best-case values for rarity of occurrence.

TABLE N.2. Probability Calculation (Jude || 2 Peter, best case)

No.	EM	DI	IP_{dir}	IP_{ndir}	CP_{ndir}	CP_{dir}
					1	0
1	0.027	0.558	0.023	0.977	0.977	0.023
2	0.098	2.069	0.086	0.914	0.893	0.107
3	0.045	0.977	0.041	0.959	0.856	0.144
4	0.018	0.374	0.016	0.984	0.843	0.157
WC1	0.036	0.570	0.024	0.976	0.823	0.177

TABLE N.2. *continued*

No.	EM	DI	IP_{dir}	IP_{ndir}	CP_{ndir}	CP_{dir}
5	0.036	0.531	0.022	0.978	0.805	0.195
6	0.054	0.957	0.040	0.960	0.773	0.227
7	0.054	0.683	0.028	0.972	0.751	0.249
8	0.054	1.007	0.042	0.958	0.719	0.281
WC2	0.036	0.429	0.018	0.982	0.706	0.294
9	0.045	0.662	0.028	0.972	0.687	0.313
10	0.143	3.071	0.128	0.872	0.599	0.401
11	0.098	1.730	0.072	0.928	0.556	0.444
12	0.125	2.549	0.106	0.894	0.497	0.503
13	0.134	2.794	0.116	0.884	0.439	0.561
14	0.161	3.198	0.133	0.867	0.380	0.620
15	0.107	2.096	0.087	0.913	0.347	0.653
16	0.089	1.760	0.073	0.927	0.322	0.678
17	0.045	0.961	0.040	0.960	0.309	0.691
18	0.054	1.232	0.051	0.949	0.293	0.707
19	0.036	0.691	0.029	0.971	0.285	0.715
WC3	0.089	1.429	0.060	0.940	0.268	0.732
20	0.116	2.427	0.101	0.899	0.241	0.759
21	0.071	1.538	0.064	0.936	0.225	0.775
22	0.045	1.034	0.043	0.957	0.215	0.785
WC4	0.027	0.402	0.017	0.983	0.212	0.788
23	0.134	2.078	0.087	0.913	0.193	0.807
24	0.089	1.364	0.057	0.943	0.182	0.818
25	0.071	1.467	0.061	0.939	0.171	0.829
WC5	0.027	0.321	0.013	0.987	0.169	0.831

NOTE: Calculation uses the best-case values for rarity of occurrence.

APPENDIX O

Probability of Borrowing
(Jude)

TABLE O.1. Indicator Scores (Jude)

No.	DL	DS	DM	DF	CL	CS	CI	CF	PL	PS	PT	PF	ES
1	0	0	0	0	0	0	0	0	0	0	0	0	0
2	0	0	0	0	0	0	0	0	0	0	0	0	0
3	0	0	0	0	0	0	0	0	0	0	0	0	0
4	0	0	0	0	0	0	0	0	0	0	0	0	0
WC1	0	0	0	0	0	0	0	0	0	0	0	0	0
5	0	0	0	0	0	0	0	0	1	0	0	0	0
6	0	0	0	0	0	0	0	0	0	0	0	0	0
7	0	0	0	0	0	0	0	0	1	0	0	0	0
8	0	0	0	0	0	0	0	0	1	0	0	0	0
WC2	0	0	0	0	0	0	0	0	1	0	0	0	0
9	0	0	0	0	0	0	0	0	0	0	0	0	0
10	0	0	0	0	0	0	0	0	0	0	0	0	0

TABLE O.1. *continued*

No.	DL	DS	DM	DF	CL	CS	CI	CF	PL	PS	PT	PF	ES
11	0	0	0	0	0	0	0	0	0	0	0	0	0
12	0	0	0	0	0	0	0	0	0	0	0	0	0
13	0	0	0	0	0	0	0	0	0	0	0	0	0
14	0	0	0	0	0	0	0	0	0	0	0	0	0
15	0	0	0	0	0	0	0	0	0	0	0	0	0
16	0	0	0	0	0	0	0	0	0	0	0	0	0
17	0	0	0	0	0	0	0	0	0	0	0	0	0
18	0	0	0	0	0	0	0	0	0	0	0	0	0
19	0	0	0	0	0	0	0	0	0	0	0	0	0
WC3	0	0	0	0	0	0	0	0	0	0	0	0	0
20	0	0	0	0	0	0	0	0	0	0	0	0	0
21	0	0	0	0	0	0	0	0	0	0	0	0	0
22	0	0	0	0	0	0	0	0	0	0	0	0	0
WC4	0	0	0	0	0	0	0	0	0	0	0	0	0
23	0	0	0	0	0	0	0	0	0	0	0	0	0
24	0	0	0	0	0	0	0	0	0	0	0	0	0
25	0	0	0	0	0	0	0	0	0	0	0	0	0
WC5	0	0	0	0	0	0	0	0	0	0	0	0	0

TABLE O.2. Probability Calculation (Jude)

No.	BI	IP_{bor}	IP_{nbor}	CP_{nbor}	CP_{bor}
				1	0
1	0	0.00	1.00	1.00	0.00
2	0	0.00	1.00	1.00	0.00
3	0	0.00	1.00	1.00	0.00
4	0	0.00	1.00	1.00	0.00
WC1	0	0.00	1.00	1.00	0.00
5	1	0.08	0.92	0.92	0.08

TABLE O.2. *continued*

No.	BI	IP_{bor}	IP_{nbor}	CP_{nbor}	CP_{bor}
6	0	0.00	1.00	0.92	0.08
7	1	0.08	0.92	0.85	0.15
8	1	0.08	0.92	0.79	0.21
WC2	1	0.08	0.92	0.73	0.27
9	0	0.00	1.00	0.73	0.27
10	0	0.00	1.00	0.73	0.27
11	0	0.00	1.00	0.73	0.27
12	0	0.00	1.00	0.73	0.27
13	0	0.00	1.00	0.73	0.27
14	0	0.00	1.00	0.73	0.27
15	0	0.00	1.00	0.73	0.27
16	0	0.00	1.00	0.73	0.27
17	0	0.00	1.00	0.73	0.27
18	0	0.00	1.00	0.73	0.27
19	0	0.00	1.00	0.73	0.27
WC3	0	0.00	1.00	0.73	0.27
20	0	0.00	1.00	0.73	0.27
21	0	0.00	1.00	0.73	0.27
22	0	0.00	1.00	0.73	0.27
WC4	0	0.00	1.00	0.73	0.27
23	0	0.00	1.00	0.73	0.27
24	0	0.00	1.00	0.73	0.27
25	0	0.00	1.00	0.73	0.27
WC5	0	0.00	1.00	0.73	0.27

APPENDIX P

Probability of Borrowing
(2 Peter)

TABLE P.1. Indicator Scores (2 Peter)

No.	DL	DS	DM	DF	CL	CS	CI	CF	PL	PS	PT	PF	ES
1	0	0	0	0	0	0	0	0	0	0	0	0	0
2	0	0	0	0	0	0	0	0	0	0	0	0	0
3	0	0	0	0	0	0	0	0	0	0	0	0	0
4	0	0	0	0	0	0	0	0	0	0	1	0	0
WC1	0	0	0	0	0	0	0	0	0	1	0	0	0
5	0	0	0	0	0	0	0	0	0	0	0	0	0
6	0	0	0	0	0	0	0	0	0	0	0	0	0
7	0	0	0	0	0	0	0	0	0	0	0	0	0
8	0	0	0	0	0	0	0	0	0	0	0	0	0
WC2	0	0	0	0	0	0	0	0	0	0	0	0	0
9	0	0	0	0	0	0	0	0	0	1	0	0	0
10	0	0	0	0	0	0	0	0	0	0	0	0	1

TABLE P.1. *continued*

No.	DL	DS	DM	DF	CL	CS	CI	CF	PL	PS	PT	PF	ES
11	0	0	0	0	0	0	0	0	0	0	0	0	0
12	0	0	0	0	0	0	0	0	0	1	0	0	0
13	0	1	0	0	0	0	0	0	0	0	0	0	1
14	0	1	0	0	0	0	0	0	0	1	0	0	0
15	0	0	0	0	0	0	0	0	0	1	0	0	0
16	0	0	0	0	0	0	0	0	0	1	0	0	0
17	0	1	0	0	0	0	0	0	0	1	0	0	0
18	0	0	0	0	0	0	0	0	0	1	0	0	1
19	0	0	0	0	0	0	0	0	0	0	0	0	1
WC3	0	0	0	0	0	0	0	0	0	1	0	0	0
20	0	1	0	0	0	0	0	0	0	0	0	0	0
21	0	0	0	0	0	0	0	0	0	0	0	0	0
22	0	0	0	0	0	0	0	0	0	0	0	0	0
WC4	0	0	0	0	0	0	0	0	0	1	0	0	0
23	0	0	0	0	0	0	0	0	0	0	0	1	0
24	0	1	0	0	0	0	0	0	0	1	0	1	0
25	0	0	0	0	0	0	0	0	0	0	0	0	0
WC5	0	0	0	0	0	0	0	0	0	0	0	1	0

TABLE P.2. Probability Calculation (2 Peter)

No.	BI	IP_{bor}	IP_{nbor}	CP_{nbor}	CP_{bor}
				1	0
1	0	0.00	1.00	1.00	0.00
2	0	0.00	1.00	1.00	0.00
3	0	0.00	1.00	1.00	0.00
4	1	0.08	0.92	0.92	0.08
WC1	1	0.08	0.92	0.85	0.15
5	0	0.00	1.00	0.85	0.15

TABLE P.2. *continued*

No.	BI	IP_{bor}	IP_{nbor}	CP_{nbor}	CP_{bor}
6	0	0.00	1.00	0.85	0.15
7	0	0.00	1.00	0.85	0.15
8	0	0.00	1.00	0.85	0.15
WC2	0	0.00	1.00	0.85	0.15
9	1	0.08	0.92	0.79	0.21
10	1	0.08	0.92	0.73	0.27
11	0	0.00	1.00	0.73	0.27
12	1	0.08	0.92	0.67	0.33
13	2	0.15	0.85	0.57	0.43
14	2	0.15	0.85	0.48	0.52
15	1	0.08	0.92	0.44	0.56
16	1	0.08	0.92	0.41	0.59
17	2	0.15	0.85	0.35	0.65
18	2	0.15	0.85	0.29	0.71
19	1	0.08	0.92	0.27	0.73
WC3	1	0.08	0.92	0.25	0.75
20	1	0.08	0.92	0.23	0.77
21	0	0.00	1.00	0.23	0.77
22	0	0.00	1.00	0.23	0.77
WC4	1	0.08	0.92	0.21	0.79
23	1	0.08	0.92	0.20	0.80
24	3	0.23	0.77	0.15	0.85
25	0	0.00	1.00	0.15	0.85
WC5	1	0.08	0.92	0.14	0.86

Works Cited

Primary Sources

Aland, Kurt, Barbara Aland, Johannes Karavidopoulos, Carlo M. Martini, and Bruce M. Metzger, eds. *Novum Testamentum Graece (BNT)*. 27th ed. Stuttgart: Deutsche Bibelgesellschaft, 2001. BibleWorks, v. 10.

BibleWorks Greek Apostolic Fathers Morphology (APM). Norfolk: Bible-Works, LLC., 2012. BibleWorks, v. 10.

BibleWorks Greek New Testament Morphology (BNM). Norfolk: BibleWorks, LLC., 2001. BibleWorks, v. 10.

BibleWorks LXX/OG Morphology and Lemma Database (BLM). Norfolk: BibleWorks, LLC., 2001. BibleWorks, v. 10.

Borgen, Peder, Kåre Fuglseth, and Roald Skarsten. *The Philo Concordance Database in Greek (PHI)*. n.p.: n.p., 2005. BibleWorks, v. 10.

——— . *The Philo Concordance Database in Greek with Lemmatization and Morphological Tagging with Corrections (PHM)*. Edited by Jean-Noel Aletti and Andrzej Gieniusz. n.p.: n.p., 2007. BibleWorks, v. 10.

Codex Alexandrinus. BibleWorks, v. 10.

Codex Bezae. BibleWorks, v. 10.

Evans, Craig A. *The Greek Pseudepigrapha (OPG)*. n.p.: OakTree Software, 2008. BibleWorks, v. 10.

Greek New Testament and LXX Database (BGT). Norfolk: BibleWorks, LLC., 1999. BibleWorks, v. 10.

Greek New Testament and LXX Morphological Database (BGM). Norfolk: BibleWorks, LLC., 1999. BibleWorks, v. 10.

Josephus, Flavius. *Flavii Josephi opera edidit et apparatu critico instruxit Benedictus Niese (JOS)*. Translated by Benedictus Niese. 6 vols. Berlin: Weidmann, 1887. BibleWorks, v. 10.

—————. *Flavii Josephi opera edidit et apparatu critico instruxit Benedictus Niese: Greek Morphology (JOM)*. Norfolk: BibleWorks, LLC., 2003. BibleWorks, v. 10.

Koivisto, Rex A. *The Greek Pseudepigrapha Morphologically-tagged Text (OPM)*. n.p.: OakTree Software, 2008. BibleWorks, v. 10.

Lightfoot, J. B. *The Apostolic Fathers (APF)*. Edited by J. R. Harmer. 2nd ed. London: Macmillan, 1898. BibleWorks, v. 10.

Perseus Digital Library. Edited by Gregory R. Crane. Medford, MA: Tufts University. www.perseus.tufts.edu.

Rahlfs, Alfred. *Septuaginta: Id est Vetus Testamentum iuxta LXX interpretes edidit Alfred Rahlfs (LXT)*. Stuttgart: Deutsche Bibelgesellschaft, 1935. BibleWorks, v. 10.

Thesaurus Linguae Graecae: A Digital Library of Greek Literature. Irvine, CA: University of California, 2014. www.tlg.uci.edu.

Westminster Leningrad Codex (WTT). Philadelpha, PA: Westminster Theological Seminary. BibleWorks, v. 10.

Other Sources

Achtemeier, Paul J. *1 Peter: A Commentary on First Peter*. Hermeneia: A Critical and Historical Commentary on the Bible. Minneapolis, MN: Fortress, 1996.

Aland, Kurt, and Barbara Aland. *The Text of the New Testament: An Introduction to the Critical Editions and to the Theory and Practice of Modern Textual Criticism*. 3rd ed. Translated by Erroll F. Rhodes. Grand Rapids, MI: Eerdmans, 1989.

Attridge, Harold W. *The Epistle to the Hebrews: A Commentary on the Epistle to the Hebrews.* Hermeneia: A Critical and Historical Commentary on the Bible. Philadelphia, PA: Fortress, 1989.

Ayles, H. H. B. *Destination, Date, and Authorship of the Epistle to the Hebrews.* London: C. J. Clay & Sons, 1899.

Barnett, Albert E. *Paul Becomes a Literary Influence.* Chicago, IL: The University of Chicago Press, 1941.

Barth, Markus. "Traditions in Ephesians." *New Testament Studies* 30 (1984): 3–27.

Bartholomä, Philipp F. "Did Jesus Save the People out of Egypt? A Reexamination of a Textual Problem in Jude 5." *Novum Testamentum* 50, no. 2 (2008): 143–58.

Bauckham, Richard J. *Jude, 2 Peter.* Word Biblical Commentary 50. Nashville, TN: Thomas Nelson, 1983.

Beetham, Christopher A. *Echoes of Scripture in the Letter of Paul to the Colossians.* Biblical Interpretation Series 96. Leiden, The Netherlands: Brill, 2008.

Berding, Kenneth. *Polycarp and Paul: An Analysis of Their Literary and Theological Relationship in Light of Polycarp's Use of Biblical and Extra-Biblical Literature.* Supplements to Vigiliae Christianae 62. Leiden, The Netherlands: Brill, 2002.

Best, Ernest. "Who Used Whom? The Relationship of Ephesians and Colossians." *New Testament Studies* 43, no. 1 (January 1997): 72–96.

Bigg, Charles. *The Epistles of St. Peter and St. Jude.* International Critical Commentary. Edinburgh: T&T Clark, 1901.

Bird, Michael F. "The Reception of Paul in the Epistle to Diognetus." In *Paul and the Second Century,* edited by Michael F. Bird and Joseph R. Dodson, 70–90. New York: T&T Clark International, 2011.

Black, David Alan. *New Testament Textual Criticism: A Concise Guide.* Grand Rapids, MI: Baker Books, 1994.

Burge, Gary M., Lynn H. Cohick, and Gene L. Green. *The New Testament in Antiquity: A Survey of the New Testament within Its Cultural Contexts.* Grand Rapids, MI: Zondervan, 2009.

Clarke, W. K. Lowther, ed. *The First Epistle of Clement to the Corinthians.* London: Society for Promoting Christian Knowledge, 1937.

Coutts, John. "The Relationship of Ephesians and Colossians." *New Testament Studies* 4 (1958): 201–7.

Crossan, John Dominic. *The Birth of Christianity: Discovering What Happened in the Years Immediately after the Execution of Jesus*. New York: HarperSanFrancisco, 1998.

Daube, David. "Appended Note: Participle and Imperative in 1 Peter." In *The First Epistle of St. Peter: The Greek Text with Introduction, Notes and Essays*, edited by Edward Gordon Selwyn, 467–88. London: Macmillan & Co. Ltd., 1955.

Davids, Peter H. *The Epistle of James: A Commentary on the Greek Text*. New International Greek Testament Commentary. Grand Rapids, MI: Eerdmans, 1982.

————. *The Letters of 2 Peter and Jude*. The Pillar New Testament Commentary. Grand Rapids, MI: Eerdmans, 2006.

————. "The Pseudepigrapha in the Catholic Epistles." In *The Pseudepigrapha and Early Biblical Interpretation*, edited by James H. Charlesworth and Craig A. Evans. Journal for the Study of the Pseudepigrapha Supplement Series 14, 228–45. Sheffield: Sheffield Academic, 1993.

DeMaris, Richard E. *The Colossian Controversy: Wisdom in Dispute at Colossae*. Journal for the Study of the New Testament: Supplement Series 96. Sheffield: Sheffield Academic, 1994.

Donaldson, Terence L. "Parallels: Use, Misuse and Limitations." *Evangelical Quarterly* 55 (October 1983): 193–210.

Donker, Gerald J. *The Text of the Apostolos in Athanasius of Alexandria*. Society of Biblical Literature: The New Testament in the Greek Fathers 8. Atlanta, GA: Society of Biblical Literature, 2011.

Ellingworth, Paul. *The Epistle to the Hebrews: A Commentary on the Greek Text*. New International Greek Testament Commentary. Grand Rapids, MI: Eerdmans, 1993.

————. "Hebrews and 1 Clement: Literary Dependence or Common Tradition?" *Biblische Zeitschrift* ns 23, no. 2 (1979): 262–69.

Elliott, John H. *1 Peter*. Anchor Bible 37B. New Haven: Yale University Press, 2001.

Evans, Craig A. *Ancient Texts for New Testament Studies: A Guide to the Background Literature*. Peabody, MA: Hendrickson, 2005.

Fee, Gordon D. *Paul's Letter to the Philippians*. New International Commentary on the New Testament. Grand Rapids, MI: Eerdmans, 1995.

Fishbane, Michael A. *Biblical Interpretation in Ancient Israel*. New York: Oxford University Press, 1985.

Fossum, Jarl. "Colossians 1.15–18a in the Light of Jewish Mysticism and Gnosticism." *New Testament Studies* 35, no. 2 (April 1989): 183–201.

———. "Kyrios Jesus as the Angel of the Lord in Jude 5–7." *New Testament Studies* 33, no. 2 (April 1987): 226–43.

Fung, Glenn. "The Disputed Federalist Papers: SVM Feature Selection Via Concave Minimization." In *TAPIA '03 Proceedings of the 2003 Conference on Diversity in Computing, Atlanta, GA, October 15–18, 2003*, 42–46. New York: The Association of Computing Machinery, 2003.

Gilmour, Michael J. *The Significance of Parallels between 2 Peter and Other Early Christian Literature*. Academia Biblica 10. Leiden, The Netherlands: Brill Academic, 2002.

Gloer, Hulitt W. "Homologies and Hymns in the New Testament: Form, Content and Criteria for Identification." *Perspectives in Religious Studies* 11, no. 2 (Summer 1984): 115–32.

Goodacre, Mark S. *The Case Against Q: Studies in Markan Priority and the Synoptic Problem*. Harrisburg, PA: Trinity Press International, 2002.

———. *Goulder and the Gospels: An Examination of a New Paradigm*. Journal for the Study of the New Testament: Supplement Series 133. Sheffield: Sheffield Academic, 1996.

———. *The Synoptic Problem: A Way Through the Maze*. New York: T&T Clark International, 2001.

Goppelt, Leonhard. *A Commentary on 1 Peter*. Edited by Ferdinand Hahn. Translated by John E. Alsup. Grand Rapids, MI: Eerdmans, 1993.

Grässer, Erich. "Der Hebräerbrief, 1938–63." *Theologische Rundschau* ns 30, no. 2 (1964): 138–236.

Green, Gene L. *Jude and 2 Peter*. Baker Exegetical Commentary on the New Testament. Grand Rapids, MI: Baker Academic, 2008.

Green, Michael. *The Second Epistle General of Peter and the General Epistle of Jude: An Introduction and Commentary*. Grand Rapids, MI: Eerdmans, 1968.

Gregory, Andrew F. "1 Clement and the Writings That Later Formed the New Testament." In *The Reception of the New Testament in the Apostolic Fathers*, edited by Andrew F. Gregory and Christopher M. Tuckett, 129–57. Oxford: Oxford University Press, 2005.

Gregory, Andrew F., and Christopher M. Tuckett. "Reflections on Method: What Constitutes the Use of the Writings That Later Formed the New Testament in the Apostolic Fathers?" In *The Reception of the New Testament in the Apostolic Fathers*, edited by Andrew F. Gregory and

Christopher M. Tuckett, 61–82. Oxford: Oxford University Press, 2005.

Hagner, Donald Alfred. *The Use of the Old and New Testaments in Clement of Rome*. Supplements to Novum Testamentum 34. Leiden, The Netherlands: E. J. Brill, 1973.

Hartog, Paul Anthony. *Polycarp and the New Testament: The Occasion, Rhetoric, Theme, and Unity of the Epistle to the Philippians and Its Allusions to New Testament Literature*. Wissenschaftliche Untersuchungen zum Neuen Testament 2.134. Tübingen: Mohr (Siebeck), 2002.

Hawthorne, G. F. "Philippians, Letter to the." In *Dictionary of Paul and His Letters*, edited by Gerald F. Hawthorne, Ralph P. Martin, and Daniel G. Reid, 707–13. Downers Grove, IL: InterVarsity Press, 1993.

Hays, Richard B. *Echoes of Scripture in the Letters of Paul*. New Haven: Yale University Press, 1989.

Head, Peter M. *Christology and the Synoptic Problem: An Argument for Markan Priority*. Society for New Testament Studies Monograph Series 94. Cambridge: Cambridge University Press, 1997.

Hengel, Martin. *The Four Gospels and the One Gospel of Jesus Christ: An Investigation of the Collection and Origin of the Canonical Gospels*. Harrisburg, PA: Trinity Press International, 2000.

Hill, Charles E. *The Johannine Corpus in the Early Church*. Oxford: Oxford University Press, 2004.

Hoehner, Harold W. *Ephesians: An Exegetical Commentary*. Grand Rapids, MI: Baker Academic, 2002.

Holmes, Michael W. "Paul and Polycarp." In *Paul and the Second Century*, edited by Michael F. Bird and Joseph R. Dodson, 57–69. New York: T&T Clark International, 2011.

Holtzmann, Heinrich Julius. *Einleitung in das Neue Testament*. Freiburg: Mohr (Siebeck), 1886.

Horrell, David G. *The Epistles of Peter and Jude*. London: Epworth, 1998.

Hurst, L. D. *The Epistle to the Hebrews: Its Background of Thought*. Society for New Testament Studies Monograph Series 65. Cambridge: Cambridge University Press, 1990.

Jobes, Karen H. *Letters to the Church: A Survey of Hebrews and the General Epistles*. Grand Rapids, MI: Zondervan, 2011.

———. "Quantitative Methods for Exploring the Relationship between Books of the Septuagint." In *The Bible As Book: The*

Transmission of the Greek Text, edited by Scot McKendrick and Orlaith A. O'Sullivan, 73–95. New Castle, DE: Oak Knoll Press, 2003.

Johnson, Luke Timothy. *The Letter of James*. The Anchor Yale Bible 37A. London: Yale University Press, 1995.

Kahmann, Johannes. "The Second Letter of Peter and the Letter of Jude: Their Mutual Relationship." In *The New Testament in Early Christianity: La réception des écrits néotestamentaires dans le christianisme primitif*, edited by Jean-Marie Sevrin. Bibliotheca Ephemeridum Theologicarum Lovaniensium 86, 105–22. Leuven: Peeters & Leuven University Press, 1989.

Kelly, J. N. D. *A Commentary on the Epistles of Peter and of Jude*. Black's New Testament Commentaries. London: Adam & Charles Black, 1969.

Kenny, Anthony. *A Stylometric Study of the New Testament*. New York: Oxford University Press, 1986.

Koch, Dietrich-Alex. *Die Schrift als Zeuge des Evangeliums: Untersuchungen zur Verwendung und zum Verständnis der Schrift bei Paulus*. Beiträge zur historischen Theologie 69. Tübingen: Mohr (Siebeck), 1986.

Koester, Craig R. *Hebrews: A New Translation with Introduction and Commentary*. Anchor Bible 36. New York: Doubleday, 2001.

Koester, Helmut. "Written Gospels or Oral Tradition?" *Journal of Biblical Literature* 113 (1994): 293–97.

Köhler, Wolf-Dietrich. *Die Rezeption des Matthäusevangeliums in der Zeit vor Irenäus*. Wissenschaftliche Untersuchungen zum Neuen Testament 2.24. Tübingen: Mohr (Siebeck), 1987.

Kümmel, Werner Georg. *Introduction to the New Testament*. Rev. ed. Translated by Howard Clark Kee. Nashville, TN: Abingdon, 1975.

Landon, C. *A Text-Critical Study of the Epistle of Jude*. Journal for the Study of the New Testament: Supplement Series 135. Sheffield: Sheffield Academic Press, 1996.

Lane, William L. *Hebrews 1–8*. Word Biblical Commentary 47A. Nashville, TN: Thomas Nelson, 1991.

Leonard, Jeffery M. "Identifying Inner-Biblical Allusions: Psalm 78 as a Test Case." *Journal of Biblical Literature* 127, no. 2 (Summer 2008): 241–65.

Lincoln, Andrew T. *Ephesians*. Word Biblical Commentary 42. Dallas, TX: Word Books, 1990.

Lincoln, Andrew T., and A. J. M. Wedderburn. *The Theology of the Later Pauline Letters*. New Testament Theology. Cambridge: Cambridge University Press, 1993.

Lindemann, Andreas. *Die Clemensbriefe.* Handbuch zum Neuen Testament 17. Die Apostolischen Väter 1. Tübingen: Mohr (Siebeck), 1992.

———. *Paulus im ältesten Christentum.* Beiträge zur historischen Theologie 58. Tübingen: Mohr (Siebeck), 1979.

Longenecker, Richard N. "Christological Materials in the Early Christian Communities." In *Contours of Christology in the New Testament,* edited by Richard N. Longenecker, 47–76. Grand Rapids, MI: Eerdmans, 2005.

Luther, Martin. "Sermons on the Second Epistle of St. Peter" and "Sermons on the Epistle of St. Jude." Translated by M. H. Bertram. In *The Catholic Epistles,* edited by J. Pelikan and W. A. Hansen. Luther's Works 30. St. Louis, MO: Concordia Publishing House, 1967.

MacDonald, Margaret Y. *Colossians and Ephesians.* Sacra Pagina 17. Collegeville, MN: The Liturgical Press, 2000.

Marshall, I. Howard. *New Testament Theology: Many Witnesses, One Gospel.* Downers Grove, IL: IVP Academic, 2004.

Martin, Troy W. *By Philosophy and Empty Deceit: Colossians as Response to a Cynic Critique.* Journal for the Study of the New Testament: Supplement Series 118. Sheffield: Sheffield Academic, 1996.

Masterman, John Howard Bertram. *The First Epistle of S. Peter: Greek Text, with Introduction and Notes.* London: MacMillan & Co., Ltd., 1900.

Mayor, J. B. *The Epistle of St. Jude and the Second Epistle of St. Peter.* London: Macmillan, 1907; reprint, Grand Rapids: Baker, 1965.

Mealand, D. L. "The Extent of the Pauline Corpus: A Multivariate Approach." *Journal for the Study of the New Testament* 59 (1995): 61–92.

Mees, Michael. "Die Hohepriester-Theologie des Hebräerbriefes im Vergleich mit dem Ersten Clemensbrief." *Biblische Zeitschrift* ns 22, no. 1 (1978): 115–24.

Melick, Richard R. *Philippians, Colossians, Philemon.* New American Commentary 32. Nashville: Broadman & Holman, 1991.

Metzger, Bruce M. *The Text of the New Testament: Its Transmission, Corruption, and Restoration.* 3rd ed. New York: Oxford University Press, 1992.

———. *A Textual Commentary on the Greek New Testament.* 2nd ed. Stuttgart: Deutsche Bibelgesellschaft, 1994.

Metzger, Bruce M., and Bart D. Ehrman. *The Text of the New Testament: Its Transmission, Corruption, and Restoration,* 4th ed. New York: Oxford University Press, 2005.

Michaels, J. Ramsey. "Catholic Christologies in the Catholic Epistles." In *Contours of Christology in the New Testament*, edited by Richard N. Longenecker, 268–91. Grand Rapids, MI: Eerdmans, 2005.

Miller, Robert J. "Is There Independent Attestation for the Transfiguration in 2 Peter?" *New Testament Studies* 42 (1996): 620–25.

Mitton, C. Leslie. *Ephesians*. New Century Bible. London: Oliphants, 1976.

——— . *The Epistle to the Ephesians: Its Authorship, Origin and Purpose*. Oxford: Clarendon, 1951.

Moffatt, James. *An Introduction to the Literature of the New Testament*. The International Theological Library. New York: Charles Scribner's Sons, 1911, reprinted 1929.

Moo, Douglas J. *2 Peter and Jude*. NIV Application Commentary. Grand Rapids, MI: Zondervan, 1996.

——— . *The Letter of James*. The Pillar New Testament Commentary. Grand Rapids, MI: Eerdmans, 2000.

——— . *The Letters to the Colossians and to Philemon*. The Pillar New Testament Commentary. Grand Rapids, MI: Eerdmans, 2008.

Myers, Elizabeth A. *Authorship of 1 Peter and Hebrews: New Evidence in Light of Probable Intertextual Borrowing*. Cody, WY: Pistos Ktistes Publishing LLC, 2020.

——— . *Intertextual Borrowing between 1 Peter and Hebrews: Probability of Literary Dependence and the Most Likely Direction of Borrowing*. Cody, WY: Pistos Ktistes Publishing LLC, 2020.

——— . "Probability of Intertextual Borrowing." In *Exploring Intertextuality: Diverse Strategies for New Testament Interpretation of Texts*, edited by B. J. Oropeza and Steve Moyise, 254–72. Eugene, OR: Cascade Books, 2016.

Neville, David J. *Arguments from Order in Synoptic Source Criticism: A History and Critique*. New Gospel Studies 7. Macon, GA: Mercer University Press, 1994.

——— . *Mark's Gospel — Prior or Posterior? A Reappraisal of the Phenomenon of Order*. Journal for the Study of the New Testament: Supplement Series 222. London: Sheffield Academic, 2002.

Neyrey, Jerome H. *2 Peter, Jude*. Anchor Bible 37c. New York: Doubleday, 1993.

O'Brien, Peter T. *Colossians and Philemon*. Word Biblical Commentary 44. Nashville, TN: Thomas Nelson, Inc., 2000.

————. *The Epistle to the Philippians: A Commentary on the Greek Text.* New International Greek Testament Commentary. Grand Rapids, MI: Eerdmans, 1991.

O'Day, Gail R. "Jeremiah 9.22–23 and 1 Corinthians 1.26–31: A Study in Intertextuality." *Journal of Biblical Literature* 109 (1990): 259–67.

Orchard, Bernard, and Harold Riley. *The Order of the Synoptics: Why Three Synoptic Gospels?* Macon, GA: Mercer University Press, 1987.

Osburn, Carroll D. "The Text of Jude 5." *Biblica* 62 (1981): 107–15.

Oxford Society of Historical Theology. *The New Testament in the Apostolic Fathers.* Oxford: Clarendon, 1905.

Pakkala, Juha. *God's Word Omitted: Omissions in the Translation of the Hebrew Bible.* Forschungen zur Religion und Literatur des Alten und Neuen Testaments 251. Göttingen: Vandenhoeck & Ruprecht, 2013.

Pearson, Sharon Clark. *The Christological and Rhetorical Properties of 1 Peter.* Lewiston, NY: Edwin Mellen, 2001.

Porter, Stanley E. "The Use of the Old Testament in the New Testament: A Brief Comment on Method and Terminology." In *Early Christian Interpretation of the Scriptures of Israel: Investigations and Proposals*, edited by Craig A. Evans and James A. Sanders, 79–96. Sheffield: Sheffield Academic, 1997.

Reicke, B. *The Epistles of James, Peter, and Jude.* Anchor Bible 37. Garden City: Doubleday, 1964.

Robinson, John A. T. *Redating the New Testament.* London: SCM Press Ltd., 1976.

Sanders, E. P. *The Tendencies of the Synoptic Tradition.* Cambridge: Cambridge University Press, 1969.

Sandmel, Samuel. "Parallelomania." *Journal of Biblical Literature* 81, no. 1 (March 1962): 1–13.

Schreiner, Thomas R. *1, 2 Peter, Jude.* New American Commentary 37. Nashville, TN: Broadman & Holman, 2003.

Schutter, William L. *Hermeneutic and Composition in 1 Peter.* Wissenschaftliche Untersuchungen zum Neuen Testament 2.30. Tübingen: Mohr (Siebeck), 1989.

Selwyn, Edward Gordon. "Essay II: Bearing of Evidence on the Supposed Dependence of 1 Peter on Other Epistles." In *The First Epistle of St. Peter: The Greek Text with Introduction, Notes and Essays*, 365–466. London: Macmillan & Co. Ltd., 1955.

Shimada, Kazuhito. "The Formulary Material in First Peter: A Study According to the Method of Traditionsgeschichte." Ann Arbor, MI: Xerox University Microfilms, 1966.

————. "Is 1 Peter Dependent on Romans?" Annual of the Japanese Biblical Institute 19, 87–137. Tokyo: Yamamoto Shoten, 1993.

Silva, Moisés. Philippians, 2nd ed., Baker Exegetical Commentary on the New Testament. Grand Rapids, MI: Baker Academic, 2005.

Spicq, Ceslas. "La Iᵃ Petri et le témoignage évangélique de Saint Pierre." Studia Theologica 20 (1966): 37–61.

————. Les Épîtres de Saint Pierre. Sources bibliques. Paris: Gabalda, 1966.

Stein, Robert H. The Synoptic Problem: An Introduction. Grand Rapids, MI: Baker Books, 1987.

Swinburne, Richard. The Existence of God. 2nd ed. New York: Oxford University Press, 2004, first published 1979.

Thompson, Michael. Clothed with Christ: The Example and Teaching of Jesus in Romans 12.1–15.13. Journal for the Study of the New Testament: Supplement Series 59. Sheffield: Sheffield Academic, 1991.

Thurén, Lauri. "The Relationship between 2 Peter and Jude — A Classical Problem Resolved?" In The Catholic Epistles and the Tradition, edited by Jacques Schlosser, 451–60. Bibliotheca Ephemeridum Theologicarum Lovaniensium 176. Leuven: Peeters, 2004.

Tyson, John R., ed. "Blaise Pascal (1623–62)." In Invitation to Christian Spirituality: An Ecumenical Anthology, 292–301. New York: Oxford University Press, 1999.

Wand, J. W. C., ed. The General Epistles of St. Peter and St. Jude. Westminster Commentaries. London: Methuen & Co. Ltd., 1934.

Watson, Duane Frederick. Invention, Arrangement, and Style: Rhetorical Criticism of Jude and 2 Peter. Society of Biblical Literature Dissertation Series 104. Atlanta, GA: Scholars Press, 1988.

————. "A Rhetorical Analysis of Philippians and Its Implications for the Unity Question." Novum Testamentum 30 (1988): 57–88.

Webb, R. L. "Jude." In Dictionary of the Later New Testament and Its Developments, edited by Ralph P. Martin and Peter H. Davids, 611–21. Downers Grove, IL: InterVarsity Press, 1997.

Witherington, Ben, III. "The Influence of Galatians on Hebrews." New Testament Studies 37 (1991): 146–52.

————. Paul's Letter to the Philippians: A Socio-Rhetorical Commentary. Grand Rapids, MI: Eerdmans, 2011.

Index of Scripture
and Other Ancient Sources

New Testament Apocrypha and Pseudepigrapha

Apostolic Fathers

OTHER ANCIENT SOURCES

Index of Modern Authors